Florence Morse Kingsley

The Cross Triumphant

Florence Morse Kingsley

The Cross Triumphant

ISBN/EAN: 9783744692663

Printed in Europe, USA, Canada, Australia, Japan

Cover: Foto ©Thomas Meinert / pixelio.de

More available books at **www.hansebooks.com**

THE CROSS TRIUMPHANT

BY

FLORENCE MORSE KINGSLEY

Author of
"Titus," "Stephen" and "Paul."

———

Philadelphia
HENRY ALTEMUS
1899

HENRY ALTEMUS, MANUFACTURER,
PHILADELPHIA.

CONTENTS.

CONTENTS.

CHAPTER I.

JESUS, a carpenter of Galilee, who also was called the Christ by certain Jews who followed him, had been dead full seventeen years—dead, and already put out of mind and forgotten by many who had both seen him and heard him speak, when a man-child was born in the little mountain village of Aphtha. Many months before the child opened his eyes in the cold gray of a winter dawn his father had closed his forever. They laid him, swathed hand and foot in spiced linen, in a narrow niche cut deep in the rocky hillside.

His young widow lived on alone in a tiny cottage on the opposite side of the valley. From her doorway she could see the great stone which lay across the narrower doorway. She thought in those days that if she also might dwell in that other house—from whose doorway one never passed out—she would be content, quite still and content. Later she remembered the child. When she looked upon the fatherless one she said, "He shall be called Phannias."

(9)

The child's first conscious memory was that of the face of his mother, dark with passionate sorrow, shining with love, solemnly beautiful as a storm-cloud rent with lightning yet touched with the clear light of the sun. As he gazed into this face, whereon love and sorrow were so wondrously blended, thoughts began to grow within him. His eyes answered her eyes. After a time he came to understand the words which fell from her lips; but he made no haste to use his own tongue. Long after the little head, running over with curls of midnight blackness, came to be seen here and there about the house and garden, he was still silent.

The neighbors were not slow to observe this. "The child hath a dumb devil," they whispered among themselves, and made ostentatious room for the widow when she came to the fountain, the child perched upon her shoulder, or later, clinging shyly to the folds of her robe.

Rachel, wrapped in the impervious garment of her sorrow, paid no heed to either looks or whispers, returning the reluctant salutations that greeted her appearance with dropped lids and the formal "Peace be with thee." She had come to Aphtha a bride and a stranger; widowed within the month of her arrival, she was a stranger still. Her nature, rich, generous, abundant, a bright river of gladness, had on a sudden plunged into black silent depths, to emerge no more save in one sparkling fountain. Henceforth she lived for her child alone.

Phannias dimly comprehended this before he spoke. He also understood that he himself was not like the other children, who noisily laughed and cried, played and quarreled about the village streets. For himself he seldom either smiled or wept, nevertheless he was happy as an angel. The garden, with its terraced steeps, whereon the vine was wedded to the olive with eastern thrift and beauty; the luxuriant tangle of almond and oleander, whose blossoming branches wrapped the low-walled cottage in a bower of fragrant silence; the stream twinkling pleasantly over its smooth round pebbles; tall lilies, pouring forth odorous secrets at dawn and at twilight; pigeons circling in blue air like nearer clouds; bird voices loud and jubilant with the new day, or drowsily sweet and tender in the purple evenings—all these and others innumerable, changing from wonder to wonder with the changing seasons, made of the child's narrow world no less than heaven. In this heaven his mother reigned supreme; of all things beautiful, lovely and adorable, she was to the child the most beautiful, the most lovely, the most to be adored.

When Phannias was three years old his mother told him of God. He had already learned to pray, as the bird learns to sing. The nestling listens to the song of its mother and twitters its joy aloud; so Phannias babbled sweetly to his mother's eyes words which she taught him evening by evening. But one day a new thought came to him, and with the thought a question. "Who is God, my mother?"

Rachel trembled—angels also tremble when they teach a white soul of God. "God is the holy, invisible One who made the whole earth," she said slowly. "He made all things that thou dost see, child,—thyself also. Thou must love—adore him."

"Did he make thee?"

"Yes, truly, he made me."

"Then I will love him, for I love thee."

To love the maker of his mother, of the stars and the lilies, was not difficult; it was indeed quite as easy and inevitable as breathing. The child breathed and loved, and was happy for a whole year; then his mother told him of The Law. He quickly learned that The Law was far more difficult to understand than God. The Law had made nothing pleasant or beautiful. The Law did not love him, yet it required of him many things, some of them strange and hard to understand.

In the joyous days of the grape harvest, when all the other children of the village frolicked in the vineyards from dawn until evening, their hands and faces stained purple with the luscious juices of the fruit, Phannias stood sad and silent beside the door of his mother's cottage. The Law forbade him to touch, much less taste, a single berry of all the tempting clusters ripening fragrantly in the warm shadows of the vines.

"Did The Law make the vines, my mother?" he

asked, leaning his round cheeks in his palms, and
staring wistfully at the heaped-up clusters of red,
purple and white which the young men and maidens
were carrying with shouts of happy laughter to the
vintage.

"No, my son," answered Rachel, smiling into
the questioning dark eyes upturned to hers. "God
made the vines ; the fruit also is good and pleasant.
But thou art vowed unto God a holy Nazarite, as I
have already told thee many times. Thou wilt be
beloved of God, as was Samuel, the prophet ; the
angels also will love thee."

Phannias had learned from his mother's lips many
wonderful stories concerning the unseen God, and
his dealings with men and women long since vanished from off the earth. She was accustomed to
read these tales from a scroll, which was kept between whiles in a box of fragrant wood. This scroll
had once belonged to his father, she told him ; it
would one day be his. The child regarded it with
awe, the spicy odor of the parchment unfolding
strange meanings beyond the tales of love and hate,
obedience and rebellion, mercy and terrible retribu-
tion, which his mother recited in her low, passionate
voice.

As for the story of Samuel, the prophet, he
knew it by heart ; nor was he ignorant of the vow
which bound him. The Nazarite must abstain from
three things : the fruit of the vine, either fresh or
dried, in old wine and new ; vinegar also, and the

pleasant molasses made of grapes which the children ate upon their bread in the cold days of winter. He must refrain from cutting the hair of his head. He must avoid contact with things dead.

Grapes were undoubtedly beautiful to look upon, and the fragrance of the new wine was sweet as it was borne past on the slow, creaking ox-carts ; but there were also compensations.

"Shall I live in the temple, as did Samuel ?" he asked, after a short period of reflection ; "and will God speak to me in the night-time ?"

Rachel regarded her child in silence. No angel could be more pure and beautiful, she thought, with an exultant swelling at heart. She remembered her vow, the vow of Hannah, the mother of Samuel, a vow made in bitterness of soul and with strong crying in the first days of her desolation : "If thou wilt look upon the affliction of thine handmaid, O Lord of Hosts, and wilt give unto thine handmaid a man-child, then will I give him unto the Lord all the days of his life, and there shall no razor come upon his head."

"My Phannias," she said slowly, "thou shalt indeed dwell in the temple ; and—God will speak to thee."

CHAPTER II.

THE MAKING OF A RABBI.

A S Phannias grew older the thing called The Law waxed increasingly insistent; it entered into every moment of his waking life, filling his ears with a never-ending clamor of "thou shalts" and "thou shalt nots." Thus and so must he wash, eat, drink, stand, sit and walk; thus and so must he pray, think, love and hate. The list of forbidden things and of things unlawful and unholy grew and lengthened day by day till it seemed to the bewildered child that the lawful, the holy, the permitted were quite lost sight of and forgotten.

His mother had long ceased to be his only teacher; the ruler of the synagogue and the ten Batlanin,—or men of leisure who constituted the legal congregation,—beholding a Nazarite for life growing up in their midst fatherless, had early constituted themselves fathers in Israel to guide his young steps in the slow and difficult path of ceremonial holiness. Day by day these zealous teachers riveted to the child's tender soul heavier and yet heavier lengths of that galling chain of rabbinical laws and precepts which the blind centuries had welded to the ten strong links forged on Sinai.

The child dragged his chain patiently. To be holy, to be beloved of God, appeared to him ever more and more desirable, but alas, ever more difficult and remote. He longed for the time when he should go up to the temple in Jerusalem. Once there, he thought, surrounded by all the beauty and the glory of the house of Jehovah, breathing as it were the very air of heaven, it would be both easy and delightful to please God.

In the satisfied eyes of his mother he grew in grace even as he grew in stature. She was both glad and afraid when Ben Huna, the excellent rabbi who taught the village school, told her that her son possessed a brilliant mind and would one day be a great scholar. To be a scholar meant chiefly to know the law as it was laid down in the Bible and in the holy books of the learned, the Talmud and the Mishna. Already the lad had been taught to thank God that he had not been made a woman. He must also learn that "the mind of woman is weak;" that "blessed is he whose children are sons, but woe to him whose children are daughters;" that "as children and slaves so also is woman, devoid of understanding and wisdom." Therefore while Rachel looked forward with joy to the day when her child should sit among the great rabbins at Jerusalem, she knew right well that the first stones were being laid in an impassable wall which should divide them forever.

In secret Phannias hated both the Talmud and

the Mishna, with their endless obscurities, ambigui-
ties, expositions, arguments and illustrations ; the
distracting babel, as it were, of the myriad voices
of half a thousand years. But he found in the
Bible a spring of living water, fresh and delightful,
which comforted him in the arid desert of man-
made wisdom.

Also, and chiefly, because the lad loved his
master, he remained human and sane during this
period of his life. The Rabbi Ben Huna was truly
a wise man. Not only was he possessed of great
learning—a good thing in itself, but of small moment in a world wherein there are only degrees of
ignorance—but beyond and above his knowledge
of the Bible, the Mishna and the Talmud, he was
possessed of a soul of rare gentleness. To Ben
Huna a spirit created of God was the most wonderful thing in all the universe. He bowed himself
before the meanest pupil who sat in his presence,
believing that through each pair of childish eyes
looked forth a sacred intelligence, each differing
from every other with all the infinite variety of omnipotence. He was therefore never angry or impatient
because of apparent dullness or lack of understanding. Nor did he at any time make use of the rod, or
even of the leathern strap, for chastisement; wherein
he differed from the custom laid down by Solomon
and practiced by most instructors of youth.

"God created man in his own image," he was
wont to say ; "moreover, he breathed into the

2

body so created his own spirit; is it meet then to disfigure with stripes the image of the Most High? or to pour contempt upon the breath of God which animates it?"

If, during the hours devoted to mastering the knottier portions of the law, this wise master observed a drooping of some curly head, or caught a sigh of weariness from one of the smaller or duller children, he would straightway propound some curious riddle, or relate a marvelous legend, which effectually opened every languid eye; whereat the lesson would be resumed and carried to a triumphant finish.

"Truly the children are like the tender plants in our gardens," he would say, with a wise shake of his gray head; "there must be more sunshine than cloud, more pleasant warmth than winter cold to bring them to their fruitage."

As for Phannias, he came in time to understand that all created things were under the law; that The Law was, in a word, *El Shaddai*, the Almighty. Ben Huna bade the children observe the mother bird, that throbbing bit of fire and air, fettered to her narrow nest through the long hours and days of incubation. He pointed out to them the eager labors of the bee, the unflagging industry of the ant, the patient unfolding of leaf and stalk of every smallest seed hid in the broad bosom of the fields. He made plain how that in all the realm of nature, from the humblest blossom of earth to the brightest

star of heaven, there was nothing purposeless, nothing idle, nothing lawless.

He also set forth at length that The Law was a
great wall and bulwark, whereby Israel was bless-
edly set apart in the green pastures of the Creator's
love and favor ; dwelling learnedly on the fact that
of the six hundred and thirteen laws of the Mosaic
code, the two hundred and forty-eight "thou shalts "
corresponded wondrously to the two hundred and
forty-eight members of the human body; and that the
number of the negative precepts, the " thou shalt
nots," beautifully equaled the three hundred and sixty-
five days of the solar year. Hence, if on each day
each member of the body should keep one of the af-
firmative precepts, and abstain from one of the things
forbidden, unholy and unclean, the whole law would
be safely accomplished within the circle of the year.

" Surely not a difficult thing for God to require
of us, my children," he would conclude, with a
slow wave of his hand about the listening group.

The good rabbi did not neglect to add that if one
man could for one day perfectly keep the whole
law—not neglecting the smallest jot or tittle—on
that blessed day the Messiah, the anointed of Jehovah, the glorious redeemer of Israel from suffering and bondage, would surely come. Indeed, Ben
Huna began and ended every homily with tales of
this long-awaited Messiah and his kingdom. Some
of these tales were exceeding strange, some beautiful, others marvelous beyond belief.

The children straightened their small shoulders
valiantly, like mighty men of war, when their gentle master told them how the King Messiah would
gird himself with a sword forged of the lightning
and go forth against his enemies, attended by the
conquering hosts of Israel, overthrowing walled
cities and slaying the armies of the foe, with the
chief captains and princes and warriors thereof, till
the garments of the Anointed One were dyed purple, like to the skins of grapes ; while the mountains around Jerusalem poured down rivers of iniquitous Gentile blood.

In the jubilant days of the vintage he related the
old rabbinic legend of how, when Messiah's kingdom should be established upon earth, all trees and
vines would be laden every month the whole year
round, and that with fruit the like of which the
earth had never yet produced. In those days a
single grape would load a wagon or a ship, so that
the wine press and the labor thereof would be no
more required ; men would draw the sparkling new
wine from one of these glorious fruits as from a
cask.

In the time of the barley harvest he repeated
the prophetic words of the sacred poet, David :

"There shall be an handful of corn in the earth upon the
    top of the mountains ;
The fruit thereof shall shake like Lebanon !"

This corn—a single grain of which would be

greater than a man's clenched fist—would not, he
assured them, be reaped with the sickle and beaten
out with the hard labor of the flail, as they now beheld it; for God would send a mighty wind from
his chambers which would blow down the white
flour into the vessels made ready to receive it.

As for Jerusalem, the holy city, the desire of nations, the joy of the whole earth, the chosen of Jé-
hovah, " In the days to come," he declared, " Jerusalem will be the centre of Messiah's kingdom. It
will be so great that its walls will reach even to the
gates of Damascus. Its palaces and dwellings will
be more lofty than high towers, piercing even to the
distant clouds, and shining splendidly by night with
a light beyond the light of the sun. Its gates will
be builded of pearls and of stones exceeding precious; thirty ells long will they be, and as broad.
The mountains, moreover, round about the city will
abound in gold and silver and jewels of price, and
every child of Israel may take of them as he
will."

All of these tales and legends, gleaned from the
writings of the ancients, did the good Ben Huna
relate to his pupils; but best of all he loved to
break forth with the inspired cry of Isaiah : " Look
upon Zion, the city of our solemnities ! Thine eyes
shall see Jerusalem a quiet habitation, a tabernacle
that shall not be taken down ; not one of the stakes
thereof shall be removed, neither shall any of the
cords thereof be broken. But there the glorious

Lord will be unto us a place of broad rivers and streams, whereon shall go no galley with oars, neither shall gallant ship pass thereon. For the Lord is our judge, the Lord is our lawgiver, the Lord is our king ; he will save us.—And the inhabitant shall not say, I am sick. The people that dwell therein shall be forgiven their iniquity !"

Then all the children would be very quiet, their round eyes fixed in reverent silence upon the face of their master. At such times he seemed to them no less than a prophet.

On one of these occasions Phannias, bolder than his fellows, ventured to pluck Ben Huna by the sleeve as he mused with bent head. " Tell me, my master, will the king Messiah come on a sudden from out the heavens, clothed with purple and girt with the lightning ?"

"Not so, my son," said Ben Huna gravely. " How is it that thou hast forgotten the word of the sure prophecy of Jehovah, ' Behold the days come, saith the Lord, that I will raise unto David a righteous branch, and a king shall reign and prosper, and shall execute judgment and justice in the earth.' Also it is written that the prince shall appear in the town of Bethlehem, situate not ten furlongs distant. Hear now the word of the prophet Micah : ' But thou, Bethlehem, though thou be little among the thousands of Judah, yet out of thee shall he come forth unto me that is to be ruler in Israel ; whose goings forth have been from of old, from everlasting.' "

The children, one and all, knew this right well; they had heard it from their cradles, and no less than their elders they thought and talked and dreamed of the wonderful holy prince, whose coming heralded all imaginable delights.

Phannias was silent, but his dark eyes, fixed full upon his master's face, were both eager and questioning. Ben Huna observed this. " Hast thou also another question, my son?" he asked, with a benignant smile.

" I would tell thee one thing," said the boy modestly, " that befell me yesterday."

" Say on, my son."

" At the sixth hour," continued the lad, " it happened that my mother sent me to Jabez, the innkeeper in Bethlehem, to fetch oil which she had bought for our lamps. Jabez bade me rest in the shadow of the khan, and also fetched out to me cakes of fine meal and goat's milk in a wooden bowl."

Ben Huna nodded his head approvingly. He was well pleased at the token of respect shown his favorite pupil,—for whom, in his heart of hearts, he already hoped great things. " The innkeeper is a man of wisdom and discernment," he said, "in that he showeth honor to whom honor will one day be due."

Phannias' dark sensitive face flushed. " He told me a strange story," he said, looking down upon the ground with a troubled air.

The rabbi frowned. " What did he tell thee,

child?" he said quickly, a note of anxiety in his gentle tones.

"Jabez is an old man," said Phannias, thoughtfully; "perchance the mists of age have clouded his understanding. This is the story that he told me. Threescore years ago, when all the world was taxed according to the decree of Cæsar, every man went up to his own city that he might pay his tribute. To the city of Bethlehem also came a multitude of them that were of the house and lineage of David. 'The inn was full,' quoth Jabez; 'and my pouch was swollen with coin. It was a good time and a profitable; indeed, for my part I could not regret the taxing, though not a few of the tribute-payers cried out that it was woe and iniquity; also they cursed the Gentile, Tiberias, and his brood of evil-doers, both loud and deep.

"'Towards evening, when, as I have said, the inn was already filled to overflowing, there came a man from Galilee and besought of me a place to eat and sleep. Thou art welcome, even as my earliest guest, I told him; but what then shall I do? Every stall hath already its beast of burden, and as for the sleeping-places, thou mayest look for thyself and see that there is no room for so much as the sole of a man's foot. At this the stranger was greatly troubled, and said that while for himself he could make shift with his woolen cloak and a pillow of earth, his young wife was ill and must tarry no longer in the chill of the winter night.

"'Come thou in, I cried, and rest, if thou wilt, in the cave yonder where my oxen are feeding; there will be a roof at least betwixt thee and the naked heavens ; I will fetch a bundle of straw for the woman. It was a poor place enough, but the man seemed grateful for it. He brought in the woman, a blue-eyed slip of a thing, tottering for very weariness as her husband lifted her across the threshold.'

"Jabez showed me the place"—and Phannias dropped his voice almost to a whisper—"a stall hollowed out in the hillside !"

"Go on with thy tale," said Ben Huna, sternly ; "I will hear it as he told thee."

Phannias fixed his great black eyes on his master's face with manifest amazement. "I have told thee the tale even as he told me, my master," he said. Then he went on slowly, as if careful to remember every smallest word. "The innkeeper tarried before the gate that he might guard those within, but about the fifth hour of the night he laid himself down upon a truss of straw and, being very weary, soon fell sound asleep. How long he slept he knew not, but he was suddenly awakened by a sound of loud knocking at the door, and voices calling to him to open.

"At first he would not, saying that the inn was full and the door fast, according to the law. But looking out from the postern and seeing, among them that tarried before the gate, certain honest shepherds of his acquaintance, he opened.

"'Peace be unto thee, thou son of Abraham, and peace be to this house!' cried the chief shepherd; and by the light of the torch which he carried the innkeeper saw that the man trembled like one who was afraid, yet his face shone with a strange joy. 'Show us the holy babe, I beseech thee, that we may worship him; for verily He is come that was promised!'

"Whereat the innkeeper was astonished. 'There is no babe,' he said; 'Jehovah help thee, man, thou art distracted with wine!'

"But they insisted, saying that as they watched their flocks on the hillside, a great light shone about them, and in the midst of the light appeared a mighty angel, who declared to them that the Christ was born."

Ben Huna laid an authoritative hand on the child's shoulder. He perceived that the youthful Nazarite was trembling with excitement. "I will finish the tale, my son," he said gravely. "The son of Eliphaz hath strangely forgotten the wisdom which his years should have taught him, else he would not have told thee this thing. The time is not yet for teaching thee the false, the evil, the accursed. Woe is me, that one so guiltless must needs learn aught of the guilty! But know this much, that while Israel hath waited patiently for her Deliverer through the slow ages, many false prophets have appeared—yea, and shall appear till the promised day of blessing.

" The babe which was born in the khan yonder
grew to be a man, dwelling quietly enough in the
Galilean village of Nazareth, where both he and
his father followed the honest trade of carpenter.
During these years it is said of him that he observed
the law and dwelt blameless among his fellows.
Then on a sudden a mad hermit arose out of the
desert, one John, called also of the people the
Baptist, because he would have no other followers
save those who consented to be plunged by him
into some stream or river—a thing not enjoined by
the law of Moses. This man proclaimed himself
the prophet of the Messiah ; much people followed
him, and there was a great stir of the excitable
rabble through all the land. In the midst of the
tumult the carpenter, Jesus Ben Joseph—who also
was of near kin to the Baptist—laid down his tools,
and, taking to himself certain ignorant and unlearned fishermen of Galilee, began to go about
the provinces, haranguing the people and cunningly
working pretended marvels among the superstitious
folk of the country-side.

" At the first the learned paid little heed to either
the sayings or doings of the Galilean, but when it
came to the ears of the council at Jerusalem that
he taught the people to despise the customs, declar-
ing that he had come to fulfill the law and the
prophets, it seemed wise to look to the matter. I
was a young man in those days and tarried in the
schools of the rabbis at Jerusalem." Ben Huna

paused abruptly and arose to his feet. " The hour
grows late," he said. " Go your ways, my lambs,
lest your parents chide me for a careless shepherd."

In truth, the good rabbi was not minded to relate the undeniably strange facts in this history
of the man of Galilee to these wide-eyed listeners
of his, without time for due thought and reflection. He knew also that there would be questions
to answer.

" The words of a teacher," he said within himself,
" are like the seed which a man casts into his field ;
they must be sifted with jealous care lest a hidden
germ of evil be mingled therewith to bear fruit unto
destruction. To-morrow I will tell them what
befell the carpenter who called himself the Son of
Jehovah."

The children, many of whom had already heard
the story, ran joyfully away to their play. But
Phannias, walking slowly homeward, thought of
the dark manger which he had seen in the ancient
khan, and of how the gloomy place shone with
unearthly brightness in that black midnight sixty
years ago. He wandered dreamily to the verge
of the hill on which the village stood and looked
down into the storied valley beneath. There were
shepherds yonder, watching the flocks which wandered on the hither side of the stream. Beyond
the smooth green slopes stood the hoary pile of
the *Migdol Eder,* the watch-tower, all unchanged
since the mysterious night when angels burst the

starry walls of heaven to herald the coming of the babe of Bethlehem.

As he gazed, Phannias was seized with a strong desire to learn more of the strange story. Why might he not find the very shepherds who had seen the vision! Without stopping to consider that the sun was already dropping behind the western horizon, the child ran swiftly down the rugged path which led to the valley.

CHAPTER III.

THE SHEPHERD'S STORY.

THE shepherds lay wrapped in their warm abbas watching the flocks as they cropped the green pastures beneath the shelter of the hill. It was the time of year when the sheep were suffered to feed by night as well as by day, that they might be sleek and well-nourished by Passover time. For these flocks of Bethlehem were sacred to the service of the great temple at Jerusalem, and every spotless lamb which frolicked joyously at its mother's side in the soft spring grass was destined to pour out its innocent life into the golden bowl of sacrifice.

The men had eaten their frugal supper of bread and olives, and had cast lots for the night-watches, a duty which in these troublous times was not without its positive perils to shepherds as well as to flocks. The chief shepherd, one Enoch, a stout, middle-aged man, was speaking; he had a long tale to tell of the day's doings in Jerusalem.

"The High Priest, Ananus," this worthy was saying, with an air of relish, " hath burned his holy fingers in the Roman torch. Nothing pleases the

multitude better than blood, as his sacred highness
knows right well, and the multitude was clamorous
and must needs be appeased. There being no
procurator in Jerusalem since the death of our excellent Festus, there was no one to say him nay
when he laid hold on three of the chief men of the
Nazarenes. Look you," he continued, frowning
and raising his voice excitedly, as he perceived significant glances pass betwixt the men. "I am no
believer in the false Messiah, as ye well know, but
one of them, the man James, called also the Just,
is not unknown to me, and I say that the condem-
nation was unlawful. He is a Nazarite—for more
than fifty years, and a righteous, law-abiding man,
save for his one folly in confessing the crucified
carpenter. He was condemned to be stoned because, forsooth, he perverted the multitude ; am I
not of the multitude, and did he pervert me ?"

One of the under-shepherds whispered something
to his neighbor with a sly chuckle, whereat Enoch
pounded irritably upon the ground with his staff.
" Hold thy peace, fellow, till I have had my say.
The Nazarenes were condemned, and the temple
guard dragged them off to the place of death. I
myself saw them as they were haled through the
streets after their sentence, a great multitude following, some wailing and beating upon their breasts,
others crying out curses upon the crucified Galilean
and his followers. Into the midst of the tumult
rode a detachment of the Roman guard bearing a

command from the newly-appointed procurator,
Albinus, to release the prisoners at once. The cunning Nazarenes had sent a fleet messenger to meet
the Roman as he journeyed toward Jerusalem."

"Holy fire! so the rascals escaped after all!"
cried out one of the listening shepherds.

"They were loosed from their bonds," said his
chief grimly; "what befell them afterward at the
hands of the multitude I know not. It was said
that Ananus would be at once degraded from his
office as a punishment for his part in the infringement of Roman law."

"That were small wonder," commented one of
the group, shrugging his shoulders, "and welcome
news to our worshipful Agrippa, who makes high
priests that he may also have the pleasure of un-
making them."

"Sedition! Sedition!" shouted another, beating his horny palms together. "The air is full of
it; the very sheep yonder will shortly refuse
their fodder and cry out for the fruit of the vine!"

"Ay, comrade, it is well spoken," said an aged
man who had been listening quietly, shaking his
head from time to time with the grave and sorrowful air of a man who listens to a tale of long-expected disaster. "Ay, the times are ripe for marvels; and who should know it better than I, who
have already seen prodigies past the telling? Strange
things have come to pass in yonder guilty city—
strange things and terrible; and stranger things

and things yet more terrible are to come. Ye shall
see them, but perchance I shall be spared, for the
tale of my days is nearly told. Hear ye, one and
all, the man of Nazareth was of the house and lineage of David! He was born in the khan yonder,
beneath a star—a blazing star! *I* saw it! *I*—in
the flesh, I saw it!"

The trembling tones of the old man's voice rose
to a shrill cry. He flung his arms high above his
head with a gesture of unutterable longing. The
shepherds looked at one another with meaning
smiles.

"The dotard will rave of the star, the babe and
the angels till dawn," muttered one of the younger
men, sneering openly. "I, for one, will not hear
it." With that he arose, and flinging his abba
across his shoulders strode away toward the watch-
tower.

One by one the other shepherds followed his example till the old man was left alone with his mem-
ories beside the dying fire. He did not seem to
notice that his comrades had left him, but sat motionless, staring into the luminous dusk of the early
twilight. Suddenly his dim eyes brightened; he
rose trembling to his feet and stood with bowed
head, awaiting the approach of a figure, clad all in
white, which came swiftly toward him down the
steep hillside. To the worn vision of the aged
shepherd the beautiful child-figure, with its light
fluttering garments, seemed no other than an angel,

floating adown the steeps of heaven to console him
in his grief and loneliness.

As for Phannias—for it was Phannias who ran
lightly down the rugged path—no sooner did his
eyes light on the bowed figure of the shepherd than
he knew with a child's beautiful prescience that he
had found what he sought.

"Wilt thou tell me, good sir," he cried in his
clear sweet voice, "of the visit of the angels, and
of the child—the little child—Jesus, in the manger
of the khan?"

"Blessed be Jehovah! Praised be his holy
name!" murmured the shepherd, folding his withered hands. "Men will neither heed nor believe
me; but, lo! thou hast sent an angel to hear my
witness before I go hence!"

Phannias regarded the old man with awe, his
large serious eyes shining with eager joy. He but
half comprehended his words. "Didst thou indeed
see him?" he asked wistfully, "and wilt thou tell
me how it all befell? I have already seen the dark
manger; the keeper of the inn told me that the
light from the star above streamed through the
earthen roof."

"It did!—it did!" cried the shepherd, tears of
pure joy coursing down his withered cheeks. "The
star and the light from the wings of unseen angels
filled the place with the radiance and warmth of
heaven. Ah, the glory of it all! What joy beyond the telling for mortal eyes and ears and

tongues, and what blackness of despair and grief in the sad years to come. I will not tell thee of that, but only the beautiful beginning of it all.

"Look you, child of the Highest, we guarded the flocks in this very place threescore years ago, a goodly company, devout and prayerful, looking for the fulfillment of the promise. I was but a lad —no higher than my staff here. As we kept the midnight watch, making mention of the Lord's anointed, as was our wont, on a sudden there was a light,—a great light, and in the midst of it there appeared the figure of a man, clad in shining raiment. And when we were all fallen on our faces to the earth,—being sore afraid because of the vision, the angel spake graciously to us.

"'Fear not!' he said, 'for behold, I bring you good tidings of great joy which shall be to all people. For unto you is born this day, in the city of David, a Saviour, which is Christ the Lord. And this shall be a sign unto you : ye shall find the babe wrapped in swaddling-clothes, lying in a manger.'

"When the angel had said this there was a sound, sweet and awful, as of mighty silver trumpets, and with the trumpets the voices of a great multitude of them that sang gloriously. Yet was the multitude as one voice crying,

"'Glory to God in the highest !
On earth peace,—good-will to men !'

"I heard it ! *I*—in the flesh—*I* heard it ! Also

I beheld with these mortal eyes the host of the blessed—rank upon rank of shining ones; some floating just above the ground, their dazzling garments shedding a silver light over all the valley and the stream and the flocks, so that one could see the tiniest lamb nestling by its mother's side; while beyond and above the earth, shining rank upon shining rank, wing folded to wing, the singing angels filled the heavens, a cloud of glory! *I* saw it! I—in the flesh! And I live to bear witness that it is true!" The shepherd turned his face toward the stars, stretching out his arms with a long, quivering sigh.

Phannias regarded him with a pure delight not unmixed with fear. After a time he ventured to lay his hand on the old man's sleeve. " And afterward, good shepherd," he urged timidly—" what happened afterward?"

The shepherd dropped his arms and fixed his dim eyes upon the child. " Who and what art thou?" he said faintly. " Art one of them—or do I but dream of the angels? For the shining ones went away again into heaven, one and all,—ay, they went away. And though I have longed and prayed during all these weary years for but a whisper of the celestial voices the door is fast shut. And the babe? Ah, dear God, it was peace, goodwill that he brought to men, but men would none of it; and few believed our witness of the things which had come to pass. ' There was no angel,' they said, and laughed us to scorn. 'As for the babe, he is but the son of a carpenter.'

"Alas, alas, for babe and mother! Alas, for the tree of blood—the accursed tree! But hark you, child, and remember what I shall say to thee is God's own truth. The babe of Bethlehem was the Messiah of Israel, the Anointed of Jehovah; and of yonder guilty city, Jerusalem, will God require his blood! Ay, the avenging sword of Jehovah of Hosts hangs above it like a devouring flame! I saw the Prince of Heaven wrapped in swaddling-clothes and lying in the manger, even as the angel declared unto us. *I*—I in the flesh! And I bear witness that it is true—true—all true!"

"What, raving yet, dotard?" cried a harsh voice. "Come, have done with thy senile madness and drive up the flock from beyond the stream. Sacred fire! but thou hast frightened the ewes from their pasture! Who is this?" And the owner of the voice, a big burly shepherd, turned suddenly upon Phannias.

"I pray thee to leave the little one in peace," besought the old shepherd earnestly, laying a protecting hand on the child's head. "Jehovah hath sent him that he might hear my true witness of the things that have happened in this place. He will also witness to the truth, as I have told it to him, when I shall go hence."

"Jehovah smite me," roared the other, "but I hope that will be soon! Get thee about thy business, dotard !" With that he raised his thick oaken staff and shook it threateningly in the old man's face.

The aged shepherd staggered back as though he had received a mortal wound, and with a low gasping cry fell to the ground.

" I did not strike him—I swear I did not strike him !" cried the other, aghast at the effect of his brutal words. " Thou knowest, boy, that I did but remind the laggard of his duty !"

But Phannias neither heard nor heeded. He was bending over the fallen shepherd. " Water— quick !" he cried in an agony, for even to his childish eyes the look on the gray, worn face was not to be mistaken.

The old man's eyes opened ; they were full and bright, like the eyes of youth. " The angels !" he cried once in a loud, exultant voice—and was silent.

An hour later Rachel and Ben Huna found the child ; he was sitting flat upon the ground, holding the shepherd's head upon his knees, his face not less white than the peaceful face of the dead. He looked up at them with a radiant smile. " He saw the angels," he whispered. " It is true—true—all true !"

CHAPTER IV.

THE CHILD AND THE LAW.

PHANNIAS opened his eyes the next morning with the earliest twitter of half-awakened birds, to find the dawn flooding the white walls of his chamber with rosy light, while the blossoming boughs of the great almond tree just outside his window stirred fragrantly in the fresh breeze. The child had slept dreamlessly, and his soul unfolded like a flower to greet the rising sun. Springing from his bed he lifted his face to the glowing heavens, repeating softly the beautiful prayer to the Creator of light with which every devout Israelite was wont to greet the new day :

" Blessed art thou, O Lord, our God, King of the universe !
Who createst light and formest darkness !
In mercy thou causest the light to shine upon the earth
and the inhabitants thereof,
And in goodness renewest every day the work of creation !
Blessed art thou, Creator of light !"

The world was so beautiful, thought the child, in a rapture of gratitude. He remembered, with a sudden bounding of the heart, the strange story of the shepherd.

" It is true !" he said joyfully. " He saw the

angels ; and last night they took him, because he
was poor and old and lonely."

Full of these thoughts and eager to know more
of the wonderful babe, angel-heralded, yet so meanly
cradled in the ruinous old inn, the child flew to the
door of his chamber. He was met at the threshold
by his mother, pallid, sad, her eyes swollen as if
from sleeplessness and prolonged weeping.

" Mother !" he cried aghast, " mother !" and
would have thrown his arms about her neck, but
she repulsed him gently.

" Thou must remain within thy chamber, my
son," she said gravely, " till the hour is come for
thy departure for Jerusalem."

" But why——"

" I cannot talk with thee ; it is forbidden. Thou
hast touched the unholy dead, and art thyself unholy and polluted. Alas, thou hast broken thy
vow ! Abase thyself before an angry Jehovah, for
thou hast grievously trespassed against his holy
law."

An hour later, lying prone upon the earthen
floor of his chamber, crushed beneath a load of
misery, immense, heart-breaking, intolerable, Phannias became dimly aware of a clamor of voices
without."

" Woe, woe !" wailed the voices. " Heaviness
is come upon this house, and mourning doth cover it
like a garment ! For the law—the law of Jehovah
is broken ; his statutes are defiled and trodden under

foot. Verily, we had hoped for a blessing because
of this child! We had expected great things of
Jehovah because of the undefiled! But now is his
body polluted; his vow also hath he despised and
set at naught. Woe! Woe!"

Phannias held his sobbing breath to listen. He
had heard sounds like this but once before in his
short life; that was when the son of their neighbor
had died of a fever, and the mourners had bewailed
him during thrice seven days. He covered his ears
with his hands to shut out the gruesome clamor,
only to hear his mother's parting words: "Thou
hast touched the unholy dead, and art thyself unholy and polluted."

He sprang to his feet in a sudden frenzy of grief,
and laying hold of his linen tunic tore it in an instant from top to bottom. This rending of one's
garments, he had been told, was a peculiarly pious
act, well pleasing to God; it signally displayed
one's contempt for self, and a holy indifference to
bodily comfort which could not fail to gratify the
always observant deity. That it furnished a certain
relief to overcharged feelings the child straightway
discovered, and tore again and again at his clothing
till it hung in ribbons about his body.

Somewhat calmed by this religious rite, he presently ventured to peep out through the lattice, and
was overwhelmed afresh with poignant humiliation
to behold the ten Batlanin and the ruler of the
synagogue, in company with certain pious women

of the village, all beating dolorously upon their breasts, and casting the earth of his mother's garden upon their uncovered heads; the chanting going on meanwhile with undiminished vigor.

"They would not do this thing for Jacob, the potter's son," muttered Phannias, shaken with unreasoning anger; "as for David, the herdsman's son, he may do what he will and there is no one of them all to cry in his ears, 'The Law,—The Law;' I would that I were a boy, and not a Nazarite."

Smitten with instant remorse, he fell to repeating the psalms and prayers of the synagogue service with zeal and energy, resolutely closing his ears to the dismal noises without; this took a long time. Later he discovered that he was hungry. As the slow hours of the morning dragged out their weary tale of minutes, the child concluded that his mother had forgotten him, and this thought was so terrible that he fell to weeping again.

Rachel had not forgotten her disgraced child. His painful sobbing pierced her tender soul. She longed to carry the burden of his sin on her own strong shoulders, to comfort him in her warm arms, to fetch him food and drink, lovingly prepared by her own hands; and all this she would have been swift to do, had she been left to follow the instincts of her heart. But in vowing her child to the service of God she now discovered that she had bound him to the altar of sacrifice, while Israel, stern priest of Jehovah, already stretched forth an authoritative hand toward the victim.

Before dawn the ruler of the synagogue and the Batlanin, together with certain rigid and unbending "mothers in Israel," had gathered at the widow's house to bewail with her, and to counsel, direct and restrain her in this the sad hour of her affliction. They decided in solemn conclave that the disgraced Nazarite must fast from sunrise to sunset during thrée days; and, further, that he must be left in absolute solitude until the day of his separation, when Ben Huna should take him up to Jerusalem to receive the prescribed cleansings with the bitter waters of purification. The conduct of the remaining ceremonials necessary to restore him to the holy state of the Nazarite, from which he had so grievously fallen away, they left to the care of the learned rabbi.

The good Ben Huna was profoundly disturbed by the grave misfortune which had befallen his favorite. He was, indeed, disposed to take upon himself the reproach of the whole matter. "It is I who have erred," he said, "and in no small measure; I should have told the lad the whole story of the false Messiah. Alas, that angelic innocence must learn the dark ways of earth!"—and he shook his gray head mournfully. "I had the intent to explain the matter in good time; but in truth I wished first to consider in mine own heart how best to reveal to him that certain, even from the blessed

fold of Israel, have gone astray after the man. For
all of these things must the boy learn, that he may
also teach others to distinguish betwixt the true and
the false."

The ruler of the synagogue frowned and plucked
angrily at his beard. "It was a dark day for Bethlehem yonder—ay, and for Jerusalem, and for all
Israel—when the Galilean carpenter came thither
with his wife," he said in a loud voice. "Verily,
I have it on good authority that there be many in
the town below who do secretly believe the idle
tale bruited abroad by the shepherds, and that
despite the accursed end of the Nazarene !"

"It was a strange story, neighbor, say what you
will," ventured one of the Batlanin, pursing up his
mouth. "I have heard my father declare that the
man, Joseph, and his wife tarried in the khan during twoscore days after the birth of the child.
There was no end to the wonderful sayings noised
abroad concerning the child and his mother. I
remember me well how that——"

"'T were best forgotten, son of Abraham," interrupted the ruler of the synagogue, with an authoritative wave of the hand ; "—ay, best forgotten.
Let us the rather remember that Jehovah brought
confusion upon the Nazarene and upon multitudes
of his deluded followers. Yea, even Nero, the sinful ruler of the Gentiles, hath of late become a
scourge in the hands of an offended God to utterly
destroy them that confess the accursed name in

Rome.   It were well also to remember that this is
a house of mourning because of the false prophet."

It was decided that Jabez, the aged keeper of
the inn at Bethlehem, should be visited and sternly
admonished against a repetition of his offence.   He
had been more than once forbidden to recount the
story of the birth in the manger, it having been long
since decided by the sapient authorities in Jerusalem
that legends and stories relating to the life and sayings of the malefactor, Jesus, were blasphemous,
and therefore unlawful.

Toward evening these excellent neighbors left
Rachel alone in her house.   With trembling hands
she made haste to prepare the poor food she was
allowed to offer her child, shutting her eyes to the
fact that the sun was yet an hour above the western
horizon.

"He is but a babe," she whispered to herself;
"and, after all, it was I who made the vow when the
poor child knew nothing of it.   Jehovah impute
the sin to me.   An infringement more or less can
make little difference to any one of us who has
grown old under the law."

Treading softly lest she disturb the meditations
of "the separated," she approached the door of his
chamber.   Phannias was curled up in the window-
seat, his face pressed close against the lattice.   Something in his attitude reminded the mother painfully
of an imprisoned bird clinging to the bars of its
cage.   She hastily set down the loaf and the pitcher

of water and was about to. withdraw noiselessly
when the child turned his head.

"Mother," he said softly, fixing his great eyes
upon her face, "where is the Messiah? I wish to
go to him; I wish to tell him just how it all happened; I know that he will not be angry with me.
The shepherd had seen the Prince, thou knowest;
he told me how the angels came down from heaven
and sang—thousands upon thousands of them!
And one angel, brighter than them all, declared
that the Messiah had come, and that they would
find him wrapped in swaddling-clothes and lying in
a manger. And, oh mother, they did find him! I
have seen the very spot where he lay in the khan
yonder—so cold and dark a place, with the manger
cut from the rock of the hillside! The shepherd
was old and lonely, dearest mother; I think the
angels took him away with them. If I should tell
this to the Prince, surely he would forgive——"

Rachel raised her hand imperatively, the while
she sternly repressed a desire to take the child in
her arms and cover his beautiful serious face with
kisses. Never had he seemed more holy, never
more angelically pure, than at this moment, when
the law declared him unclean, unholy, polluted.
What if the law was wrong? She thrust the
thought from her with instant self-reproach.

"My son," she said sorrowfully, "I cannot talk
with thee now of this matter; but thinkest thou if
Messiah had come we would have kept thee in ig-

norance of it these ten years of thy life? To-morrow the good rabbi, thy master, will take thee to Jerusalem, there to be cleansed of thy grievous pollution; and where haply thou mayest be permitted to renew thy vows before the merciful God of Israel. Ben Huna will tell thee all that is best for thee to know of the man called Jesus of Nazareth, who unhappily saw the light in yonder city of David. Think no more of the wild tale of the shepherd, but dwell only on thy guilt, that thou mayest purge thy soul before God, to the end that he graciously restore thee to his favor."

"But why may I not already be forgiven, my mother?" asked the child, laying a caressing little hand upon her robe; "I have repeated the Sabbath psalms thrice over, the commandments also and the benedictions, the Hallel, and——"

"Alas, my son!" cried the mother in poignant distress, "he who lifts polluted hands to Jehovah hath committed a deadly sin!—But the sin is mine, since I did not warn thee," she made haste to add, seeing the deadly pallor that stole over her child's face. "Look, I will fetch sackcloth straightway and ashes, that thou mayest abase thyself. I also will lie in sackcloth, and cry unto God all the night for thee and me."

An hour later, when Rachel crept quietly to the chamber of her son, bearing the symbols of woe, she found him quietly asleep upon his bed. Tears hung on his long lashes, but he smiled as he slept.

She could not know that the black mists of the day's sordid sorrow had lifted, and anon became radiant with angelic figures, mingling and inter-mingling in cloudy glory, shining rank upon shin-ing rank, wing folded to wing ; while sweet and far the melodious thunder of trumpets preluded the triumphant chorus of " Peace on earth ! Good-will to men !"

Half-ashamed—though why she knew not—the woman spread the rough sackcloth over the round limbs of the sleeper, and strewed the ashes, sad symbols of sin and impurity, on the fair young head. But in his dreams the angels sang on.

CHAPTER V.

AT THE FOUNTAIN.

D URING the short journey from Bethlehem to
the holy city it seemed to Phannias that
Ben Huna, his kind, affectionate master, had under-
gone a terrible transformation ; that he had become,
in effect, The Law itself—stern, pitiless, unloving.
The child hung his head as he walked apart, slow
tears of misery forcing their way from beneath his
swollen eyelids. He understood in the fulness of
its bitterness what it meant to be "separated." The
days spent in his little chamber had been long and
lonely, but he now wished that he might have remained there forever.

As the two, walking slowly as befitted so solemn
an occasion, passed through the village streets,
curious eyes stared at them from doors and
windows ; wayfarers drew aside with ostentatious
care to give them room ; while Jacob, the potter's
son, busy gathering sticks for his mother's fire,
paused in his occupation long enough to cry out
derisively :

"Ah-i, Nazarite ! Who now is so much holier
and wiser than others ? Thou art unclean as yonder
dog—ah-i !"

Phannias' eyes flashed and his brown fists
clenched themselves. " Raca !" he muttered ;
" what knows he of the law !"

As for Ben Huna, he lifted his staff threateningly,
vowing in his heart of hearts that upon his return
not only the strap but also the rod should be visited
upon the son of the potter, and that to the limit of
the law. The worthy rabbi was secretly overflowing with compassion for his charge, but he considered that the abundant nature of the child needed
pruning, and what better instrument for the purpose
than the sharp blade of the law ? He resolved
therefore to omit no smallest detail in the impres-
sive ceremonial of legal purification, and to vigor-
ously enforce the last requirement of the Mosaic
Code and the Talmud. For the time being he resolutely forced down both his sympathies and his
affections behind the strong wall of rabbinical pre-
cept and tradition.

He briefly explained to his pupil, in cold, measured tones, that inasmuch as he had been polluted
with the foul and terrible uncleanness of death—
which was in truth the last appalling consequence
of sin, and therefore doubly abhorrent to the pure
and deathless Jehovah—he must walk, eat and
sleep, solitary and alone, during the seven days of
his separation. He added that when the days were
accomplished he would relate to him the history of
the false Messiah—a story which it was painful to
recall, but which was assuredly instructive, since it

furnished undeniable proof of Jehovah's abiding wrath upon them that trespassed against the laws of Moses.

To all of which Phannias listened in meek silence.

When at midday the pair approached Jerusalem, despite his present misery and his vague apprehensions for the future, the child's eyes brightened as they rested upon the magnificent city, lying white and beautiful as a holy dream in the arms of its green, encircling hills.

Ben Huna straightened himself exultantly. "Awake, awake!" he cried aloud; "put on thy strength, O Zion! Put on thy beautiful garments, O Jerusalem, the holy city; for henceforth there shall no more come into thee the uncircumcised and the unclean. Shake thyself from the dust and arise, O Jerusalem! Loose thyself from the bands of thy neck, O captive daughter of Zion!"

The head of Phannias sank upon his breast. It seemed to him that the distant temple gleamed coldly from awful, unattainable heights of holiness, steep as high heaven. He buried his face in his hands, feeling to the least atom of his small, wretched body that he was unworthy even to look upon "the city of solemnities."

Ben Huna's eyes dwelt proudly upon the bowed head. "He understands," he thought, "as no other child of them all could understand;"—and reflected, not without satisfaction, on the hour when

he should bring the beautiful boy into the temple
before the eyes of the great rabbins and doctors of
the law.

"Remain here, my child," he said, insensibly re-
lapsing into his tone of affectionate comradeship;
"I will go into the city and fetch the water of separation, that thou mayest receive the first sprinkling
at my hands. While I am absent thou mayest eat
bread, and drink from the spring yonder."

Phannias had no wish to eat, but the cool ripple
of the fountain drew him to its brink. It was a
quiet spot, quiet and green and cool. After a time
the child ventured to dip his burning forehead into
the sparkling water, which welled up, clear as air,
in its worn limestone basin, to slip away to the valley amid a lush tangle of grass and brilliant flowers.
Overhead, in the rosy thicket of wild almond and
pomegranate, a bird called aloud. A butterfly,
fanning lazily by, dropped softly to his motionless
brown hand and rested there for an instant, its jeweled wings waving slowly in the warm sunshine.
Phannias sighed, a long sigh of relief and happiness;
for the moment the cold, inexorable face of The
Law withdrew itself behind a veil of love and beauty.

A woman, ascending with her water-jar from the
village below the spring, stopped short on beholding the gleam of white drapery between the green
leaves. She leaned forward, noiselessly parting the
branches, that she might obtain a better view of the
wayfarer.

"A child!" she said to herself, with a smile at her caution, and came briskly forward.

Phannias lifted his eyes at her approach. "Peace be with thee," he said simply; then bethinking himself, he drew back. "I—I am unclean!" he stammered.

The woman stared aghast. "Surely not a leper?" she cried.

Phannias shook his head. "I have broken the law," he said mournfully. "I am a Nazarite. I have touched the dead."

The woman lifted her eyes in pity and amaze. "Dear Lord, who also died and art alive again," she murmured, as if to some unseen bystander, "surely the child is clean in thy sight!—Where dost thou dwell, little one?" she asked, setting down her pitcher and advancing to the rim of the fountain; "and how camest thou to break thy vow?"

The voice of the questioner was low and sweet. Phannias, regarding her with shy curiosity, observed that when she smiled her eyes shone with a gentle radiance pleasant to behold. Insensibly he drew nearer, that he might warm his chilled heart in the genial glow.

"It was the shepherd who died," he said, half under his breath. "He told me a strange story of angels who came to the earth to sing of peace and good-will—a long time ago. There was a babe born in the khan at Bethlehem. I saw the place where it lay, wrapped in swaddling-clothes."

He stopped short to look at the woman ; she had uttered some inarticulate sound, which he took to be an expression of anger or reproof. " Yes, I know that thou wilt say it is not true," he said quickly. "No one believes it, the shepherd him-self said so. It was that, I think, that made him sick and sad—yes, and killed him at the last like a blow."

" But I do believe it !" cried the woman, her face shining with so wonderful a light that Phannias stared at her in silent astonishment. " It is all quite true !" After a little time she turned her deep eyes full upon the child. " Did the shepherd tell thee the name of the babe who lay in the manger ?" she asked, smiling into his serious face.

" He said," whispered Phannias, "that the babe was the Messiah !"

" Ay, verily ! and who should know this better than he to whom the angel of the Lord declared it face to face. And did he tell thee what happened afterward ?"

The child's sensitive face quivered. " The shep-herd died," he said, looking away toward Jerusa-lem; " I could not ask him more. But Ben Huna, the wise rabbi, who also is my master, said that the babe grew to be a man—a carpenter, in the village of Nazareth ; and that he kept the law until one John, a wild hermit out of the desert, aroused the people with strange ravings of a coming Messiah. In those days the carpenter, whose name was Jesus, also arose and went about among the people, working pretended marvels and teaching unlawful things. I—I do not yet know what became of him; my master will—will tell me afterward," he faltered, shrinking back before the sudden fire of wrath that leapt up in the eyes of the woman.

"I am not angry with thee, child," she said passionately, "but only with the wise rabbi, as thou callest him, who hath told thee the half-truth, more accursed than a lie, which withers in the telling. Look at me, child, and listen well!—He would have loved such an one as thou; and thou—ah, if thou couldst but see him! I knew this Jesus when he lived upon earth, and I declare unto thee God's truth concerning him, as did also the shepherd in his last hour upon earth. He was verily the Promised of Israel, royal Prince of David, born in David's city, according to the ancient promise.

" It is true that he lived in Nazareth and labored with his hands, meek, obedient to the law as thou thyself; but when his time was come he received baptism from the hands of John and from on high. Afterward he went about among the poor, the sick, the afflicted, proclaiming the love and mercy of the Father; healing the lame, the blind, the leprous, with word or touch, and even raising them that were dead to life again. Yes, it is true! And I speak not of things which I have heard only, but of things which I have seen—ay, seen and touched and handled. I am Mary, of Bethany—in the

wooded hollow yonder. Jesus of Nazareth was
our friend—our own familiar friend ; he tarried with
us often." She paused, smiling dreamily, as one
whom the impetuous current of her thought had
carried far away into some sweet day of the past.

"Our own familiar friend—our dear, familiar
friend," she repeated the words softly, caressingly ;
then sighed and smiled, and sighed again. "My
brother, Lazarus, fell ill," she said, her deep eyes
bent upon the gurgling water. "We sent for our
friend, Jesus, once,—twice,—thrice ; but he tarried.
I could not understand ; I knew that he loved my
brother—that he loved us all. Lazarus died at
dawn of the third day. My sister and I watched
beside his body. ' He will come at noon,' I said.
But the sun looked down from mid-heaven, and there
was neither word nor sign. ' He will surely come
before evening !' wailed my sister. But he came not.

"At sunset we buried our dead. They rolled
the stone before the door of the tomb. All was
now ended—finished. He had not come. Others
of our friends and acquaintance gathered about us ;
the mourning went on drearily through the long
hours. He did not come. Four long, black days,
and still he did not come. My heart grew sick in
my bosom and, at the last, lay cold and heavy as
the dead, bound in his grave-clothes. When one
told us, ' Behold the Master is at hand,' I could
not rise to meet him. ' Nay, he loved us not,' I
said ; ' I will not look upon his face.'

"My sister, Martha, stronger or more faithful than I, went out to meet him. Anon she returned, her face aglow. 'The Master is come,' she whispered urgently; 'he calleth for thee.'

"At that word my sick heart leapt in my bosom. I rose up and slipped away with all haste. I saw him! Ah, he knew all; he loved us! Yet I fell down at his feet straightway and cried out the bitter thought that had devoured my soul in secret, during the long hours of watching and weeping: 'Lord, if thou hadst been here my brother had not died!'

"I reproached him to his face—the Lord of glory! Blinded with bitter tears I could no longer see him, but I knew that he was weeping, that he asked, 'Where have ye laid him?'

"Some one—my sister, I think—raised me to my feet. 'What need,' I whispered, 'to look upon his tomb!' Others also of our friends who followed us said openly, 'Could not He which opened the eyes of the blind have caused that even this man should not have died?'"

The low passionate voice trembled into silence; the dark eyes were fixed upon a green hillside which rose from the wooded hollow near the village.

Phannias' gaze followed; he perceived that the sunny slope, niched with gray, rough-hewn slabs, was no other than the place of tombs—a place of dread, they had taught him, death-polluted, demon-haunted, to be feared and shunned above all other plague-spots of the evil earth. He stared curiously

at the woman. She was not weeping; she seemed
not even sad; the wide eyes brimmed over with
the strange radiance which he had observed upon
her face as she spoke of the shepherds. It was
assuredly a strange world—the child decided—
wherein they wept who should laugh, and rejoiced
who should the rather lament. He sighed deeply.

"An over sad tale for young ears, sayst thou,
little one?" Phannias looked up; the woman was
regarding him steadily. The strange lovely light
had spread over all her face now, so that it glowed
like a rich landscape beneath the summer sun.
"Yet not sad, as thou shalt hear, but most beautiful, most wonderful, most happy. So it seems to
me as I tell it—and I have told it many times since
then.

"Thou seest the hillside yonder—the place of
tombs; and thou art not ignorant concerning them
that enter, pale and silent, into the black door of
the sepulcher, how that they come forth no more
into the light? Yet I say to thee with all verity
that I have seen the grave give up its dead. The
babe of Bethlehem's manger, grown to manhood,—
the Friend of sinners,—the Prince of Israel stood in
yonder place of tombs. Look, child, there is an
empty sepulcher, midway on the hill, beneath the
shadow of the tamarisk. It was to that tomb,
closed, silent, foul with the damps of corruption,
that we came that day, hopeless and heavy-hearted.

"'Take ye away the stone!' He commanded.

" My sister laid her hand upon his arm. ' It is already four days,' she whispered.

" He turned to her. ' Did I not tell thee that if thou wouldst believe, thou shouldst see the glory of God ?'

" Then certain of the men who had followed us, in obedience to her signal, rolled away the stone. A great stillness fell upon us all ; within the black hollow we could see the dead, lying white and rigid in his narrow prison. The breath of the grave, heavy with spicery, stole out chill and damp into the quiet sunshine, like a stealthy ghost.

" He stood before the open door, his eyes lifted to the blue heavens. After a time he spoke, very softly, as one would speak to a friend who leaned close to listen. ' Father, I thank thee that thou hast heard me. I know that thou hearest me always ; but because of these who stand by I say it, that they may believe that thou hast sent me.'

" When he had thus spoken, he cried with a loud voice, ' Lazarus, come forth !'

" Then he that was dead—our brother—our be-loved—came forth, stumbling, as one suddenly aroused from a deep sleep ; bound, moreover, hand and foot with his grave-clothes. How shall I tell thee, child, of the moments that followed, of the terror and the joy that seized upon us all, so that we were dazed and helpless like the newly-awakened dead. It was the Master who brought us back to

ourselves, reminding us gently that there was something that we might do for our beloved.

"'Loose him,' he said to me quietly, 'and let
him go home.'"

The woman stooped and dipped her pitcher in
the spring; she was still smiling, as one who car-
ries about a joyful secret. "I think," she said,
"that the wise rabbi is returning from Jerusalem.
He will tell thee more of this Jesus; he will tell
thee that the wise and learned council at Jerusalem
caused him to be put to death not many days after
he called my brother from the tomb. But know,
child, that the grave had no power to hold the
Anointed of the Highest. He became alive again!
He lives to-day—to-day and forever! Do not
forget!"

She turned and hurried away down the steep
pathway, her dripping pitcher poised lightly on her
head.

Phannias stared after the retreating figure in
dazed silence, then he started to his feet. "Where,
oh, where is he?" he cried passionately. "Tell
me; I want to find him—I must find him!"

The woman had already gained the terraced
street of the village. She turned for an instant and
pointed upward, then disappeared behind the high
wall of a garden.

Below, coming with long strides along the dusty
highway, was Ben Huna. He carried in both hands
with jealous care a silver vase. The vase contained

the ashes of a red heifer, burned beyond the city gates with pomp and show of priestly ritual. These ashes had been justly commingled with pure water from the great laver of the sanctuary ; the mixture was called the Water of Separation. It cleansed from sin—according to The Law.

CHAPTER VI.

EXPIATION.

TO Phannias, the days that followed appeared like a strange dream, wherein the harsh realities of the known and visible world mixed and commingled with cloudy influxes from the infinite and invisible, which girds us about one and all with mystery, never entirely shut out from the most sordid soul, often opening in strange, enchanting vistas before the prescient eyes of innocence.

Ben Huna observing the still look of peace upon the face of the child, and perceiving moreover that the silence and aloofness of his separation irked him not at all, was divided in his mind betwixt amazement and displeasure. He was conscious of a keen desire to write with the sharp stylus of the law an ineffaceable lesson upon the white soul of the youthful Nazarite. This desire was rooted—or so the good rabbi assured himself—in pure love for the child. If beneath all this recognized benevolence there lurked a secret ambition to be known in days to come as the guide and instructor of a most holy Nazarite, a wise and mighty rabbi, a high priest, perchance—nay, who could tell—the ambition itself was laudable.

On the seventh day, the final sprinkling with the water of separation having been duly accomplished, the child's long silken hair was cut off and solemnly buried in the earth, in token that all the past years of his vow were as though they were not. On this occasion Ben Huna devoted the better part of the twenty-four hours to a learned and vastly comprehensive discourse on the nature of the contaminating uncleanness incurred by touching the dead. He also explained the legal process by which ·the cleansing water of separation was prepared, dwelling with enthusiasm on the wisdom and graciousness of the Creator in thus providing a loophole of escape for the guilty.

Phannias listened in silence, the while Ben Huna drew out the fine-spun thread of legal disquisition, waxing eloquent and eager as he mingled aphorism and parable, monstrous extravagance and profound allegorical truth, with the hair-splitting finesse of the accomplished scholar. The child thought dreamily of the man of Galilee, standing in the dismal place of tombs and calling to the unholy dead with a voice of power. The last words of the woman of Bethany, and her strange gesture in answer to his wild cry of appeal, haunted him. "The grave could not hold him : he lives to-day and forever." He longed with a great longing to behold this Jesus, the Prince of Israel and of death.

On the eighth day Ben Huna brought his charge

to the temple, there to offer to the priest the two
young pigeons, prescribed by the law, the one a
sin-offering, the other a burnt-offering. The child
looked about him with wide wondering eyes. The
solemn ranks of carven pillars, beneath whose
mighty feet shone marble floors, stretching away in
echoing vistas to distant gleaming gates; the pun-
gent breath of incense mingling with the smoke of
the never-dying fire upon the great altar of sacrifice; the white figures of priest and Levite, gliding
noiselessly here and there upon their holy errands;
the scattered worshipers, standing motionless with
bowed heads, or lying prostrate in agonized suppli-
cation before the Jehovah, who inhabited eternity,
but who also dwelt in the awful darkness of the
Holy of Holies—all this pressed hard upon the
sensitive soul of the child. He would fain have
hidden his shorn head from the insupportable
glories of the place; but Ben Huna led him steadily
forward, through the wonderful brazen gate Beautiful; across the vast glittering court of the women;
up the shining circular steps, worn smooth with the
feet of countless worshipers. Mechanically the
child counted them, remembering that they were
numbered for the fifteen Psalms of degrees.

When they stood at last in the Court of Israel,
which enclosed in cloistered calm the shining soul
of the sanctuary, he lifted his eyes with difficulty to
the marvelous structure, towering into the brilliant
blue of the midday heavens, as it were a mountain

of fire and snow. He had been told many times of the exceeding beauty of this habitation of the Most High; how that it was builded of great blocks of marble, overlaid with gold of dazzling brightness; how that kings and princes and mighty men had for ages brought of their riches and treasure for its adorning. He trembled to think that within the gleaming walls, behind the double veil of scarlet and purple and gold, brooded the awful presence of the Shechinah, that ineffable glory of the Godhead, which had led the children of Israel through the wilderness, a pillar of cloud by day, a pillar of fire by night.

Absorbed in these meditations he did not hear the words of the priest who advanced to confer solemnly with Ben Huna, but he started violently when the pitiful quavering bleat of a lamb broke the silence which followed. His eyes grew dark with fear as the priest seized the little creature from the hands of the attendants, examined it perfunctorily, then with a muttered accompaniment of ritual led it away toward the place of sacrifice. Ben Huna signed to the child to follow; he obeyed blindly. The loud frightened bleating of the lamb pierced his heart; it was so white, so innocent, and life was sweet in the wide flowery fields. For an instant a fierce unreasoning hatred of the glittering temple, of the white-robed muttering priest— yes, of the God, hid within the gorgeous sanctuary, whose anger could be appeased by so

5

piteous a sacrifice—swelled his heart almost to
bursting.

In obedience to a peremptory gesture from the
priest, he laid his trembling hands upon the soft ·
white head of the lamb, responding with faint amens
to the loud chanting of the ritual of Atonement.
The priest hastily muttered a benediction, then with
the practiced swiftness of the priestly butcher he
seized the animal by the throat; a single thrust of
the sacred knife and the red life-blood flashed into
the golden bowl of sacrifice.   Phannias glanced up
timidly into the cold, grim face of the priest; then
his head dropped upon his breast and he turned as
if to go away.

A watchful Levite seized him by the shoulder.
"Wouldst turn thy back upon the altar?" he
whispered, with an angry frown.   "Stand where
thou art till the sprinkling be done!"

The child paid but scant heed to the service which
followed, the while the pitiful little body of the
lamb, laid in order upon the undying fire of the
vast altar, slowly consumed away.   He stared with
wide eyes at the slender cloud of smoke, which
bowed and wavered spirit-like before the dazzling
front of the sanctuary.   He wondered if the sharp
odor of the burning flesh was indeed a sweet savor,
pleasing and acceptable to the King of kings throned
in the veiled place.   Could it be that the awful
hidden Presence regarded him with gracious eyes,
as he stood without, clean once more and sanctified,

because the lamb had died? A single drop of the sacrificial blood gleamed red upon the snowy skirt of his tunic; the child touched it timidly; how was it that the dead shepherd—to whom angels had spoken—was unclean, while the lamb—which had eaten grass in the meadows—was holy? And all the while his lips repeated mechanically the yearning prophetic words of the sacrificial liturgy:

"Return, O my soul, to thy rest,
For Jehovah hath requited me!
Surely thou hast delivered my life from death,
Mine eyes from tears, and my feet from falling.
Praise, O ye servants of Jehovah,
Praise ye the name of Jehovah!
Blessed be Jehovah's name,
Henceforth and forever!
From sunrise unto its setting,
Praised be Jehovah's name!
Halleluiah! Amen and Amen!"

CHAPTER VII.

IN THE TEMPLE.

ALL at length was finished. The priest had pronounced him clean, forgiven, sanctified, and restored to grace and favor with God and man. Then it was that a great wave of joy swept over the soul of Phannias. The color flowed back into his pallid cheeks; his eyes sparkled; he could have danced, as did King David before the ark.

Ben Huna perceived his exultation and smiled—a wise smile. "Now thou shalt look upon the glories of the temple, my son," he said indulgently, "and delight thine eyes with the beauty of Zion."

Phannias looked up joyfully into the face of his master; it was no longer averted, cold, unloving, like the grim face of the offended Law. "Nay, he was more kind"—thought the child in a rapture of gratitude—"more loving, more wonderfully wise than ever before."

"I am already full of joy," he murmured.

"Thou art filled with joy, my son, because thou hast satisfied the requirements of *the law*," said Ben Huna, astutely; "and thus only may happiness be found. Call to thy mind how that David rejoiced and sang aloud of the pleasure to be found in keeping the precepts of the Most High. '*The law* of thy mouth,' he declared, 'is better unto me than thousands of gold and silver. Unless thy *law* had been my delight, I should have perished in my affliction. I will never forget thy *precepts;* for with them hast thou quickened me.' Remember this thing that hath befallen thee, my child ; write it upon the tables of thy heart, for so shalt thou inherit the reward of the righteous, even length of days, riches also and honor, at the hands of Jehovah. Verily, he delighteth in the obedience of Israel ; but the unruly and froward of heart he utterly destroys."

Phannias' bright face clouded ; he remembered the mysterious man of Galilee, put to death—the woman had said—by the wise and learned Council at Jerusalem. "My master," he ventured, after a timid pause, "is it true that every one who pleases God and keeps the law is honored, and rich, and of many days ?"

Ben Huna pursed up his lips with an air of pride ; verily, this child was destined to sit one day among the askers of deep questions. "God showeth mercy unto thousands of them that love him and keep his commandments," he answered conclusively ; "he also visiteth the iniquity of the fathers upon the children, unto the third and fourth generation of them that hate him. So it is that if a man who seemeth to be righteous suffers evil, who shall say whether it be his sin or the sin of his fathers which causeth him to be punished ?"

Phannias sighed deeply. " The Law is a strange thing," he said under his breath, "—strange and terrible."

Before the setting of the sun the twain had looked upon the "Mountain of the House" in all its glory. They had stood in the lofty vaulted chamber of Council, wherein the judges of Israel were wont to convene. The central seat, Ben Huna informed the lad in a reverent whisper, was the throne of the president of the Sanhedrim; on either side were ranged the semicircular benches of the seventy judges, chosen from among the priests, the elders and the scribes of Israel.

" I would not have you ignorant, my son, that thou also art of the priestly line," said the rabbi, as the two passed down one of the stately marble stairways which led from the sacred enclosure into the spacious court of the Gentiles. " At no distant day thou wilt come to thine own ; here shalt thou dwell, holy unto the Lord."

" Will the Messiah come to this place ?" asked Phannias, staring thoughtfully at a wretched beggar who lay asleep in the shadow of the sacred wall.

" Assuredly he will come to this place !" cried the rabbi with exultation. " The Messiah will visit this holy mountain, and the light of it shall extend to the ends of the earth, even as the light of a jasper stone, exceeding precious."

The worthy man was silent for a space, then he looked down at the child. He had turned once more toward the shining tower of the sanctuary, which gleamed within its fair setting of cloistered courts like a jewel of price. " To think that thou, even thou, my son, couldst bring that blessed day to pass !" he cried yearningly.

" If I could keep the six hundred and thirteen laws," murmured Phannias, hanging his head ; " but I have already sinned grievously——"

" Thou shalt sin no more because of the false Messiah," said Ben Huna, his face hardening. " Come, we will walk in Herod's portico yonder, and I will speak to thee of the matter, as I promised."

The child followed the long strides of his master in silence, and found himself presently in the most wonderful cloister in all the world ; more than a hundred feet in breadth, and a clear thousand in length ; its lofty roof of carven cedar supported by four rows of mighty Corinthian pillars, cut and polished from precious marbles of varying tints. The floor of this vast columned court rested upon vaulted substructures, built up at uncounted cost from the wild valley of Jehoshaphat, hundreds of feet below. Ben Huna, seeing the look of wonder in the eyes of the child, vouchsafed this explanation. He also bade his charge observe how, from either side of this so-called Herod's porch, there extended a triple line of Corinthian columns, forming a cloister nearly four thousand feet in length, which enclosed the whole area of the temple mount; the cloister in turn being surrounded with a wall of enormous strength and thickness.

"The temple," he declared, waxing warm with the matter in hand, "is in truth a sacred fortress, splendid, impregnable. It commands not only the holy city but the heights around. God will never allow it to be removed; it is eternal as the rock upon which it stands!"

The worthy rabbi dilated at great length upon the subject, it being indeed a favorite theme among all patriotic Jews, to whom the temple was not less precious than their own souls. "Thou hast seen the glory and the might of this habitation of the Most High," he concluded, fixing his keen eyes on the child's attentive face. "What now wouldst thou think if I should declare to thee, 'I am able to destroy this temple and build it again in three days?'"

Phannias looked his astonishment at this strange question. Then seeing that his master's face was stern and grave, he answered straightway, "I should think that it could not be true."

"The babe of Bethlehem's manger, grown to manhood, beheld this place, even as thou hast beheld it," said Ben Huna slowly; "and, standing in the midst of its eternal glories, spake this foul lie. Afterward, when he had blasphemed repeatedly against the law and the prophets—yea, and this holy place also, he declared openly that *he was the Christ.*"

The voice of the speaker sank to a hoarse whisper, as though he feared to profane the air with the terrible words.

Phannias looked down at the marble pavement in trembling silence.

"The outraged chiefs of the nation brought the man before the holy tribunal of the Sanhedrim," continued Ben Huna, in measured tones. "He was found—guilty."

"And what—" faltered the child—"became of him ?"

"He was nailed to a cross, hand and foot,—crucified," said Ben Huna coldly ; "a blasphemer fitly tortured betwixt two common criminals on the accursed mount of death yonder."

"And—and afterward ?"

"*Afterward!* Nay, what more of this demon's web of falsehood hath blown about thine ears ? Afterward he was buried. The tomb was sealed and guarded by order of the Roman governor, who had been forewarned of treachery by the watchful priests. The Gentile soldiers drenched themselves with wine, after their heathen custom ; and while they slept their drunken sleep certain ignorant peasants—who had followed the man for years, gaping at his false miracles—stole the body. Anon these declared that the crucified blasphemer was risen from the dead—risen and ascended into heaven !"

"Didst *thou* see this man ?" demanded Phannias, after a long silence.

"Thanks be to Jehovah—no!" I was in Alexandria during the days of that abomination."

"Then how—" and the child's timid voice gained strength—"how is it that thou dost know that he was not—the Messiah?"

Ben Huna looked down into the clear questioning eyes upraised to his. He was neither angry nor alarmed at the question. He fancied that he detected here the budding Haggadist, who would, in wise conclaves of the future, determine abstruse points of sacred law and doctrine in such wondrous fashion that men would ask: "Who and what manner of man was the instructor of this mighty scholar; and at whose feet did he sit, who hath this excellent wisdom?"

"Thou art not in the wrong, my son, in thy desire to penetrate to the very uttermost of this matter," he said, drawing his beard through his hand with an argumentative air. "How to recognize the Messiah through a study of the law and the prophets is a most worthy task, and one which haply shall fill thy days during many blessed years. This crucified carpenter of Galilee was not the Messiah—nay, it were almost blasphemous to couple his name with the blessed name of the Prince of Peace. None, save the unlearned and superstitious, could possibly regard him as such; and for this I could name thee a thousand reasons. At this moment I will propound to thee one question. If the man of Galilee actually arose from

his dishonored tomb—as his followers impudently
claim to this day—why did he not reveal himself
in this holy place, crowned, triumphant? Who
then could have doubted of all the wise and
mighty and godly men who here assemble themselves? But not one of all these—*not one*, mark
you—saw him. The witnesses of the alleged miracle were his chosen followers; and of these the
chief disciple, to my certain knowledge, denied the
man with curses on the night of his trial before the
Sanhedrim. But, come, it is already the ninth
hour; we must get us down to the city, where there
are divers things I would show thee before we
sleep. To-morrow's dawn must find us well on our
way toward Bethlehem."

As the man and the child emerged from a maze
of narrow streets into the great square which lay
before the Roman tower, Antonia, they found
themselves in the midst of an excited multitude,
which filled the place to overflowing.

"What has happened?" asked Ben Huna, addressing a Jew who had drawn himself up into an
embrasure of the wall that he might look over the
heads of the crowd.

"They are scourging the knave in the castle
yard!" replied the man with an air of fierce delight. "May the lash silence his blasphemous
tongue!—Ah, look; he is coming out!"

The crowd opened like the jaws of an animal,
and Phannias saw the tall, emaciated figure of a

man emerge from the castle gate, which closed behind him with a clang. He who had been thrust out stood for an instant looking about him with dazed eyes, then, drawing himself up to his full height, flung his lean arms above his head.

"Woe to Jerusalem! Woe! Woe!" His voice, curiously muffled and dull, struck ominous echoes like the blows of a hammer from the frowning walls of the castle. "Woe to Jerusalem! Woe!"

The crowd moaned and shuddered; cries and curses arose from single throats, but not a hand was raised to seize the man who had been scourged. He walked slowly through the swaying multitude, his bright eyes fastened upon some point high above their heads, his face drawn and fixed in ghastly semblance of a smile. Suddenly he broke into a run, swaying his terrible face from side to side, like one who flees from an unsupportable horror; the strange dead voice beat the air in fainter and ever fainter reverberations. "Woe! Woe to Jerusalem! Woe!"

The man who had spoken to Ben Huna drew a sharp breath and flung his hand across his eyes. "May Jehovah destroy the prophet of evil!" he groaned.

"Who is the fellow?" demanded Ben Huna with indignation. "Why has he not been dealt with after the law? I have seen men stoned for less!"

The Jew shrugged his shoulders. "He has been scourged thrice at our instance—with what result, thou seest. Our masters,—curse them, will permit us nothing further." He cast a look of venomous hate at the Roman guard, standing stolidly at their posts before the castle gate. "Night and day for more than a twelvemonth, in the streets, in the synagogues, in the very temple itself, that accursed note of evil has sounded in our ears. My God, I will hear it no longer!"

With that the Jew thrust his fingers in his ears and fled away like one demented. Ben Huna stared upward in horror and amaze. The mysterious voice seemed to drop from the air above their heads; it beat upon the writhing multitude like the hailstones of an angry God. "Woe to Jerusalem! Woe! Woe!"

"'Tis the voice of a demon!" cried Ben Huna. "Come, we will go!" And grasping the child's hand, he hurried away toward the gate Miphkad.

CHAPTER VIII.

CONCERNING THE PRINCE.

THE Phannias who returned to Bethlehem was no longer a child. Rachel perceived this, and insensibly bowed herself before him after the fashion of women. The intimate mother-love, warm as the breast of a brooding dove, gave place to a more distant but not less passionate affection, which consoled itself with endless renunciations, labors, vigils, prayers, wordless and well-nigh unceasing.

The boy, after the manner of youth, grew and expanded in this atmosphere of love and abnegation like a sturdy tree, which, embraced and nourished by the puissant forces of nature, comprehends them not at all, save as things necessary for its good. Into his studies concerning the Messiah he threw himself with an ardor which astonished even Ben Huna. During these quiet years, peacefully like the one to the other as the sunshiny days of midsummer, the strange tale of the shepherd and the yet stranger words of the woman of Bethany well-nigh faded from his mind.

Ben Huna had not again referred to the crucified Nazarene. "The mind is a treasure-house," he was

wont to declare; "if it be small, or if it be great,
it is one, since God hath set bounds to its capacity.
Seek therefore to fill thy treasure-house, whether .
small or great, with that which is good, that thou
mayst delight thyself therein, when the evil days
come and the windows thereof be darkened." Believing this, the worthy rabbi set himself the more
diligently—though in all simplicity of heart—to fill
the boy's mind to overflowing with the worthless
husks of living truth which the slow-passing generations had heaped to themselves through the ages.
Yet ever amidst the dusty heaps of futile wisdom
there gleamed here and there shining fragments of
truth, dropped as it were in pity from the generous
hand of infinite wisdom.

Searching his parchment roll of the Mishna,
Phannias chanced one day upon a strange prophecy
concerning the days of the Messiah; he carried it
straightway to his master. "What sayst thou to
this?" he asked, and read:

"In the time of the Messiah the people will be
impudent and given to drinking; wine shops will
flourish; and the fruit of the vine will be costly.
None will care for punishment. The learned will
be driven from one place to the other, and none
will have compassion on them. The wisdom of the
scribes will be an abomination. Fear of God will
be despised; truth will be trodden under foot, and
there will be few that are wise. The son will not
reverence his father; the daughter will rise against

the mother, the daughter-in-law against the mother-in-law, and a man's foes shall be they of his own household. The face of that generation is as the face of a dog!"

Ben Huna knit his grizzled brows. " It is a hard saying, my son," he said gravely ; " yet when shall the coming of the Prince be glorious if not at a time when judgments are ripe against the doers of evil ? Doth not Jeremy the prophet declare the word of the Lord concerning him : ' Behold the days come that I will raise unto David a righteous Branch,*and a king shall reign and prosper, and shall execute judgment and justice in the earth'?   So also hath the prophet Isaiah spoken : ' With righteousness shall he judge the poor and reprove with equity for the meek of the earth : and he shall smite the earth with the rod of his mouth, and with the breath of his lips shall he slay the wicked.' "

Phannias stared thoughtfully at the parchment. " ' The fear of God will be despised,' " he repeated slowly; " ' truth will be trodden under foot, and there will be few that are wise.' What—if—the foolish people reject their Prince, and the generation ' with the face of a dog ' turn against him to rend him ?"

Ben Huna raised his hand in solemn protest. " To question thus were to doubt the eternal purpose of Jehovah !" he cried in a trembling voice. " Thinkest thou that the God of Israel would suffer his own Anointed, ordained from the foundation of

the world, to be despised of the unrighteous?
Verily 'He will smite the earth with the rod of his
mouth, and with the breath of his lips shall he slay
the wicked. And the whole earth shall be filled
with the glory of the Lord !' "

As Phannias made his way thoughtfully homeward he became aware of a stranger, who sat by
the wayside as if to rest after the steep climb from
the valley below. This man, who was old and
poorly dressed, rose upon his approach and stepped
forward. "Canst thou direct me to the khan?" he
said, a certain ring of authority in his deep tones.
Then, as his eye traveled slowly over the white
garments of the youthful Nazarite, resting at length
on the dark, eager face, framed in its loose locks of
curling hair, his worn face brightened into a smile
of singular sweetness.

"Surely, like to thee must he once have been,
who walked the earth in the beauty of his holiness," he said meditatively. "—Thou art vowed to
holiness, my son; dost thou know the holiest?
Thou art studying the wisdom of the ancients; hast
thou discerned the wisdom of God unto a life that
endeth not?"

Phannias regarded his questioner with frank
amazement. "I can tell thee where the khan is,
good sir," he said. "But who on the earth below
or in the heavens above is holiest, save the God
who changes not, and who can be known by no ·
man? As for the wisdom of the ancients, I have

6

learned nothing from the wisest of them all of a life which endeth not."

"Wouldst thou also taste of that bread of God, whereof he that eateth lives forever?" asked the stranger, studying the serious face of the lad, beautiful as that of some listening angel.

Phannias made no answer; and after a pause his questioner continued, with a gesture full of benignity, "Sit by me on the bank here, my son, and I will tell thee of this bread of God, which came down from heaven no less truly than did the manna in the desert of Sinai, and by which a man may live forever." .

Phannias obeyed, wondering and still silent. The stranger made no haste to speak again; he was looking thoughtfully down the steep path which wound up from the storied valley below. There Ruth, the faithful Moabitess, had gleaned among the shining sheaves; and David, the poet king, had watched the flocks in his marvelous boyhood. The sheep still fed on the smooth green slopes, and on the further side of the stream the garments of the gleaners shone gay between the shocks of yellow corn. "They have told thee of the child born in the khan yonder, and of his shameful death," he said at last, quietly and without turning his head. "What knowest thou more of Jesus of Nazareth?"

Phannias started violently; then the hot color flamed up in his brown cheeks. "I know this of

the man," he said coldly; "he once stood in the
holy temple in Jerusalem, and, looking about upon
its eternal glories, declared that he was able both
to destroy it and to raise it up again within the
space of three days. This was an idle boast, as
the event proved. I would know no more of the
boaster."

The stranger's lips moved in silence for an instant; then he turned his gentle eyes full upon his
companion. "If the saying had concerned Herod's
temple it would have been not the less true; for he
spake as never man spake—even the winds and the
waves obeyed his voice; yet he spake not save of
the temple of his body. On that day his enemies
surrounded him, demanding a sign, and he, knowing that he was come from God and in what manner also he must go to God, said to them: 'Destroy this temple, and in three days I will raise it
up.' And verily it came to pass; that evil generation which knew not the face of its Prince slew
him with murderous hands. Then was fulfilled
that which he had spoken; on the third day God
raised him from the dead with power, and he became alive again, and living, ascended before our
eyes into the heaven from which he came."

"But why," asked Phannias, trembling, "did he
not reveal himself in the temple,—crowned, triumphant? Then they which were wise in Israel would
have believed in him."

"'The face of that generation was as the face of

a dog,'" said the stranger, quietly. "Is it not so written in thy parchment roll? And was it meet that God's Anointed should discover his glories before them that had rejected and despised him—yea, that had spit upon him, and scourged him, and mocked him, hanging upon the cross. So also he said—and the saying is just and true—'Give not that which is holy unto the dogs, neither cast ye your pearls before swine, lest they trample them under their feet, and turn again and rend you.'"

"But the cross—the awful tree; it is written in the law that he that is hanged thereon is accursed of God."

"Is it not also written," answered the stranger— and a sweet and terrible light shone from his worn face—"'Cursed is every one that continueth not in all things which are written in the book of the law to do them.' And what man is there who can be justified by the law in the sight of God? Christ therefore hath redeemed us from the curse of the law, being made a curse for us. For God so loved the world that he gave his only begotten son, that whosoever believeth in him should not perish, but have everlasting life."

"Nay, but God would not suffer the Messiah to fall under the feet of his enemies, as one accursed of God and despised of men?" cried Phannias, his eyes aflame. "I cannot believe it!"

"He was despised and rejected of men," murmured the stranger, bowing his head; "a man of

sorrows and acquainted with grief; and we hid, as
it were, our faces from him. He was despised and
we esteemed him not."

Phannias started at sound of the familiar words.
"Isaiah wrote not of the Messiah—the Prince!" he
urged vehemently. "'Behold the King shall reign
and prosper; he shall execute judgment and justice
upon the earth.—The wicked shall he destroy with
the breath of his mouth.' No—no, it cannot be
that he hath already come! What would be the
fate of Israel if such a frightful thing were true?
It is not true—it cannot be true! I will never believe it!" The boy cast a shuddering glance upward, as if he feared to behold the naked weapon
of God's wrath, already outstretched to destroy.

The stranger had risen to his feet; he also was
looking up into the radiant heavens, but with love
and yearning, as one who looks beyond a veil
scarce drawn over longed-for and transcendent
glories. He was silent, yet involuntarily Phannias
bowed his head, waiting, though for what he knew
not.

After a time he became aware of a light touch
upon his shoulder. The stranger was regarding
him with a melancholy smile. "They have wrought
well who have sought to blind thine eyes to the
light which hath shined in the darkness," he said
gently; "yet I have prayed for thee, and when God
wills thine eyes shall be opened; thou shalt see the
light, and the grace of the Lord Jesus Christ shall

come upon thee there to abide." With a gesture
of farewell, he turned away. Phannias watched him
as he toiled painfully up the rugged path which led
to the ancient khan, a long shaft of sunlight falling
in sudden glory upon his bowed figure.

CHAPTER IX.

A QUESTION AND AN ANSWER.

HAD the Messiah already come, and had he been rejected and put to death by a blind and maddened people?

This terrible question pursued Phannias through tortured hours and days. He turned to the prophets with feverish energy, reading again and again the solemn sayings of Isaiah, which the stranger had repeated.

" It cannot—cannot be !" he cried aloud, tears of anguish starting to his eyes. But like a strain of melancholy music the prophetic words rang continually in his ears ; he could not but listen :

" Surely he hath borne our griefs, and carried our sorrows ; yet we did esteem him stricken, smitten of God and afflicted. But he was wounded for our transgressions, he was bruised for our iniquities : the chastisement of our peace was upon him ; and with his stripes we are healed."

Rachel was not slow to perceive that something was amiss with her son. Anxiously she prepared the most tempting foods, and made all possible haste in the fashioning of certain garments which the lad, human enough in his boyish likings, had coveted. But none of these things sufficed to draw from him so much as a glance of surprise or approval. And when for the third time he left his favorite doves unfed, and in his distraction trampled a blossoming lily under foot, she resolved to penetrate his reserve and find out for herself the nature of those absorbing studies, which she had begun to regard with alarm and disapproval.

"Surely the child must eat," she said resolutely. "Even the great prophets could not live by fasting alone. As for the priests in the temple, do they not continually feast upon the fat of the land till they be sleek and flourishing.—And such also is God's good will concerning them that do his pleasure."

Full of these thoughts she approached Phannias, who sat, musing with cloudy brows, on his favorite bench beneath the fig tree.

"My son," she began timidly, "wilt thou not take of the bread which I have baked for thee? Here also is a savory dish of the lentils, which thou art wont to eat with pleasure. See now, I have made them ready for the third time."

Phannias looked up with a shadowy smile. "I am not hungry, my mother," he began, a faint note of apology in his voice.

"Nay, son, but thou art hungry; rise, therefore, and eat, lest thou become faint and overborne.—Much learning is not good for thee, who art yet but a child," she added, with a hostile glance at the scroll which lay beside him on the bench. " Thrice in the days past have I been minded to take from thee the parchments and bestow them in a place which thou wottest not of. Must I see thee perish before my eyes like a leaf that withereth ? For what then have I lived all these years, if I must behold this evil come upon me ?"

Phannias stretched out his arms with a great choking sob ; for the moment he was a little child again, and his mother, full of authoritative love and wisdom, seemed, even as of old, the sure refuge from the poignant misery which he had borne in silence till he could bear it no longer. " Mother !" he cried, "what if the Messiah has come and we knew him not !"

Rachel drew back in horror and amaze. " Nay, now I know that thou art ill ! Much study hath well-nigh destroyed thy understanding. Come, now, eat of the meat which I have made ready for thee, and afterward sleep ; thou wilt awake to wonder at thy sick fancies."

But Phannias was not to be comforted with savory dishes, nor soothed with sleep. " Listen," he said imperatively, "I will tell thee all ; then thou mayst judge for thyself whether I be mad.—Nay, if all Israel be not mad—doomed !" In rapid, disjointed sentences he poured out all that he had heard concerning Jesus of Nazareth,—the shepherd's tale, the strange words of the woman of Bethany, and the meeting with the traveler beside the road

leading to the khan. More than once his mother
made as though she would have interrupted the
fiery torrent of his words; almost roughly he bade
her hold her peace till he should have finished.
At length his head sank upon his breast and he was
silent.

His mother gazed through her tears at her child's
downcast face and bowed figure. "It is no less
than the Evil One," she cried, "who also desires to
pervert thee from thy holy calling! · Yes, truly,"
she went on, her voice gaining strength with her
righteous wrath, " has he not thrice attacked thee
in hours of weakness? First, when thine ears were
filled with the mad tale of the dotard at yonder
inn—may Jehovah requite him! Again, when thou
wast weak and ill because of the fasting, as thou
wast going to Jerusalem to be cleansed, and
now——"

" Nay, my mother," said Phannias wearily, "thou
hast not seen these witnesses of the past; they
were godly in speech and conduct even as thyself."

"Who art thou that judgest?" said Rachel
boldly. "Art thou not still a child; and hath not
the Evil One power to assume what semblance he
will? See now, thou shalt eat, as I have bidden
thee; afterward we will talk further of this matter."

An hour later, having seen her beloved wrapped
in the profound slumber of exhaustion, she slipped
away to find Ben Huna. The rabbi heard her story

without question or comment. But it was evident that he was neither seriously alarmed nor angry at what had happened. "Thou art quite in the right, my good woman," he said, with that amiable condescension which marked the intercourse of the learned with an inferior creation—"quite in the right; the Evil One goeth about openly, like a roaring lion; and anon, thinly disguised in the robe of righteousness, that he may entrap the unwary and innocent of heart. These mischief-making Nazarenes swarm in our midst like the devouring grasshopper; they go from place to place diligently spreading what they are pleased to call 'the good tidings,' even as did their master, before his career was fortunately cut short by death."

The rabbi lapsed into silence for a time; then he went on argumentatively, more as if speaking with himself than with the distressed mother, who hung upon his words with the utmost anxiety. "The lad is a good scholar—learned in the law beyond his years. Nay, there is no one like him, even in the great schools of Jerusalem. I, Ben Huna, have said it. Even so, great scholars and those learned in the law have been entrapped by this heresy; witness Nicodemus, one of the holy Sanhedrim, and Joseph of Arimathea also; yea, and Saul of Tarsus, —Lord, Jehovah! why permittest thou such things!"

"What of these men of whom thou hast spoken?" interrupted the mother, leaning forward breathlessly.

Ben Huna lifted his eyebrows and shrugged his shoulders. "They were drawn away after the false Messiah, woman; blasphemously accepting the accursed fruit of the tree as the Anointed of Jehovah. And why they did this—how it was accomplished, I swear I cannot understand!"—drawing his beard meditatively through his large wrinkled hand. "I have heard these Nazarenes prate of a mysterious power which came upon them from above, which compelled them to believe. Verily, there must be some diabolic power at work here. These miracles of the so-called apostles now, they are undoubtedly strange—strange. In my opinion the Sanhedrim pays too little heed to this matter; 'tis more than a sect, in my opinion; 'tis a sword, menacing the life of the nation."

"But Phannias," cried the mother, venturing to interrupt the current of these sapient meditations—"what must I do with my son? He is even as a young eaglet, struggling in the snare of the fowler!" and she wrung her hands weakly. "If these Nazarenes have diabolic powers, as thou hast said —nay, I also have said it—have they not already drawn their invisible meshes about the child? And if my child is undone, I am ready to die; there is no good thing left to me in all the world!"

"Hold thou thy peace, woman!" said Ben Huna, with a large gesture, expressive of a patient tolerance, which is yet not to be trifled with. "There shall no evil befall the lad. Have I not

already enriched his mind with the wisdom of the
ancients; and shall I not presently pluck out these
evil sayings from his heart, even as a wise husband-
man plucks out the noisome weeds from his fair
garden spaces? Behold how the winds in their
wanderings waft viewless germs of evil even from
the ends of the earth; they fall hither and yon, on
the field of the diligent man and on the vineyard
of him that despiseth labor. God wills it so. But
the diligent man will straightway pluck up the evil
growth before it bear the fruit of mischief, while the
vineyard of the idler is choked. Look you, the lad
is no longer a child, that thou, a woman—albeit a
godly and diligent woman—mayst guide and direct.
The hour has struck when he must leave thee and
go up to Jerusalem, there to abide. And this
should have been long since; verily I was not slow
to perceive it; yet I had compassion on thee in thy
lonely estate and said nothing of it. If now thou
wouldst behold thy son honored in Israel, thou
wilt not open thy mouth to say me nay."

Rachel bowed her head. She had lived through
this hour in the silence of her shrinking soul a
thousand times. "I have already given my son to
the service of God," she said with resignation. But
two large tears silently arose and looked out from
her sorrowful eyes.

CHAPTER X.

JESUS IV.

THE tree of Israel was dead. The fiat had gone forth : " Cut it down ; why cumbereth it the ground ?" But though the ax was already lifted, the tree stretched its meager branches to the threatening heavens, its withered foliage shivering in ghastly semblance of life.

The strange question which fell from the lips of a rejected king as he walked the streets of Jerusalem for the last time was about to be answered. " If they do these things in a green tree, what shall be done in the dry ?"

Israel had forgotten the question. But the answer, prepared from the foundation of the world, was at hand.

In all the doomed nation no prophet with tongue of fire called the people to repentance ; no yearning message of love and pity fell from the darkened windows of heaven ; no angel embassy, clad in the shining insignia of Jehovah, chanted of " Peace, good-will, to men."

From time to time the far-reaching echoes of the gathering hosts of heaven struck faint notes of fear from the sacred mountains round about Jerusalem. At such times the people would pause in their occupations and gaze at one another with furtive eyes. Yet for the most part men laughed and wept; ate and drank; made merry at weddings and feasts; wore sackcloth for their dead; vowed solemn vows; prayed long prayers; fetched tithes of mint and anise—all in the old, old fashion; the while the undying fire burned in the vast, shining temple, and the smoke of countless sacrifices arose to the nostrils of an angry God.

In the year 66—counting from the birth of the man of Galilee—Phannias the Nazarite came to Jerusalem. In those days he possessed the body of a warrior, the face of an angel and the soul of a child. His master, Ben Huna, bent and powdered with the rime of years, but scarce less a child in the guileless candor of his heart, came with him.

" This youth is destined to great things in Israel," he declared boldly to the chief priest—one Jesus, fourth of his name in the high-priestly line. " I, Ben Huna, for many years now a member of the lesser Sanhedrim, have instructed him both in the wisdom of the law and the prophets; he will shine as a lamp in the sanctuary of the Most High, even as did the Nazarite, Samuel, in days of old."

The high priest turned his impenetrable front full upon Phannias; the young man stood up boldly under the cold gray eyes, which peered out at him from a network of crafty wrinkles. " There is already no lack of light in the dwelling-place of *El*

Shaddai," he said in measured tones ; "who also
hath created the light to enlighten his people
Israel—Blessed be his righteous name ! The young
man will find full employment for his powers in the
service of the temple, if haply he be accepted of
the holy Sanhedrim."

Ben Huna, who was openly disappointed with
the cool reception accorded his favorite, would have
spoken further ; but before he could determine which
were most cogent and convincing of the many words
which crowded hotly to his lips, he found himself
in the anteroom of the audience chamber, the in-
terview plainly at an end. Two days later the
worthy rabbi, who still lingered in Jerusalem, was
again commanded to appear in the palace. This
time he was admitted alone to the august presence
of the potentate.

"Concerning this Nazarite, who is of the seed of
Aaron," began the high priest without preamble ;
"what of the record of his genealogy ?"

Ben Huna turned pale to the lips. "We have
found an irregularity in the line of descent," he
faltered—"in the ninth generation of the mother,
but——"

"Thou must search out this irregularity and
make it good," interrupted the high priest peremptorily. "The youth shall serve as I will direct until
the matter be established beyond a peradventure."

Ben Huna opened his lips to reply, but on second
thought he remained silent.

After a brief pause the high priest continued ju-
dicially, "I learn that the candidate is unpolluted
by any one of the one hundred and forty-four phys-
ical blemishes which would have invalidated him
from service. This is well."—Then with a keen
glance into the downcast face of the rabbi, "The
single missing name in the ninth generation of the
female line might well have clad the youth in the
sable garments of disgrace and eternal banishment,
but that I willed it otherwise. Yet the irregularity
is a stigma not to be tolerated ; it must be removed
ere we can receive him into the full fellowship of
our holy calling."

After he had dismissed the worthy rabbi with a
muttered benediction, Jesus IV. sank back upon the
richly embroidered cushions of his divan with a
languid sigh. "It were well," he thought, "to hold
in check such youthful aspirants to the priesthood ;
these are no times for would-be prophets ; we may
have other and better use for this gigantic Nazarite." Further desultory reflections on this unim-
portant theme were cut short by the announcement
of a messenger from the temple. At sight of the
terrified face of the man who entered his presence,
the high priest started up from his recumbent position. "What now, Phinehas?" he demanded
sharply. "Hast thou fetched me the moneys?"

"Alas, my good lord !" gasped the custodian of
the temple treasure—for it was no less a person who
stood trembling in the high-priestly presence. "Woe

is me, revered servant of Jehovah ! how shall I tell
thee of what has happened !"

"Tell it with thy tongue, blockhead," cried the
priest wrathfully. "What is it that hath happened ?"

"The treasure—the sacred treasure," wailed the
man—tearing at his garment; "the accursed Gentile hath laid violent hands upon the treasure, and
hath taken away seventeen talents of gold !"

"What is this thou art saying ?" cried the high
priest, starting to his feet; "hath the procurator,
Florus, dared to do this thing ?"

"I was about my duties in the temple," said
Phinehas, growing somewhat more composed,
"when on a sudden a file of Roman soldiers—may
leprosy and death seize upon them ! burst into the
sacred enclosure. What could I do ? They demanded—and took—seventeen talents !"

"What of the guard ?"

"The guard fled, your highness."

"But the Levites—what of them ? Was there
no one of all the thousands employed about the
place to raise a hand in defence of the treasure ?"

"Those who remained in the enclosure stood as
if turned to stone, my lord ; all save one, a stranger,
who chanced to be separating the sacred wood from
certain knotty and imperfect sticks hard by. He
smote the centurion, and would have felled him to
the earth had not the soldiers beat him off with the
flats of their swords."

"What was the name of this priest?" said Jesus
sharply.

"I did not wait to ask, my good lord."

"Go back; find him, and send him hither."

The custodian of the temple treasure hesitated.
"It appeared to me, my good lord," he said cring-
ingly, "that the youth was dying; I therefore bade
the Nethenim remove his body to the vaults, that
the temple might not be defiled. He was a Nazarite—by his hair I judged it, and had not received
ordination."

The high priest lifted his eyebrows. "A pious
end," he said indifferently. Then he turned sharply
to Phinehas. "This thing must not come to the
ears of the people, else there will be a tumult, and
mischief beyond the reckoning." He ground his
teeth in impotent fury. "To lose seventeen talents
is a terrible disaster; but more and worse will come
if the people openly rebel."

"Unfortunately, revered servant of the Most
High, a number of persons who were in the court
at the time witnessed the occurrence."

"Get you back to the temple without delay," interrupted the high priest. "Assemble every priest
and Levite in the Court of Israel; I will follow."

CHAPTER XI.

THE REJECTED.

IF Ben Huna was bitterly disappointed in the circumstance which debarred his favorite from
the full functions and honors of the priesthood, it
was far otherwise with Phannias. The dream of
his life was at length realized; he was to dwell
perpetually in the shining courts of Jehovah, whose
every service was fraught with mysterious possi-
bilities. He would have accepted the meanest
duty of the lowliest of the Nethenim—or servants of
the Levites—with joyful alacrity. To stand twice
each day in the Court of Israel—the while the
singing Levites emerged in solemn white-robed
procession from the subterranean music rooms, to
assemble in serried ranks upon the Steps of Degrees;
to hear them call, one company to another, in their
sweet, musical voices :

"Holy! Holy! Holy! Lord God of Sabaoth!"

the harps, the cithems and the cymbals clashing
in silver ecstasy—was to thrill with a joy un-
speakable. And when, in the intervals of the
chanting, the priests blew mightily upon the sacred
trumpets, and at the sound the whole congregation

fell down, worshiping upon their faces—Phannias
lifted his glowing face to the white walls of the
sanctuary, his soul swelling with a passion of
gratitude. To be born a Jew, he thought at
such times, was to inherit a wondrous past and
a yet more wondrous future ; to be born a priest
of Jehovah, was little short of being made an
angel !

In these first days of his novitiate he looked joyously into the faces about him ; surely all who
served in the Mountain of the Lord's House were
his brothers beloved. Here he would discover
tranquil lives, reflecting the face of God, as still
pools reflect distant stars ; and mingling with them
in familiar intercourse he would find deep answers
of peace to all the burning questions which had
vexed his soul.

On the third day of his service he ventured to
speak of his thoughts to the priest, whom he had
been set to assist in the task of selecting un-
blemished wood for the sacrificial fire. This priest
was old, bent and wrinkled, as Phannias had already observed ; he moved stiffly and scarce lifted
his eyes from his work. The two were busy in
one of the chambers of the Women's Court.

" Hast thou served long in this holy place, good
master ?" asked Phannias, making haste to relieve
his companion of a heavy load of knotted and
worm-eaten sticks which were to be cast into " the
closet for rejected wood."

The old man lifted his dim eyes. "Who calls me master?" he said frowning—"Nay, if thou wilt make a jest of my infirmities, I must bear it. Yet thou also hast been set aside or thou wouldst not serve here."

"How then shall I call thee?"

"Call me Jachin," said the old priest shortly, turning a stick over and over in his withered hands. After a little he spoke again, fixing his dull eyes upon his companion with a faint show of curiosity. "Why art thou sorting wood for the sacrifices, who hast a comely face and an upright body? For myself I was not permitted to serve at the altar because of a crooked finger; Jehovah despiseth the man or thing which hath a blemish—blessed be his holy name! So for more than forty years I have separated the spotted, gnarled and worm-eaten sticks from them which be sound and fit for the great altar. I have eaten also of the bread of the Lord's house. Yet, thrice within a moon have I been deprived of my food because I allowed a blemished stick to pass into the house of burning. Mine eyes wax dim with age and I can no longer see as I once did."

"Why dost thou not ask for thy portion and go away to thy home?" asked Phannias; "surely after forty years——"

"There be four and twenty thousand priests of Jehovah in Israel," interrupted the old man, in his high shaking voice; "and how, thinkest thou, may the great palaces of the chief priests be builded and victualed if these all receive a portion ?"

" It is the law !"

" Oh the law—the law ! There is one law for the great and rich of the earth ; there is another for them that lack. But why wilt thou hear these things from me ? Thou wilt presently know them for thyself. Verily, I have more than once remembered the saying of a certain man out of Galilee, who also visited the temple many times in his day, and whose mouth was stopped by them that were in power."

" Dost thou speak of the false Messiah ?" asked Phannias with hesitation.

The old priest shook his head. " I speak of Jesus of Nazareth," he said ; " who and what he was, God knoweth. I have thought more than once —but no, what profit in speaking one's thoughts."

" Didst thou see him ?"

" See him ? More than a score of times ! I remember once on a certain feast day when the money-changers and the sellers of sacrifices thronged the temple gates, and even pressed in beyond the limits set them into places where it was not lawful for them to be ;—for, look you, there be great gains in feast days to them that sell, and none know it better than the chief priests, whose creatures have seized upon all the temple business.

" On that day the Galilean made unto himself a scourge, and with it drove out every mother's son

of them, together with the sheep, the oxen and the
doves. Also he overturned the tables of the money-
changers, scattering the heaped-up gold and silver,
as a strong wind scatters the dust of the highway.
When the multitude stood amazed at sight of one
driving a ruck of men and animals before him with
a whip of small cords—for no one of them all,
even of the priests and Levites, durst for the moment withstand him, he turned to them and cried
aloud : ' Behold, it is written, my house shall be
called the house of prayer ; but ye have made it a
den of thieves !' Ay, verily, it was a true word ;
I could have told him so !"

"Dost thou believe that he was the Christ?"
asked Phannias, under his breath.

The old priest shrugged his shoulders. "Do I
not serve in the Mountain of the Lord's House,"
he answered, "and eat of the meat of the sacrifices ?
and shall I commit folly in my old age, as did certain others of the priesthood, who followed him
and were cast out to starve? Verily, one must
live, and what matters a belief this way or that way
to a bare back and an empty belly."

Phannias stared at his companion with frowning
brows. "What matters a bare back and an empty
belly to one who would know the truth ?" he said
loudly. "Is a man even as the beast of the field,
who lifts not his eyes from his fodder from the day
he is born till the day he falls under the knife ?"

The old man burst into a cackle of senile

laughter. "Oh, ay, thou art a brave youth and hast a nimble tongue! Such as thou art was I also ; but praise be to Jehovah, who hath given me wisdom with my years. Verily, when the children cried 'Hosanna to the son of David' in the Court of the Women yonder, I would have joined them but for my robe.—Ay, they cried 'Hosanna' from the morning until the evening sacrifice, and no man could stop their mouths! The Galilean stood yonder, where thou seest the woman with the black veil,—at my work here, I beheld it all ; and there the blind and the lame came to him to be touched. —Yes, I swear it by the great altar, the blind went away seeing, and they that were crippled cast away their beds and walked, leaping and praising God! It was a great day. These eyes have seen nothing like it."

"But the high priest and the councillors," cried Phannias ; "did they also see these wonderful things ?"

"They saw, and heard—yes, truly ; but they were angry. And where in the law canst thou find it written that a man may receive Hosannas in the temple? The Nazarene should have rebuked them."

"If he were the Prince——"

"Ay, if he had been the Prince would he not have given us a sign that we might know him?". And Jachin drew himself up with something of the pride and authority of his office. "Verily, we de-

manded such a sign and he refused it. We asked
by what authority he did these things, and he cast
the question in our teeth. 'I will also ask you one
thing,' he said, with the cunning of a more learned
than he; 'the baptism of John, whence was it,
from heaven, or of men?' What then could we
say? If we had answered, from heaven, he would
have asked, 'why then did ye not believe him?'
If we had affirmed that it was of men—or of devils,
as many of us also believed, the people would
straightway have risen against us; for they were
persuaded that John was a prophet."

"And what said ye?" asked Phannias, eyeing his
companion with interest.

This question was never answered; at that moment a sound of tumult, of clanging arms, of voices
that cried aloud, of hurrying feet startled the
laborers.

"It will be another uprising among the people!"
whispered the old priest. "Come, let us go;
there is no good thing abroad!" And seizing
Phannias by the arm, he would have dragged him
into one of the hidden stairways which led to the
underground chambers below. But the Nazarite
wrenched himself loose and darted away in the direction of the voices.

What he presently beheld was this, a file of Roman soldiers, headed by a centurion carrying a
drawn sword in his hand, in the act of emerging
from a stairway beneath the tower of the Gate

Beautiful. He had already learned of this subterranean passage, which connected the temple with the Roman garrison in the tower of Antonia; but it was with a thrill of horror that he beheld these idolatrous Gentiles close to the sacred wall, upon which, carven in letters of Hebrew, of Greek and of Latin, were inscriptions, forbidding all such to enter under penalty of death.

Observing the young man in his priest's robe of service, the centurion, who had paused somewhat uncertainly at the top of the stairway, beckoned him to approach. "Where is the treasure room, Jew!" he said peremptorily. "Lead us hither at once; we have business with the custodian."

"Knowest thou the law," cried Phannias, his face white with anger. "Get thee back to thy place or thou shalt die the death!" He advanced threateningly, lifting the knotted stick, which he had forgotten to drop as he left the wood room.

The centurion burst into a loud laugh. "By the girdle of Venus, priest, thou art bolder than thy fellows! Stand aside! if thou wilt not answer a civil question, we must even find the shekels for ourselves. Seventeen talents is the sum which our master—and yours, Jew—hath commanded us to fetch."

A sound of wailing burst forth from the cloistered corridors above the court; Phannias looked up and beheld the white faces of priests and Levites, peering down upon the scene with manifest terror.

"Come down !" he shouted angrily. "Wilt thou suffer the heathen to despoil the Lord's house without striking a blow ?" and lifting his club he rushed in blind fury upon the centurion.

He was conscious of delivering a crashing blow full on the helmeted head of the Roman ; then he fell stunned and bleeding, the glittering walls of the temple, the blue sky and the angry faces of the soldiers blending in a mad whirl before his dazzled eyes, as he sank into a sightless, soundless deep of silence and oblivion.

CHAPTER XII.

OUT OF THE DEPTHS.

PHANNIAS sat up slowly and looked about him. He beheld a great chamber, dimly lighted by certain faint beams, which, struggling through a grated opening overhead, rested like long pallid fingers upon a naked floor of stone. This floor stretched away to meet vague outlines of arch and pillar, vast, shadowy and apparently without number. Strange sounds filtered with the strange light through the grated opening ; groaning cries, frenzied shouts, the mad rush of hurrying feet mingled in a vast, discordant roar, pierced from time to time with the strident note of trumpets, calling one to the other like voices.

Phannias passed his hand across his aching forehead. He could remember nothing ; then his eye fell upon his priest's robe of service ; the fair white linen was darkly spotted and stained.

" The temple !" he cried, reeling to his feet. " My God, they are robbing the temple !"

Stumbling in the half darkness over fallen fragments of stone, he darted away among the shadowy pillars, his ears ringing with the muffled sounds of tumult. As his dazed senses gradually cleared, he

slackened his pace and finally came to a full stop.
Not far distant a shaft of sunlight fell with blinding
glory into the gloomy place and rested, a pool of
golden yellow, on the stone floor. In the midst
of this patch of sunshine knelt the figure of a priest,
his white robes shining like snow in the brilliant
light. Glancing down with shame at his own blood-
stained garments, Phannias slowly approached this
resplendent figure, his bare feet making no sound
on the dusty pavement. He had come within perhaps twenty paces of the kneeling priest, when he
again stopped, frozen with astonishment and fear.
The priest had stretched himself at full length beside an opening, which in some mysterious fashion
had yawned at his feet. He now reached down
into an unseen receptacle and produced, one after
the other, a number of glittering objects which he
heaped up beside the aperture. Golden censers,
chains, candlesticks, were added one after another to
the shining heap, with earrings, armlets and jewels
of strange barbaric design and workmanship. The
priest finally replaced the stone, glancing furtively
over his shoulder into the shadowy depths beyond ;
then he hastily bestowed the objects in a sack
which he drew from under his robe. When he
had finished his task he arose and walked slowly
away.

The Nazarite's tongue clave to the roof of his
mouth ; he knew that he had witnessed the opening of one of the secret treasure vaults of the

temple, whose whereabouts and contents were known only to the chiefs of the nation. Hot with shame and contrition he darted forward.

" Hold, servant of Jehovah !" he cried, his voice rolling in startling reverberations beneath the low-springing archways and falling in a thousand faint echoes from the vaulted roof.

The effect of these simple words upon the retreating figure was still more astonishing ; the priest dropped the sack of treasure, and falling flat upon his face, poured out a torrent of indistinguishable words mingled with frenzied prayers and entreaties.

"I will atone !" he wailed, tearing at his garments. "I swear that I will atone ! I will offer two score bullocks upon the altar, and as many fatted firstlings ; I will give to the poor a hundred shekels, and———"

"It is I who should atone," said Phannias, stooping over the prostrate figure ; " I have seen what I ought not to have seen ; yet was I innocent in the matter, for I came to this place not knowing whither I went."

Before he had uttered the last word the priest had sprung to his feet. " I know thee now ; thou art the meddlesome Nazarite who struck at the centurion," he hissed, his face distorted with rage. "And wilt thou spy upon me, while I remove the sacred utensils for the morrow's service ?" he drew back a pace, his features settling slowly into the mask-like composure of the officiating priest.

"Thou art young and impetuous, my son," he continued—his voice no less changed than his face; "thou must learn discretion with experience. I was sorely disturbed in my sacred functions by thy unexpected and unlawful presence. Yet go thy way for this time—forgiven."

"Where wilt thou that I shall go?" asked Phannias,—"for indeed I know not where I am nor how I came to this place."

The priest pointed to the soiled and blood-stained garment with a gesture of loathing. "It is not lawful for a priest to defile himself as thou hast done," he said coldly; "thou canst come no more into the temple till thou art cleansed. Turn to the right hand and walk fifty paces; thou wilt then perceive how thou shalt come out from this place. I need not say to thee, reveal to no man what thou hast discovered. Go." Checking with a frown the eager words which trembled on the lips of the Nazarite, he pointed with an unyielding finger in the direction which he had indicated.

Forty paces, and Phannias found himself in total darkness; but he went on blindly, eager to atone for his seeming fault. He began to count his steps aloud, "Forty-three—forty-four—forty-five—" another step and with a smothered cry he dropped downward into the blackness.

Phannias' first impulse, after his fearful plunge into what appeared to his dazed senses a well or pit, ankle deep with foul-smelling water, was to cry aloud for help. But when after repeated shouts the silence was broken by neither voice nor footstep, he was forced to the conclusion that he had been deliberately entrapped and abandoned, and that by a sworn servant of Jehovah. This thought was so appalling that for an instant it shut out all else from his mind.

"My God!" he groaned aloud, "what have I found in the house of thy holiness in the space of a single day. Cowardice, theft, falsehood—murder!"

With the words came a rush of fierce anger. He set his teeth hard. "I will not die in this hole like a rat in a trap!" he cried defiantly. "I will live; I will avenge myself!"

To obtain a foothold on the steep, slippery sides of the abyss into which he had fallen proved an utter impossibility; after a long and exhausting effort he abandoned the idea of escape in that direction. As he groped about in the thick darkness, he presently discovered that by reaching out his arms it was possible to touch the slimy stones on either side; while behind and in front his outstretched hand encountered nothing. The pit was therefore narrow, and longer than it was wide.

After a little he ventured to move forward a few paces; the air became perceptibly colder, and the strange, fetid odor grew almost unendurable. It occurred to him to reach up, and this time his exploring fingers met the stones of a low-swung arch, scarce six inches above his head. Still noth-

8

ing impeded his progress; he walked cautiously
forward, his bare feet slipping from time to time in
the cold slimy liquid which splashed about his
ankles. After what seemed a long time, during
which he steadily advanced, he was conscious that
his feet were slipping more and more frequently.
The passageway was ascending a sharp incline; at
the same time the walls suddenly contracted so
that he was forced to bend nearly double. After a
little he could only crawl on hands and knees, the
foul current wetting his garments to the skin.

"My God!" he murmured, "in what have I
sinned that I must perish more horribly than a
beast?"

And now a strange thing happened; the sluggish
tide flowed past him with a sudden rush of warmth,
and was gone; at the same instant his despairing
eyes caught a faint beam of light, shining like a
star in the impenetrable darkness. Light meant
life and safety. He redoubled his efforts, observing with a sense of relief that the stones upon which
he was now forced to crawl at full length were
almost dry.

Thank God, the light was near now; it was
almost overhead! He raised his head eagerly to
snuff the delicious air which blew freshly adown
the passageway. Light! Ah yes, it was there—
the blessed light, and not in one place alone; it
filtered through a dozen small grated openings set
crosswise in the stones of the archway overhead.

Turning about with the greatest difficulty—for the walls had now contracted to such dimensions that he could scarce force his body along, Phannias raised his head to one of these orifices. " Help !" he cried loudly, " Help—for the love of God ! I am perishing in this place !"

As if in answer to his cry a great chorus, softened by unknown distance into unearthly sweetness, burst forth with that angel's song of faith :

" Yea, though I walk through the vale of deep shadow
  —even the shadow of death,
I shall not fear evil;
For thou art with me ;
Thy rod and thy staff they comfort me !"

Yet further away and more faintly, like the sound of long waves on the sand-strewn beach, came the responsive " Allelujah !" of a great congregation.

Phannias stared wildly about his narrow prison. "Where am I ?" he cried. His eyes fell upon his sodden garments ; they were dyed to the waist a dull, purplish red, as he remembered to have seen the garments of the wine-makers in the joyous vintage days. He touched them shudderingly, his brain reeling with the awful conviction which had forced itself upon him.

"Surely goodness and mercy shall follow me all the
  days of my life ;
And I shall dwell in the house of Jehovah forever !"

chanted the distant voices, as if in an ecstasy of

gratitude; a clash of silver-tongued instruments answered them, mingled with great Amens.

A sound of sonorous words of benediction spoken almost above his head roused the young priest from the apathy of despair into which he had fallen. He started up, and seized the nearest grating with both hands; the golden bars yielded to his grasp like wisps of straw. "Help! Help! Help!" he shouted, and fell half fainting against the slimy stones of his prison.

The priest who was officiating at the great altar of the temple started back with an ashen face; then he bowed himself with an evil smile. "Thanks be to Jehovah that the lot fell upon no other than myself for this service!" he murmured.

Advancing to the front of the altar before the startled congregation, he lifted his arms toward heaven with a gesture of awe and adoration. " A miracle, sons of Abraham!" he cried. "Behold a voice from under the holy altar at the time of the third sprinkling; and it cried, saying, Help! What then can this portend, save that Jehovah will graciously vouchsafe the help of his arm to save his afflicted people!"

He paused, and the wondering assembly, to a man, leaned forward breathless to listen. The faint cry was presently repeated, proceeding it seemed from the very depths of the altar, where the ashes of the evening sacrifice yet smoked dully.

"Help!" wailed the mysterious voice, "in the name of Jehovah of hosts! Help!—Help!"

With a wild cry of mingled terror and joy the people fell upon their faces. Centuries had elapsed with neither voice nor sign; but now surely the God of Hosts had proven that Israel was not forgotten.

The officiating priest motioned authoritatively to the Levites, and the closing chant burst forth, blent with the silver blare of trumpets; in the midst of which, according to prescribed custom, the wondering people slowly dispersed.

An hour later, as the priest passed slowly along the corridor leading from the Hall of Robes, he was accosted by one of the chiefs of the Levites.

"A pretty diversion thou didst graciously furnish for the people to-night, my Pharez; but it will fail of its purpose. They are swarming before Antonia like angry bees. Blood will flow before morning, and in streams which will wipe out the memory of the lost treasure."

The priest stopped short with a scowl. "A pretty diversion, sayst thou?" he said angrily. "I swear to you that what I said to the people was true. Didst thou not hear the voice?"

"Ay, truly, I heard it—all who were fitly furnished with ears heard it also. But now—betwixt us; who arranged the matter? Our revered high priest is more daring than his fellows if he would meddle for political purposes with the high altar.

For myself I fear nothing—not even the Holy Place, since I helped repair the great veil ; but the altar !"

"Canst thou not see that I am absorbed in prayer ?" said Pharez coldly ; "I may not speak with thee further."

The Levite turned away with a shrug, while the priest, after watching his retreating figure till it was well out of sight, unlocked a small door to the right of the corridor. "I must see if he be there still," he muttered.

Arrived at the place of sacrifice by a secret passageway known only to the priests, he sought carefully for the broken grating in the conduit for the sacrificial blood which surrounded the great altar.

"Art thou there, Nazarite ?" he whispered loudly, applying his mouth to the spot, which he had found with ease. He repeated the question thrice, and at every opening which communicated with the subterranean drain below, but when there was neither sound nor motion, he straightened himself. "He is already dead," he muttered, with a sigh of relief.

CHAPTER XIII.

IN THE NEW OF THE MOON.

ON a certain narrow and tortuous street of Jerusalem, in that part of the city called indifferently the inner Low Town and the Agra, there once stood an ancient and shabby house. This house was by no means remarkable in its appearance, squeezed in as it was in the midst of a long row of buildings every one of which was quite as shabby and as ancient as itself. The upper stories of all of these dwellings leaned tipsily forward as if to hobnob with their venerable neighbors on the opposite side of the street; indeed, so close was their intimacy that the red eye of the sun seldom looked upon the yellow dust mingled with evil smelling refuse which paved the street level.

The Agra itself was nothing more nor less than a bewildering labyrinth of these same gloomy and crooked streets, so densely inhabited that the flat roofs of the squat houses formed, as it were, a second and airier thoroughfare on which it was possible to walk from the Broad Wall to the Temple Mount. From the frowning battlements of Antonia the Roman guard, pacing ceaselessly to

and fro, commanded alike the spacious courts of
the temple and the swarming streets of the Low
Town. The dominant Gentile looked down upon
both with the fine indifference of one who surveys
an ant hill at his feet, which he may or may not
crush into nothingness as the whim seizes him.

The inhabitants of the Agra, immersed in business, in politics, or in a stringent observance of
laws and customs, paused long enough from time
to time to breathe a comprehensive curse upon all
Gentiles; but in the main they were too much
occupied with their own affairs to waste time or
breath upon the inevitable. Rome had become the
inevitable.

Ezra Ben Ethan, owner of the ancient and
shabby dwelling already mentioned, stood upon
the roof of his house at the hour of sunset engaged in prayer. He was a small, yellow, sour-
looking Jew, chiefly furnished as to countenance
with a pair of ferret eyes and a rusty irregular
beard, which scantily clothed his prominent chin,
and over which presided a hooked nose apparently
many sizes too large for his pursed-up mouth.
Praying, according to law, with his face turned
toward the temple, he found himself unpleasantly
dazzled by the sparks of splendor which the setting
sun struck from the slow-moving shields and hel-
mets on the walls of Antonia. Whereat, having
at his command a period of leisure and a rich variety of defamatory phrases, derived about equally

from a devout study of the denunciatory Psalms
and a residence of some fifty years in the Agra,
Ben Ethan proceeded to launch a series of anathe-
mas at the offending soldiers, coupled with im-
passioned petitions to Jehovah for their general
undoing.

"How long, O Lord!" he demanded shrilly,
"how long shall yonder idolatrous Gentiles stand
upon the bulwarks of Jerusalem? How long shall
they go to and fro upon the walls of Zion? Let
them be torn limb from limb! Let them be cast
in heaps in the valley, where there shall be none to
bury them! Let their tongues dry up betwixt their
teeth, and let the young ravens pluck out their eyes
to devour them! Bring down their lying looks
unto the dust, O Lord! Give their rulers to Israel
for a prey! Smite them with the sword; send murrain and pestilence upon them! Scorch them with
the sun of thy heavens; drown them in the floods
of thy deep! Cause wild beasts to devour them;
let their bones rot within their flesh; and let—What
now, Merodah? Canst thou not leave me alone,
girl, whilst I pray for the peace of Jerusalem?"

The intruder—a maid of perhaps fifteen years,
and delicately lovely as a half-opened flower—bent
her head meekly. "I pray thee of thy goodness
that thou wilt pardon me, my father," she said; "I
did not know that thou wast still at prayer. But
it is true that one waits below who would speak
with thee on a matter of importance."

"'Twill be Simon, the publican, for the taxes," snarled Ben Ethan, wagging his beard; "but I will not pay him—I have sworn that I will not pay —until the feast of weeks."

" It is not Simon," said the girl slowly; "the man is a stranger. I think "—she continued, with a pretty air of sagacity—"that he wishes to hire our upper room."

Ben Ethan did not wait to hear more. His upper room had been unlet for more than two months already; he wished to hire it even more than he wished to pray. Having presently satisfied himself by a noiseless inspection through the peephole over his courtyard stair that the man who still waited in the street was not the despised collector of taxes, he flung wide the door. " I pray thee, worshipful stranger, that thou wilt honor my poor abode by stepping over its threshold." And he bowed himself before the man who stood without. " How is it that I, the son of Ethan, may serve thee?"

The stranger acknowledged the salutation with a grave, " Peace be with thee and with thy house." He stepped as he spoke into the courtyard and closed the door behind him. " I am told," he said, casting a pair of singularly bright dark eyes about the place, "that there is in this house an upper chamber of fair size, with an outside staircase leading to the street in the rear, and that this chamber may be hired for a reasonable sum ; am I rightly informed?"

"An upper chamber indeed, spacious beyond one's belief, honored sir," replied Ben Ethan with a comprehensive wave of the hand. He was observing with displeasure that his would-be tenant displayed no signs of opulence in his dress, and that the pouch at his girdle was unpromisingly lean. "It is true that it may be hired—yes, and for a sum—Pst, it is nothing! To the right party —thou mayst understand without offense; for myself I am a keeper of the law; I also——"

"Show me the room," interrupted the stranger, but without rudeness; "it will save us both moments which have a value beyond gold."

Ben Ethan looked hard at his visitor. "A value beyond gold," he repeated tentatively; "ah, yes, assuredly! Thou art, perchance, a merchant, seeking gain in Jerusalem. If it be a place wherein to bestow thy goods in safety, I can promise thee—But come this way, thou shalt see for thyself."

"I am not a merchant," said the stranger tranquilly, as the two men ascended the stair; "nor have I goods to bestow here or elsewhere. I will tell thee plainly the room is wanted for a meeting-place by certain godly persons, known in Jerusalem as Nazarenes, in divers other places as Christians."

Ben Ethan stopped short for an instant. "Nazarenes!" he muttered under his breath. "Now may the God of Abraham smite me if I let my room to such.—But hold, I have said nothing. This is the chamber, good sir," he said aloud; "and a more commodious, for the money, cannot be found within the walls of Jerusalem. What sayest thou?"

The other looked about him with a well-satisfied air. The room was indeed of sufficient size to accommodate quite a company; it was moreover scrupulously clean, and lighted by a large latticed window which overhung the street. "The place will serve our purpose," he said. "It is understood that we shall be undisturbed in our worship," —fixing his keen dark eyes upon Ben Ethan—"to which thou and thy household will be welcome."

Ben Ethan shrugged his shoulders and spread abroad his palms. "What with the required attendance at the temple—to make nothing of holy days and feast days and fasts and sabbaths and new moons, there be scarce hours left in the which an honest man may gain his bread. No manna drops from heaven in these hard times, and the Romans devour the land.—Not that I grudge the Almighty his dues," he added, with an obeisance templeward; "but to worship a dead man—however righteous he may have been in his lifetime! now, that appears to me a strange thing to ask of a law-abiding Jew; is it not so?"

The stranger's eye kindled. "Jesus of Nazareth was the Messiah of Israel," he declared solemnly. "Nay, more, he was the Saviour of the world!"

Ben Ethan wagged his head. "A Messiah spit

upon!" he cried shrilly. "A Messiah scourged!
A Messiah crucified!—Nay, I myself saw it, young
man, a matter of thirty years ago! But no, we
will not speak further of the matter ; it pleases thee
to believe in this man—this carpenter of Galilee,
crucified, dead and buried ; it pleases me to look
for a king who shall deliver Israel from the hand
of the Gentiles, and that right gloriously. We
will not quarrel. Thou shalt have my upper
room for the sum specified ; as for myself, I am a
poor man, the hire will pay my taxes—for heaven
bear me witness, I knew not whence the money
was to come!"

When half an hour later Ben Ethan returned to
the roof, he found his daughter perched upon the
highest ledge of the parapet. "Oh father," she
cried eagerly, without turning her head, "it is coming—I am sure it is coming! See, just behind the
hill yonder, there is a glow! Yes, truly,"—and
the girl clapped her hands ecstatically, "it is the
holy—the blessed new moon!"

"Veil of the temple!" ejaculated Ben Ethan, "it
is a good omen—a good omen! The Nazarene
and the new moon in one night!" He burst into
a cackling laugh, abruptly suppressed as he climbed
nimbly up beside the girl. "I see no moon!" he
cried testily, straining his wrinkled eyelids toward
the western horizon.

"But yes, dear father," cooed Merodah, laying
her slim hand soothingly on his shoulder ; "its

slender tip pierces yonder cluster of palms like a
silver arrow. I see it quite plainly."

"Then I shall go to the temple," said Ben Ethan
decidedly; "no need to lose a feast. God grant
that I get there in due season! I missed it last
month by a hair's breadth."

Left to herself the girl softly repeated the benedictions to the new moon, her eyes fastened upon
the slender crescent which now hung like a flaming
sickle over the brow of Olivet:

"Blessed be he who reneweth the months!
Blessed be he by whose word the heavens were created,
And by the breath of whose mouth all the hosts thereof
    were formed!
He appointeth them a law and a season, that they should
    not overstep their course!
They rejoice and are glad to perform the will of their
    Creator!
Author of truth, thy goings are truth!
He hath spoken to the moon : Be thou renewed and be the
    beautiful diadem of Israel—
Who shall herself be quickened again, like to the moon!
And praise Jehovah for his glorious kingdom!
        Amen and amen!"

The girl felt very happy when she had finished
repeating this prayer ; for did not the rabbis declare
that whoso sayeth the benediction of the new moon
in its proper time is as one who holds converse
with the shining presence of the Godhead ? She sat
for a long time in the fragrant cool of the evening,
her face turned upward to the heavens like a flower,
innocent and full of peace.

As for that excellent and law-abiding Israelite,
Ben Ethan, he was making his way with all possible speed toward the temple, where in a certain
court, called Beth Jazek, a feast was provided every
month for the devout witnesses of the new moon.

The spiritual rulers of the nation had ordained
that beside the specially appointed messengers of
the Sanhedrim, who were set to watch the sky
from commanding heights in and about the city,
any person—gamblers with dice, usurers, traders in
the produce of the Sabbatical year, women and
slaves excepted—was permitted to give evidence
of the blessed appearance of the new moon. And
not only permitted, but urged—nay, enticed by potent inducements in the shape of divers meats and
drinks, provided for the occasion by the temple authorities. It may be believed therefore that a great
concourse of the pious, who were also blessed with
good appetites, assembled on such occasions before
the gates of Beth Jazek. Indeed so great was the
eagerness to perform this act of service that of late
years it had become necessary to close the gate after
a certain number of witnesses had been admitted.

Ben Ethan licked his lips hungrily as he scuttled
along through street and alley toward the temple
mount. "Jehovah grant that the gates remain wide
till I reach them !" he ejaculated. "It will save me
a meal ; also, with his blessing, I shall be able to
fetch away under my garment enough victual for
to-morrow."

By way of further propitiating an observant deity, he repeated the benedictions to the new moon, adding with a hasty obeisance: "A good sign, good fortune be to all Israel! Blessed be thy Creator! Blessed be thy Possessor! Blessed be thy Maker! As I leap toward thee, but cannot touch thee, so may my enemies be unable to injure me! May fear and anguish seize upon them! Through the greatness of thine arm may they become as still as a stone. Fear and anguish shall seize them! Amen! Selah! Hallelujah! Peace— peace—peace be with thee!"

Arrived at the temple, Ben Ethan, with the dexterity born of long practice, proceeded to force his way through the eager multitude already assembled before Beth Jazek. Being small of stature he could dodge and double, twist and turn with extraordinary ease and agility ; also he knew to a nicety just how and when to apply a prod of the elbow, a sly kick in the calves, or a grind of the sandal heel on unprotected toes. He was therefore enabled to squeeze his lean person triumphantly inside the gates just as they were closing, his victory over adverse circumstances and the crowd of disappointed faces without only serving to whet his enjoyment.

A perfunctory examination of certain of the witnesses having confirmed the fact of the reappearance of the moon, already reported by the official messengers, the chief of the Sanhedrim pronounced

the solemn word : "It is sanctified!" Whereupon
all the witnesses, the priests and the Levites cried
aloud : "It is sanctified!"

"Alas—alas!" shrilled a strident voice. "Alas
for Jerusalem! What profiteth the blessed coming
of the new moon? What profiteth joyous feast
or solemn fast, when the holy temple is defiled with
the iniquitous feet of Gentiles, and its treasure is
seized by bloody and violent men! Sons of Abraham, the procurator, Florus, hath seized seventeen
talents from the temple treasury!"

At this word a tumult indescribable broke out.
Cries, questionings, curses, wailing, in the midst
of which the excited multitude burst out of Beth
Jazek and rushed away to the Court of Israel, un-
mindful of the heaped-up viands which they trampled under foot in their mad haste. Ben Ethan
lingered behind to stow away beneath his abba
sundry savory morsels which had escaped the general destruction.

"Veil of the temple!" he muttered, "if the times
be evil the more need to look to one's victual!"

CHAPTER XIV.

A SINGER OF HYMNS.

THE Christian—who was known as Rufus, after completing his bargain with Ben Ethan for the hire of the upper room, went quickly away, with the air of one well satisfied. He too beheld the slender horn of the new moon swimming in the dusky glow over Olivet, but he neither bowed himself nor uttered the words of the ancient liturgy. As he passed a group of Pharisees standing upon the corner of a street mouthing their prayers and gesticulating extravagantly after their custom, certain ominous words, which he had read that day from the scroll of the prophets, rushed to his lips. "Hear the word of the Lord, ye rulers of an evil generation! Bring no more vain oblations; incense is an abomination unto me; the new moons and sabbaths, the calling of assemblies I will do away; it is iniquity—even the solemn meeting. Your new moons and your appointed feasts my soul hateth. When ye spread forth your hands, I will hide mine eyes from you; yea, when ye make many prayers I will not hear. Your hands are full of blood!"

The young man lifted his eyes to the stately

mass of the temple buildings which towered above the city in solemn grandeur, and above which floated the trailing smoke of the altar fires. "What must be the end of it all?" he mused. "How shall we, who believe in the crucified Christ, have fellowship with them who slew our Lord—who would also destroy us, body and soul?"

These questions were being asked by more than one follower of the risen Jesus. They were answered in diverse fashion. Certain in Jerusalem who believed were of the strictest sect of the Pharisees; keepers of the law, loving the ritual of the temple, its sacrificial rites, its feasts and fast days; adhering rigidly to all the endless minutiæ which scribe and rabbi had laboriously fashioned from the Levitical laws.

"The Messiah has come!" cried these believers in the meek and lowly carpenter of Nazareth; "keep ye the law of Moses! Jesus is the Messiah of Israel; therefore become Jews!"

These Pharisaical Christians busied themselves devoutly in vain attempts to patch the yawning rents in the robe of Judaism with the strong new cloth of the kingdom. They traveled into far countries, visiting the scattered handfuls of believers who had been wrested from heathen darkness by the labors of a Paul or a Barnabas. "The men who have taught you are grievously mistaken," they declared; "ye cannot be saved except ye keep the law of Moses." Whereat the converts, rejoic-

ing in the beautiful simplicity of the new faith, fell
straightway into doubt and anguish of mind.

Other eyes there were which saw with a clearer
vision ; other voices, crying out a far different message. "Old things have passed away ; behold all
things are become new! Believe on the Lord Jesus
Christ and thou shalt be saved! It is not possible
that the blood of bulls and goats should take away
sin ; but this Jesus, after he had offered one sacrifice for sins forever, is set down on the right hand
of God !"

Rufus was a Jewish proselyte ; he was also a
convert to the faith of Christ ; but in Jerusalem he
had been forced constantly to remember the first
of these two facts. Therefore it was that he sighed
deeply, as he beheld the smoke of the evening sacrifice rising into the solemn heavens like a ghost of
the dead.

As the young man hastily threaded the narrow
streets, emerging now and again into the wider
market squares, he observed that these places were
unusually full of people ; and that here and there
single voices raised in excited harangue sounded
above the loud hum of the crowd. These voices
were not discoursing upon the appearance of the
new moon, but of some outrage perpetrated by the
lawless Roman, Florus, under whose rule unhappy
Jerusalem had writhed for more than a year.

Rufus would have gone his way without paying
further heed to the matter which for the moment

agitated the popular mind; tumults were common occurrences in the crowded Agra, as he was well aware. A detachment of Roman soldiers would, in all likelihood, shortly appear on the scene; arrests would follow, likewise scourgings, for which purpose a peaceable Greek would answer quite as well as a turbulent Jew. He frowned impatiently as the eddying crowd forced him back against the stall of a fruit-vender. The merchant leaned forward and plucked him by the sleeve.

"Hast thou come from Antonia?" he asked excitedly; then without waiting for an answer, "They threaten to pull the castle about the ears of the thieving Gentile unless he restores the treasure. Sacred fire! but I believe every man, woman and child in the Agra—ay, and in the whole city—is on the move! The Roman may repent him of his folly."

"To seize the treasure was an outrage," said the young Greek tranquilly; "but the people will gain nothing for themselves by making a tumult."

"A murrain on thee for an unwashed Gentile!" cried a strident voice close to his ear. "The day has come to throw off the Roman yoke! Blood! Blood! The time is ripe for blood!" The speaker —by the token of his cap and apron an apprentice in the shop of the baker hard by—clambered nimbly to the top of the stall still bellowing, "Blood—blood!" with all the strength of his lungs.

"Offspring of a mule!" cried the fruit-vender in

a rage. "Wilt thou ruin my trade with thy bray-
ing? Get thee down from my stall, or blood will
flow of a surety!—Here, you Gentile, help me
catch the knave and I will reward thee!"

But Rufus was already beyond hearing. He
reached the nearest gate without further incident;
passed through, and was presently making his way
into the deep shadows of the valley of Jehoshaphat.
Here the dull roar of the rapidly increasing mob
about Antonia was swallowed up and lost in the
large calm of the summer night. Out of the cool,
green depths rose the hoary walls of the city,
builded of "goodly stones," "compact together"
with tears and prayers and blood; crowned with
the temple as with a diadem. On the further side
of the valley lay the Mount of Olives, ascending in
gentle slopes and terraces, clothed almost to its
summit with gardens and orchards. Rufus could
already distinguish a twinkling star of light amid
the clustered olive trees, which revealed the whereabouts of the tiny whitewashed hut which he called
home.

The young Greek was a vine-dresser; he was
also, like many of his countrymen, something of a
poet. As he tranquilly pursued his way along the
narrow road which skirted the city wall, the beauty
of the rosy evening sky and the calm and peace of
the green valley filled him with happiness. He
therefore lifted up his voice, which was both sweet
and far reaching, and began to sing, or rather

chant, the words of a hymn which he had himself composed, and which was already well loved
by the Christians of Jerusalem :

> "Jesus—Christ, glad Light of the Highest!
> Light of the Father, radiant, holy!
> While the night spreads its dim mantle o'er us,
> We worship the light which hath shined—
> Which hath shined in the darkness!
> Praise to thee, Father! Praise to thee, Jesus!
> Worthy art thou to be praised of the holiest,
> Now and forever; all days and eternally,
> Beloved of God, who givest us life!"*

As the last words fell from the lips of the singer,
he stopped short and listened attentively. He
thought that a voice had called to him from above.
Looking cautiously about among the shrubs and
bushes which thrust themselves over his path out
of the gathering darkness, he wrapped his abba
more closely about his shoulder and hurried on;
reflecting, not without a sense of discomfort, on the
fact that the country had of late been plagued by
wandering bands of robbers, who made no more of
the life of a wayfarer than of a draught of sour
wine. Again he came to a standstill; the sound was
repeated, more faintly this time, but unmistakably
the cry of a human being in deep distress.

---

* An evening hymn by an unknown author; it was in use
among Christians of the fourth century, and is described by
a writer of that day (Basil) as "very ancient, handed down
from the fathers." It is the oldest hymn known. The above
is a free rendering, after Dr. J. Pye Smith.

"Where art thou?" cried the vine-dresser, turning his startled face toward the sky.

"Here!" came the answer. "In the wall!"

Rufus climbed the steep bank, staring blankly at the hoary mountain of the temple wall, which at this point struck its giant roots deep into the lap of the valley. "Call once again, that I may find you!"

"Here—here!" groaned the mysterious voice. "Help quickly, I am dying of thirst!"

"Merciful Diana!" ejaculated the startled Greek, lapsing into the vernacular of his native Athens; "how came you there? And how, in heaven's name, am I to get you out?"

His only answer was a hollow groaning sound which seemed at first to proceed from the solid wall; but which, upon further investigation, was found to issue from a triangular grated opening set deep in the stones. This grating covered a space scarce large enough to admit the head and shoulders of a man; beneath it the wall was deeply stained and discolored.

"Look you, my friend," cried Rufus in a loud, cheerful voice, albeit accompanied by a dubious shake of the head and an involuntary shudder; "these bars are too thick for one to force with his naked hands. Here is my water-bottle and a loaf; eat, drink, and have courage; thou wilt soon be released." Though he spoke thus confidently he was by no means sure of the best course to pursue in the matter. Certain dark tales concerning the cruelty and treachery of the Jewish priests, current among his own nation, came back to his mind. For himself he had long ceased to believe these things ; yet he remembered them.

Observing that his water-bottle had been drawn into the aperture, he again approached his mouth to the grating. "Who art thou ?" he urged; "and how camest thou in the wall of the temple ?"

The answer astonished him ; two large hands appeared out of the darkness ; they grasped the bars of the grating, which bent and wavered for an instant like ropes, then wrenched from their sockets fell with a clank to the stones below. Involuntarily Rufus drew back a pace, as a head covered with long matted hair was thrust out from the opening. Then he sprang forward ; the head and trunk of a man had fallen limply outward. Grasping the hanging body just underneath the armpits, the Greek bent himself with a lusty effort, with the result that both rescuer and rescued fell violently backward and rolled over and over down the steep bank into the roadway below.

Rufus was the first to recover himself. In the dim light of the evening he perceived that the body which he had pulled out from the hole in the wall lay motionless upon its face just where it had fallen.

He turned it over. "Merciful Diana !" he repeated—then correcting himself with anxious haste,

" Forgive, oh Crucified One—the man is, after all, dead."

But Rufus was mistaken ; the man who had been thrice pronounced dead within the hours of a single day had only fainted after his frightful experience. He opened his eyes presently under the somewhat clumsy ministrations of his rescuer, and sighed deeply two or three times.

" God !" he murmured, "the stars—the stars— not that horrible darkness—thank God ! Yes, I will do it—by the blood of the sacrifices—the blood —the blood." He shuddered and relapsed again into silence.

Rufus bent over him anxiously. " Canst thou arise ?" he asked ; "it is but a step from this place to a house where thou mayest find rest and re- freshment."

Somewhat to his surprise the other rose slowly to his feet. " I will go with thee where thou wilt," he said gently ; "thou hast delivered my soul from death. But listen, and bear witness to the vow which in yonder place of blood I made to the God of Israel. I, Phannias, the son of Samuel, do sol- emnly declare that I will search out to know for myself all that may be known of one, Jesus of Nazareth, who lived and died within the memory of some who are yet upon earth. If it be true that he was the Messiah, I will humble myself before him, to love him and to follow him ; but if it ap- pear that these things which men do affirm of him be false, then will I rid Israel of the memory of the man! Bear witness that I have said it."

Rufus bent his head before the stranger, who towered above him in the half light, his face drawn and haggard, his white garments purple with the blood of uncounted sacrifices. "It is witnessed," he said slowly.

CHAPTER XV.

A SIMPLE CREED.

PHANNIAS spent three days in the hut of the vine-dresser ; during these days he said little and thought much.   When one has sojourned in the valley of the shadow of death and emerged therefrom he sees henceforth with a clearer vision, whether the way be forward into the unknown country of blinding light, or along the sadder and darker ways of earth.   The hours which he had passed in that horrible place of blood and darkness were as years, and as years they left their mark upon both soul and body.

The Greek, comprehending something of all this with the facile sympathy of his race, asked no questions of his guest, leaving him to the solitude which he so evidently craved.   He had shrewdly guessed from the dress and general appearance of the stranger that he was both priest and Nazarite.   For himself he had been sufficiently imbued with Jewish prejudices to regard both offices with veneration.

" Shrine of Diana !" he muttered to himself, as he placidly dug his little patch of vineyard, " who knows but that this holy man will bring good fortune to me and mine.—Now a murrain on my un-

ruly tongue ! will I never forget the heathen gods ?
Truly I must cleanse my ways or I shall yet perish
with the ungodly !"

Whereat this strange mixture of Greek supersti-
tion, Jewish formalism and Christian faith, blended
withal in a soul of adorable simplicity and childlike clarity, proceeded to wash his hands and his
lips with Pharisaical zeal. " Beloved Jesus," he
murmured, in the tone of one who addresses a near
and familiar friend, " this stranger would learn of
thee. Now thou art aware, Lord, that I am of
small wit and less learning; wilt thou therefore
take this matter in hand for me. If the man will
be useful to thee, it will be an easy matter to reveal
to him the light which thou hast brought into the
world ! For myself, I will do as thou shalt direct."
And having thus laid the matter before his Master,
he promptly dismissed any anxiety which might
otherwise have troubled his mind.

On the morning of the fourth day Phannias
sought his host where he was at work in his garden. " I must return to Jerusalem," he said, staring abstractedly at the ground ; " I must return at
once."

" Best bide where thou art for a time," said
Rufus, surveying his guest with honest admiration.
The days of quiet had completely removed all
traces of the young Nazarite's frightful experience ;
and now clad in the spotless garments of the novitiate—garments cleansed and whitened by his own

hospitable hands, it appeared to Rufus that his
guest was more beautiful than a Greek god.   Truly,
it might be that there were no gods; but their
marble images, shining like snow in the blue air of
Athens, were still beloved in memory.   "Best bide
where thou art," he repeated; "there is tumult and
slaughter in Jerusalem.   Here thou art safe."

Phannias started violently.   "Tumult and slaughter!   But why——"

The Greek shrugged his shoulders.   "There is
always tumult," he said, showing his white teeth in
a cheerful smile.   "The Jews are never more content than when shouting and rending the garment.
—A strange custom and costly, eh?—the rending
of the garment.   But this time there is also much
more, alas!   A frightful catastrophe, in fact.   The
noble Florus took to himself seventeen talents of
sacred money from the temple coffers—An outrage?
Yes; he should smart for it, were I Cæsar.   And
when, after their custom, the people beat upon the
breast, tore the garment, and cast of the dust and
stones of the street against the gate of the castle,—
and truly what harm in all this?—the noble Florus
should have indulged them.   But no; this so
savage and implacable a Roman sends down into
the crowd soldiers with drawn swords, who shortly
disperse the multitude, leaving many dead upon the
ground both of women and men."

Phannias leaned forward breathlessly.   "And the
temple—" he urged; "is the temple safe?"

The Greek made a rapid gesture, expressive of wonderment and resignation. "The temple is so far safe," he said gravely; "but there is talk of that which threatens the whole nation. The people have arisen and swear that they will avenge their treasure and their dead. Sacred Apollo ! but there can be but one end to it all. Rome is the hand of iron ; Jerusalem the eggshell. What can happen, I ask you ?"

"I must go into the city at once," repeated Phannias, with decision. "And you, my friend— you are not of our nation, I perceive ; yet to you I owe my life !"

"Do not let that trouble you, holy Nazarite," said Rufus apologetically. "I am a Greek by birth it is true ; but I am a Jew as well, and keep the law as I am able. I am also a Christian," he added with simplicity.

"A Christian ?" repeated Phannias.

"I believe that the Jew, Jesus of Nazareth, was the Christ, sent by the true and only God to save men from their sins ; and that he will give to them a life beyond this life, which shall endure forever." Rufus recited this, his simple creed, with a joyful enthusiasm which did not escape the wondering eye of the Nazarite.

Phannias was profoundly disturbed by the terrible intelligence which he had just received, but he also remembered his vow. "Why dost thou believe that Jesus of Nazareth was sent by God ?" he asked harshly. " Did not the man perish on the cross? And does not the law teach that the fruit of the tree is accursed?"

" Truly I am not wise in matters of your law," said the Greek humbly; " but this, I know, there is no peace for him that hath sinned, either in the faith of Greece—for a god of marble cannot forgive; nor yet in the temple of the Jews. What man is there among you who are learned, I ask, who hath kept your law in the sight of God? And for us who are ignorant, what hope is there? But this Jesus was a man, as I myself; he can therefore pity, now that he lives in the heavens. He has given me peace here." And the speaker laid his hand upon his breast. " I declare to you that formerly I was of all men most unhappy. I had ceased to believe in the gods of Olympus; the God of Israel terrified me—a Gentile. But Jesus of Nazareth, I love—I adore! I am happy—I shall always be happy. In the flesh I may trust him— even for what I eat and wear. Yes, truly; is it not wonderful? He is with us always, so that if even I—a Gentile and unlearned, as you see—but whisper to him, he hears me and gives at once what I ask. You do not believe me—no; but it is quite—quite true!"

Phannias looked with amazement at the shining eyes and eloquent face of this Gentile, who spoke in so strange a fashion of a Jew, who had already been dead for a generation.

"But thou hast not even seen the man!" he said at length with a frown of incredulity; "he has been dead these many years. How is it possible to love a dead man, and a stranger? My father is dead; I would fain love him, but can one love a story—a shadow—a something which does not exist? How is it possible? Thou art beside thyself, Greek!"

Rufus shook his head. "I am not mad, holy Nazarite," he said quietly. "I have already said to you that Jesus of Nazareth is not dead; he arose from his tomb on the third day after his crucifixion and became alive again. Thou dost not believe this? No; but it is more true than any word of all the law of Moses. Speak for yourself, friend, to this Jesus, who was dead and is alive again; he will himself reveal to thee the truth so that thou canst not gainsay it."

"Dost thou mean that *I* should pray to this man?" cried Phannias; "this man who was condemned and crucified as a false prophet? Nay, was he not so convicted; and of foul blasphemy also, in presence of the wisest and holiest of Israel!"

"Do priests make no mistakes, then?" returned Rufus shrewdly. "I have asked thee no questions; but tell me how camest thou, who art also a priest, to be perishing in the wall of the temple?"

Phannias covered his face with his hands; and Rufus, perceiving that his word had smitten, continued. "Thou hast vowed in my hearing—and I

10

also have witnessed the same, that thou wilt look to the claims of this crucified Jesus. I declare to thee that he is alive and can hear thy voice, and that he will reveal himself to thee if thou wilt but see him !" In his earnestness the Greek ventured to lay his hand upon the shoulder of his guest.

The Jew drew back, all the ingrained pride of race leaping to his eyes. "I have sworn that I will investigate this matter," he said coldly; "I shall keep my vow; but I will pray only to Jehovah, than whom there is no other God in heaven or on earth."

"There is a short way and an easy into the kingdom," said the Greek sorrowfully; "there is also a way that is long and hard. Thou hast chosen, and no other may choose for thee. Pray to Jehovah that thou mayst find the truth. I also will pray for thee." He added the last words with the confidence of one who possesses royal resources upon which he may draw at will.

Phannias regarded the vine-dresser long and steadfastly. "My friend," he said at length, "I perceive that thou art true and sincere in thy belief; more than this I cannot say. For what thou hast done in my behalf—and for what thou hast promised, thou hast my gratitude. I have nothing more to give thee now; but perhaps in the future—nay, who knows." He broke off abruptly, and with no other word of farewell was gone.

Rufus looked after the tall, white figure wistfully.

"Thou wilt go with him, my Jesus," he murmured aloud. Then his face cleared as he broke into the swinging chant of his hymn :

"We worship the light which hath shined—
Which hath shined in the darkness !
Praise to thee, Father !   Praise to thee, Jesus !
Worthy art thou to be praised of the holiest,
Now and forever, on all days and eternally,
Beloved of God, who givest us life !"

CHAPTER XVI.

WITH THE CHIEFS OF THE NATION.

IN the palace of the high priest there was no decorous feast in progress, as was the custom on most days of the year. Jesus IV. and half a score of others of the high-priestly family were indeed assembled in one of the lofty rooms of the palace ; but the faces of all were grave and stern, and the wine and sweetmeats, circulated amongst them by velvet-footed servants were allowed to pass untasted.

"It were perhaps well to proclaim a solemn fast," said Ananus, who had but lately been deposed from the sacred office, and who yet in reality wielded the scant authority left to the chiefs of the Jewish nation. "A fast will at least serve to keep the people off the streets and market places."

"It is too late for that," said the high priest gloomily ; "the people are mad for blood."

"The facts are appalling enough," pursued Ananus with decision, "but they must be faced, and wisdom must prevail against madness. Look you, the Romans have slain some three thousand people ; but who and what are these people ? Jews principally, but all of the poorer classes—the malcon-

tents ; 'twill prove merely a wholesome lesson if
we can control the situation for the space of a
month. The people must be forced to submit to
Roman authority ; for on that authority rests the
peace of Israel and our own prosperity. This wild
talk of throwing off the Roman yoke is folly—
madness. Nay, 'twere as though the seamen on a
foundering ship were to cut away and cast off the
undergirding, which alone holds together the shat-
tered timbers of their vessel. This insurrection
might be laid to the doors of the Nazarenes ; by so
doing we should ourselves escape punishment, and
perchance rid the nation of a foul and blasphemous
brood."

Ananus cast his shrewd eyes about the circle of
gloomy faces and continued. "Our gracious emperor, Nero, it is said, hates and fears the Jews ;
but he hates and fears the Christians—as the Gentiles are pleased to call the Nazarenes—even more.
He has already slain three thousand of them in
Rome, including the pestilent Saul, aforetime a
Pharisee and member of the Sanhedrim ; also one,
Peter, a Galilean, who once wrought untold mischief in our midst. As I have said, this tumult
must be referred to the Nazarenes ; I will myself
look to it. In the meantime, the people must be
held in check. Better lose fifty talents from the
temple treasure than to gain the wrath of Rome."

Jesus moved uneasily in his chair. "I sent an
embassy to Florus this morning at the third hour,

according to thy counsel," he said in muffled tones.
"Simon, the son of Asaph—a Roman citizen, as
thou art aware ; also Azariah, and Joseph of Galilee, all three citizens of equestrian rank."

Ananus nodded approvingly. "It is well and
wisely done. And has the embassy returned ?"

"The embassy will not return. Simon was
scourged, and cast into a dungeon under Antonia ;
the others are crucified."

Ananus sprang to his feet with a loud cry.
" Crucified !—Impossible ! They were Roman citizens !"

" They were also Jews," said the high priest with
a despairing gesture. "Above their crosses runs
the following inscription : ' Florus, procurator, to
all the Jews which be in Jerusalem, greeting ! Such
as these will you shortly be, who have insulted the
dignity of Rome.' "

"Who then of us all is safe?" whispered Elhanan, the brother of the high priest, turning his
ghastly face from one to the other of the horrified
listeners. " I shall leave Jerusalem at once."

" Leave Jerusalem !" cried Ananus, with flashing
eyes. "If all in authority leave Jerusalem, the
people like a flock of defenceless sheep will rush
into the jaws of this wolf and perish. Jerusalem
will vanish off the face of the earth. And if Jerusalem be destroyed what place in all the circle of the
earth will be left to us ? Nay, we must remain,
one and all. This Florus is not Rome. He is a

drunken madman. He shall be punished for everything which he hath done contrary to law. Thanks
be to Jehovah, the laws of Rome are second only
to the laws of Moses. What is written is written,
and there is no man who may say : 'I am not under the law.' The procurator must be forced to
listen to reason, till we can take steps to depose
him.''

"Wilt thou thyself visit the honorable Florus?''
sneered Elhanan. "If he chance to be in a
pleasant humor, he will perhaps do no more than
scourge thee. A high priest under the lash were
a marvelous sight! But a high priest crucified!
It would amuse this humorous Roman to compose
a suitable superscription for the cross of such an
one. As for the emperor, he would straightway
banish Florus, or cause him to drink poison ; later
he would compose smooth verses to celebrate the
event.''

Ananus gnawed his beard in silence. He was
unable to disprove what sounded like a savage jest.

After a time the youngest of the group, one Eleazar, spoke. "I am with the people," he said.
"Why indeed should Israel submit herself to idolaters? Too long have our altars smoked with
heathen offerings ; too long have we been silent under outrage, till everywhere the name of Jew is
hailed with insolent laughter and hissing. There
are but a handful of the Romans ; let us slay them.
Before the news of it shall come to the ears of the

gilded popinjay, the Romans call Cæsar, we shall
have fortified our borders. As for Jerusalem, who
can prevail against it?"

Ananus shook his head. "Thy counsels, son,
are evil," he said slowly. "There is no way save
that of submission." After a pause he added,
"The sister of Agrippa is at present sojourning in
the Asmonean palace. She is more Roman than
Jew; she must be persuaded to lend us her aid in
this matter."

He would have spoken further, but at that instant an attendant parted the curtains of heavy
stuff which served to shut out the glaring light of
the court without. "A priest, my good lords," he
announced, "who insists upon being admitted."

"Bring him in," commanded the high priest,
welcoming any interruption to the dreary conference which bade fair to lead to no comfortable
conclusion. For himself he had secretly determined
to follow the advice of his brother, Elhanan, and
quit Jerusalem. To his indolent and pleasure-lov-
ing soul the present situation had become intolerable. Therefore it was that he fixed his eyes with
some eagerness upon the man who was presently
ushered into the chamber. "What wilt thou?" he
inquired; "hast thou news from Florus?"

At the question the whole circle of hierarchs fixed
their eyes upon the newcomer, observing with evident surprise his imposing stature and powerful
frame, well matched by the dignity and beauty of

his youthful face. "I know nothing of the Roman, my lord," he said, looking seriously from one to the other of the listening group. "I have come because I wish to withdraw from my service in the temple. I crave an honorable release from the duties to which I am assigned."

Eleazar's lip curled; he had readily recognized the stranger by his garb as belonging to the inferior orders of the priesthood. "The fellow is afraid," he sneered. "Nay, let him go; there are ten thousand to take his place."

But Ananus, who had been studying the face before him from under half-closed lids, raised his hand authoritatively. "Who art thou, my son?" he asked gently ; "and why is it that thou wilt desert the service of Jehovah at such a time as this?"

"My name is Phannias," replied the young man boldly. "I will serve no longer in the temple because I have seen falsehood, cowardice, murder, stalking through its courts with unveiled faces. Also, since there be many who affirm that the Messiah has already come, and that he was put to death by those who should have hailed him Prince of Israel, I have determined to know of these things for myself."

Elhanan started to his feet with an oath. "The fellow is an accursed Nazarene," he cried. "'Tis because of such knaves that Israel writhes under the lash !"

But Ananus silenced him with a word. "Let

154 THE CROSS TRIUMPHANT.

me, I pray thee, speak with this priest," he said, in a tone which those who heard were not disposed to gainsay. With a few skillfully put questions he drew from the neophyte the whole story of his experiences in the temple. "We must look to this matter," he said at length, casting a wary eye about the mute circle of listeners. "Verily, it shall be looked to; but first, there be other matters which press upon us sorely." Turning suddenly to Phannias, "My son, dost thou love thy God, thy temple, and thy nation?"

"More than life itself," was the answer,—breathed rather than spoken.

"Then putting aside all anger and malice—yea, and all questions pertaining to law and doctrine, wilt thou perform a service for thy God, thy temple and thy nation?—a service which indeed is not without great peril, as thou shalt presently hear; yet because thou art come to us in this hour I believe that Jehovah hath sent thee. Go to Florus, the procurator, and say to him such words as I shall presently teach thee. So shalt thou earn for thyself favor with God and men; for who shall question but that God will reward the labors of them that diligently serve his chosen people."

The face of the Nazarite shone. "I will perform this service," he said with simplicity; but his voice rang out in that dim chamber of luxury like the clang of a sword against the shield of an enemy.

Elhanan permitted the corners of his sensual

mouth to curl upward in a smile. " By the double veil of the holiest!" he whispered in the ear of Eleazar, "the young fool will go pleasantly to his execution. Peace be with him!"

CHAPTER XVII.

MERODAH.

TO Merodah, the daughter of Ben Ethan, immured in her father's house, had come no word of the tumult and massacre which had shaken Jerusalem to its centre. It was not indeed the custom for a law-observing Jew to hold much converse with the women of his household upon any occasion. Women, like the baser animals, were good in their place; but that place was immeasurably below the exalted position in the scale of creation occupied by their lords. The girl had observed that her father was in a sour humor, and that he spent more time than common upon the housetop, presumably engaged in prayer. In the innocence of her heart she imagined herself the sole object of his displeasure.

"Merciful Jehovah," she murmured, timidly venturing a prayer on her own account; "how is it that I do not please my father? It is true that I am ignorant; and not skillful perhaps in the baking of the bread as I ought to be."

Then she hid her face in her mantle, fearful lest she had offended the deity by the mention of her humble avocations. "How"—she asked herself

with a sigh—"shall a woman pray so that she may
find favor in the eyes of him who sitteth on the
circle of the heavens?" After mature reflection
she decided that this was indeed impossible, and
turned to the consideration of more mundane ex-
pedients. She determined at length, with a wisdom
worthy of her sex, that a certain choice dish composed of fowls and vegetables, of which her father
was inordinately fond, would most surely restore
her to the favor which she coveted. True she had
no money; but she hoped that she might barter a
coin from the necklace bequeathed her by her
mother, at the stall of a certain good-natured poulterer not three squares distant.

Full of this idea she wrapped herself in her mantle and stole out into the street, availing herself of
a moment when her father was busied with a customer in the little shop. "Good fortune!" she
murmured to herself with a happy little laugh; "he
never will know that I was away for one smallest
moment. And the fowls? It will be two of them
that I will buy; and they must be fat and good or
I will not so much as look at them. Aha! I am,
after all, wise in some ways; for this one thing my
father does not know, that to be tender and pleasant to the palate a fowl must possess a soft bone in
the breast—but I know it; yes!"

Quite absorbed in her own joyful thoughts the
girl hurried along, oblivious to certain ominous
sounds which arose from the lower city. Arrived

presently in the market place, she was amazed to
find it empty; as for the poulterer's stall, it was
quite overturned, and the vegetables and birds lay
all about in sodden shapeless heaps, as though they
had been trodden underfoot of beasts of burden.
The round, cheerful face of Bidcar, the poulterer,
was nowhere to be seen. But what was it that
protruded from under the broken timbers of the
stall?—the hand and arm of a man, partly covered
with striped drapery! Manifestly some frightful
accident had befallen the good poulterer; his stall
had fallen upon him; he was hurt—perhaps dying.
She must fetch help. There were people in the
square below; she could hear them shouting.

In another moment the mob had seized upon this
human atom, as the mad current of a swollen river
seizes the leaf which drops from an overhanging
bough and whirls it away on its wild errand. Merodah—frightened—breathless—found herself all
against her will in the midst of a seething, perspiring
mass of men, women and children, above which
hung a sullen cloud of red dust, pierced by beast-
like cries, curses, groans, imprecations. This mass
of people, as one creature, vast, mysterious, swayed
by an unknown will, moved steadily forward.

Merodah looked wildly about her, conscious only
of a desire to escape; the veil had fallen away from
her face, revealing the flower-like tints of cheek
and neck and her dark eyes, bright as those of a
frightened child. "Father!" she cried piteously,

" Father !"—not knowing that she had uttered a
sound.

A man clad in the leathern jerkin and helmet of
a soldier and carrying a short crooked sword in his
hand turned with an oath ; then stopped short.
" Wilt thou also pull down the cloisters, little one ?"
he asked, falling back a pace, and passing a grimy
finger caressingly over the smooth round cheek.

Merodah stared at him without replying.

" Sword of Mars !" muttered the soldier ; " this
is a jewel from the belt of Venus dropped into my
very hand ; I will slay the Romans later, there are
enough of them." Then, being of great stature,
he grasped the girl by the shoulder and half-guid-
ing, half-carrying her, very easily got quit of the
crowd.

Merodah drew a long sigh of relief; " Oh, sir,"
she cried, looking up into the red, bloated face of
her rescuer, " how kind of you to help me get away
from that frightful crowd ! Indeed, I know not how
I fell in with them. I must go home now ; my
father will find that I am gone and he will be more
displeased than ever."

The soldier nodded his head. " Yes, I'll warrant me that he will. Shall I take thee home to
him, little one ?"

Merodah showed her white teeth in the sweetest
of smiles. " Thou art good," she said simply ;
" but I can go quite easily by myself. See, I have
but to cross this square ; then down the street of

the brass-workers; turn a second corner; and behold—the house of my father!"

"But thou canst not go that way, my pretty,"
said the man, staring more and more boldly into
the beautiful, upturned face.

The girl drew back, her white lids fringed with
dark curling lashes drooping upon the glowing
oval of her cheek. "I am beholden to thee, kind
sir," she said tremulously. "May the God of
Israel reward thee!" With that she moved resolutely away.

The soldier burst into a roar of laughter, as
though something in her words had pleased him
through all his monstrous bulk. "The God of
Israel has rewarded me already!" he cried, with a
great oath. "And by the girdle of Aphrodite, I
want no other reward! Thou wilt come this way,
Jewess—along with me; and mind thou come
peaceably, for I have birds of other feathers to
cage."

Merodah glanced back for a brief instant into
the brutal, leering face; then obeying her instincts
turned to run.

With three long strides the soldier was at her
side. "Come, come, my pretty! Thou wilt surely
never run from one who loves thee." With that he
caught the girl in his arms, and bent his mottled
visage toward hers.

"Help—help!" she shrieked, struggling weakly
in the iron grasp of her captor.

At that moment a man in the garb of an inferior priest turned the corner of the street. He was walking swiftly, with bent head ; but at the piercing cry of the girl he stopped. " Let go the woman, coward," he called imperatively. " Let her go, I say !"

" Oh, *thou* sayst it—eh ?" roared the soldier, again mightily amused. " And who art thou to interfere betwixt a man and his rebellious wife ?"

" I am not his wife," cried Merodah. " Father— oh, father !"

Phannias caught a glimpse of the white, terrified face. " Let her go !" he repeated in a sudden fury ; and without further ado he seized the soldier about the throat with both hands.

With an inarticulate splutter of rage the fellow strove to shake off the choking grasp, reaching for his sword with one hand while with the other he still clutched the girl. Phannias perceived the motion, and let go his hold on the man's throat long enough to jerk the weapon from the unsteady fingers and hurl it far down the street.

" Curse you !" howled the soldier ; " I'll teach you to meddle with an honest man's business !" In his blind rage he loosed his grasp upon Merodah— who staggered up against the wall too terrified to fly—and lunged toward his opponent with the bellow of an infuriated bull.

Phannias was at first sight no match for his gigantic adversary ; but he was angry and sober, while the soldier was angry and drunk. Stepping lightly to one side to avoid the furious onset, he smote the fellow just under the ear. The soldier staggered to his knees; but was up again in an instant, roaring out threats and curses as he rushed upon the light-footed priest. Again Phannias avoided him, springing from side to side, as light and elusive as a flying thistle-down.

The soldier was plainly in no trim for this kind of warfare; his breath came in great gasps; his face grew purple. " Dog of a Jew !" he cried, and gathering all his forces for one last desperate effort, he hurled himself upon his enemy only to meet a stinging blow which sent him reeling back against the wall.

"Beard of Jove !" he bawled. " Thou art a sneaking coward, not fit to fight an honest man. Come on, if thou dare, and I will wrestle with thee; but may the furies smite me if I play at shuttle-cock with thee longer !"

Phannias surveyed his adversary with a scornful smile. " I have no present quarrel with thee, Gentile," he said coolly. " I commanded thee to loose the woman ; thou hast obeyed me ; the mat‧ ter is therefore finished. Go thy way in peace, and I will go mine."

The soldier shook his great shoulders, a curious mixture of admiration and malice twinkling in his small, deep-set eyes. Then the corners of his red beard lifted. "Dog of a Jew !" he exclaimed, slapping his thigh ; "for a swine eater thou art a proper youth—I swear it ! Ha, ha ! I have obeyed thee ; the matter is finished ! Thou wilt also take the woman—eh ?" He stopped short, thrusting forward his shaggy head as if listening intently ; then raising his hand to his mouth he sent forth a peculiar bellowing note, which was at once answered from a little distance.

Phannias did not wait for the half dozen men, armed with the short crooked sword of the notorious Sicars, who turned the corner of the street at a run. He seized the girl by the arm. " Come !" he whispered.

"Stop, Jew !" roared the soldier, and repeating the urgent note of summons, he gave chase.

Half way down the second street the girl stumbled and fell. " I can go no further," she moaned. " Leave me and save thyself !"

Phannias looked about him in an agony of indecision. His mission—his sacred mission, entrusted to his care by the chief of his nation ; and abandoned—for what ? He raised the girl roughly to her feet. " Art thou the wife of that man !" he said sternly. " Answer—yes or no ; they are gaining on us !"

Merodah raised her eyes to meet those of her questioner, a scarlet flush staining the whiteness of her cheek. " I am the wife of no man !" she cried, a note of anger in her tremulous tones. Then her face went white again, and she sank back half

swooning at sight of her persecutor not twenty
paces distant. Phannias' quick ear had caught the
sound of a heavy door grating on its hinges in the
wall hard by; without a word he caught up the
fainting girl and pressed boldly past the amazed
porter.

"Ah, thou dog; get thee back into the street!"
began the porter in a violent rage; then his eye
fell on the white garments of the man who had so
adroitly forced an entrance. "Why art thou here?"
he asked more civilly.

"I am pursued," said Phannias briefly. "Let
the woman rest and recover herself a little; I will
go about my business."

"This is all very well, sir priest," replied the
porter, wagging his head; "but it will not serve
in these troublous days. Thou must even explain
thyself to the captain of the guard. Follow me—
thou and the woman."

"What will he do with us?" whispered Merodah, drawing back. "Let me go—only let me go
home, kind sir! My father—Oh, what will my
father say to me?"

"Follow," repeated the gatekeeper, jingling his
keys; "or I will call the guard, who will straightway scourge ye both for thieves."

As the three traversed a large and beautiful garden,—the gatekeeper slightly in advance, they came
suddenly face to face with a group of persons.
The porter, obviously abashed, bowed himself

almost to the ground before the central figure in this group.

"Pardon, worshipful princess," he faltered apologetically; "I was not aware that your highness walked in the garden at this hour."

The person addressed made no immediate reply; her dark eyes were busying themselves with the pair who stood behind the trembling menial. "What have we here?" she asked, in a soft languorous drawl which yet conveyed unquestioned authority.

"A fellow in the dress of a priest, noble princess," began the gatekeeper eagerly, "who——"

"Let me explain our presence here," interrupted Phannias, advancing a step. "I was on my way to the palace of the procurator, bearing an urgent message from Ananus, the high priest, when I came upon this maid in the grasp of a brutal fellow; I attempted her rescue, but to escape a superior force of the enemy took refuge in an open door."

The lips of the princess curled. "A gallant priest, my lord," she observed, turning with a light laugh to the man who walked by her side. "What say you, shall we cool his ardor in our dungeon for a space?"

Phannias fixed his eyes full on the beautiful, haughty face of the lady. "Princess," he said, "I have told thee the truth. Let me, I pray thee, go my way. As for the maid, I never before set eyes

upon her; yet as I bore an honest love for my
mother I could leave no woman in such evil
plight."

" Indeed it is true—quite true !" cried Merodah,
dropping the veil which she had drawn modestly
across her face. " It is I who am at fault—I alone ;
I left my father's house, knowing nothing of the
disorder in the streets."

" A careless father to leave such a jewel unguarded," muttered the man, to whom the princess
had spoken.

" But I did not ask my father, sir," said Merodah, blushing rosily under the prolonged scrutiny
of so many eyes.

" Why then didst thou go?" demanded the
princess coldly ; " was it to meet thy lover—the
bold priest here ?   And how after all "—turning
suddenly to the gatekeeper, who winced perceptibly
under her frown, " did these persons make their
way into the palace—and into my presence ?"

" They forced their way past me, worshipful
princess ; when I but opened the door to——"

" Was the guard present when you opened—as
I have ordered ?"

" The guard stood not twenty paces distant,
your highness," stammered the man, turning white.

" Then it appears that it was our good fortune
alone which prevented a band of Sicars from sur-
prising us in the privacy of our garden.   Such in-
trusions must not be repeated.   Remove this man."

The unhappy porter, who understood too well that he had received his death sentence, ventured no word of appeal, but suffered himself to be dragged away unresisting betwixt two slaves.

The princess watched the doomed man till a clump of shrubbery hid him from her eyes; then she turned with a shiver to her women. "Merciful Diana!" she cried petulantly, "why did I make the stupid vow which binds me to this Jerusalem for thrice seven hateful days. Thirty days was it? And I have tarried but three—and every one of the three a separate age. ' 'Twill please the people,' declared my sapient brother, Agrippa; 'also thou wilt gain favor in the eyes of the priesthood.' So I made my vow. Thirty days without wine! thirty days without a coiffure! thirty days in Jerusalem! Was it not madness? And the people—what care they that Berenice plays the Nazarite? They care only for themselves and their temple. Aphrodite be my witness, I will make no more vows!"

The man at her side raised a jeweled hand to his lips to conceal a smile; then he stooped deferentially and whispered something in the ear of the princess.

"Ah, yes, the priest and the woman," she said carelessly. "Take them away and scourge them;—they deserve it, I swear, for giving us such a fright. Afterward let them go."

The man again ventured something in a low voice, at which the lady first frowned—then laughed musically. "Ah, Timones, thou art a sad flatterer!" she said, looking up from under her long lashes. "But perhaps thou art right about the priest. Let him go at once.—Ah, but stay," and she fixed her bright eyes full upon Phannias. "Is it true, priest, that thou dost also play the Nazarite?"

"I am a Nazarite for life, princess," replied the young man, who had been awaiting the result of the conference with ill-concealed impatience. "May I remind your highness that my errand with Florus is an urgent one. I would fain be allowed to depart without further delay."

"Hast thou then displeasured the high priest that he sends thee to Florus,—alone and unattended?" asked the princess. "I am told that the amiable procurator hath of late amused his leisure by crucifying every Jew who hath fallen into his hands."

"Nevertheless I must go—and at once," said Phannias firmly.

"But thou art too young to be crucified—and, yes, too beautiful," murmured the princess, dropping her lids with a sigh! Then she clapped her exquisite rose-tinted palms together with the abandon of a child. "I will go with thee!" she cried out. "Am I not also a Nazarite? I will myself plead for the people! The Roman can never say me nay. Then all this unpleasant blood and tumult will be done away with—truly I can bear it no longer!—No, I will hear no word from thee, Timones! Am I not my own mistress? I will wear a robe of purest white, with my hair unbound and streaming to its hem, and—yes, my feet unsandaled. Come—come, we will go at once!"

CHAPTER XVIII.

A RULER OF JERUSALEM.

GESSIUS FLORUS, procurator of Judæa, was a just product of his time; an ex-slave and hanger-on at the court of Nero, he had obtained his present position as a reward for a series of unparalleled crimes, committed in behalf of his royal master.

"Accept Judæa at my hands, my Gessius," quoth Nero at a banquet, and tossed a ripe plum into the hand of the sycophant; "thou wilt find it full of juice as is this fruit."

Florus had accepted the proffered honor with profuse gratitude. "If the plum be not ripe," he said sententiously, "it will ripen full soon in the sunshine of my reign."

The procurator carried with him into Judæa but one ambition. "I will return," he said, "the richest man in Rome."

His royal master heard of this saying and smiled. "The diligent bee gathereth honey," he said, affecting a yawn, "and the wise master eateth thereof."

Jerusalem was unquestionably a good field for the operations of so single-minded a ruler. By means of taxes, extortions and an occasional well-

timed removal of some rich land-owner, the worthy
Gessius amassed quite a handsome sum during the
course of his first year in office. He also succeeded in making himself unpopular to a degree
with the masses of the people. As for the priesthood, that herd of stern-faced Jews, with their
fierce eyes and their garrulous tongues, they very
quickly became a source of positive annoyance to
the diligent procurator. And when they openly
threatened to expose his dealings in Rome, he became actually alarmed. Should there chance to
be another favorite at court in need of reward, no·
one knew better than Gessius that his term of office
was likely to be terminated with unpleasant suddenness. With all his savage stupidity Florus recognized in Nero the superior brute. So it was that
he feared his subjects, and hated them no less than
he feared them.

Meantime, prodigious tales of the vast wealth
which these same Jews hoarded in their jealously
guarded temple came to his ears. His favorite
slave, Lotan, disguised in the turban and tallith of
a devout Israelite, on one occasion actually penetrated as far as the Court of Israel; from whence
he brought back marvelous reports of tables and
altars and great vessels of solid gold; fabulous
garlands and chains of wrought silver sparkling
with gems; and—most to be coveted—a mighty
grapevine, wrought of the red gold of Ophir, which
wreathed the vast façade of the Holy Place, the

branches whereof were laden with clustered grapes, every separate berry of which was a precious stone.

Florus clenched his hands longingly. "They guard their treasure like stinging wasps—these Jews," he whined.

"Destroy the nest, worshipful master," quoth Lotan, with a significant gesture, "and the wasps will shortly sting each other to the death; as for the honey, it will fall into the hands of a worthier."

"If this shall happen thou art a slave no longer; I swear .it!" cried his master. "The wasps' nest shall fall if I can bring it to pass!" So did Florus determine to fan the smoldering discontent into open warfare. It would be a simple and easy matter, concluded this intelligent ruler, to put to death every man who ventured to insult imperial Rome, as represented in his own person and dignity. To gain his magnificent ends he was willing to invite such contumely.

"These Jews," he wrote to his royal master about this time, "are traitors both in word and deed. They persistently refuse to honor thy divine image; and while intent upon worshiping a nonentity, they perpetually incite one another to discord and tumult, crying out insulting words against Rome and against thy majesty. I am determined to punish these ingrates as they deserve."

The effect produced by his first move in this game of death was greater and more far-reaching than he had anticipated; seventeen talents of gold

swelled the sum in his coffers, while three thousand
dead bodies lay in the streets and market-places of
the city. When the people in their grief and terror
shut themselves within their desolated homes they
were goaded into fresh fury by the incursions of
roving bands of soldiers, who broke into the closed
houses, plundering, torturing, killing, as their
drunken fancy dictated.

Meanwhile Florus displayed to his amazed captains the face of a religious enthusiast. "What!"
he exclaimed in a fine frenzy, "shall this conquered
people refuse to recognize the divinity of the emperor and live? Shall they heap up gold and precious stones to the honor of an unknown and un-
knowable God, whilst the gracious deities of Rome
boast not a single altar in all Jerusalem? By the
Olympian gods, I, Florus, have sworn that these
things shall no longer be!"

Florus was low in stature and possessed of a
countenance both pallid and fat, whereon the story
of his days was written sharp and clear, as one
writes with a stylus upon a tablet of wax. It
pleased him to be told that he resembled Nero;
like his royal master he affected many niceties of
speech and apparel. Since coming to Jerusalem
he had even ventured to carry the royal emerald
set in jade, which he held before his eye when he
wished to silence or intimidate those who stood in
his presence. It being the express fashion of the
moment in imperial circles to witness spectacles of

human agony, and Jerusalem being without a suitable arena for the enjoyment of such royal sports, Florus endeavored to supply the lack by planting a series of crosses about his tribunal, which was set after the custom in the open square before his palace. " These crosses "—never untenanted—" serve a double purpose," observed the sapient procurator, " since they furnish a wholesome rebuke to those of rebellious mind, as well as a much-needed diversion from the dull routine of matters of state."

Into the presence of this man, as he sat in the ivory chair of his office, came the princess Berenice, the fairest woman of her time ; with naked feet ; clad all in a robe of white, the glorious tresses of her hair streaming to its hem. Behind her followed a long train of her attendants, also barefooted and wearing the symbols of mourning and despair. At her side—for so she had willed it—walked Phannias.

" Great Florus," said the princess, advancing to the tessellated pavement, whereon all criminals and petitioners before the tribunal of Rome had stood for more than a century, " I, Berenice, princess of Israel, do beseech of thee thy august clemency in behalf of my people. If they have grievously erred in thy sight, so also have they been sorely punished. Now therefore let there be peace betwixt thee and the people of Jerusalem !"

Florus leaned forward, staring exultantly at the queenly figure which stood before him ; his sluggish soul swelled with gratified vanity. A princess, barefooted, humbled to the dust by his power! He narrowed his greedy eyes and puffed out his swollen cheeks in epicurean enjoyment of this new and delightful sensation.

Berenice, consummate mistress of fascinations, slowly lifted the fringed curtain of her lids, and permitted the mysterious splendor of her eyes to blaze full upon the fat, pallid face of the man in the chair.

For an instant Florus forgot the temple treasure; his breath came quick and fast. "Princess," he stammered, "I am—" He was about to say "I am thy slave;" but the word was bound up with hateful associations. To hide his embarrassment he raised the emerald to his eye, and the action restored him to himself. He turned his gaze upon Phannias. "Art thou also here to plead for a blasphemous and stiff-necked people?" he demanded.

"I am here to ask justice for the people of Israel," answered Phannias.

"These also asked for justice—and received it," said the procurator, pointing to the crosses with their ghastly burdens. "What canst thou say in defense of a people who refuse to worship the divinity which the gods have set up?"

"The laws of Rome permit us the enjoyment of the religion of Jehovah; the matter was settled beyond a peradventure long before thy day of power. I plead only the just observance of exist-

ing law. In behalf of the chiefs of the Jewish
nation do I stand in thy presence."

Florus threw himself back in his chair. "I am
Rome," he said loudly. "I am the law."

With an imperious gesture Berenice commanded
Phannias to be silent. "I ask not for justice, great
Roman," she cried, extending her lovely naked
arms toward the tribunal ; "I beseech thee for
mercy—mercy for an erring and rebellious people,
whose children and whose children's children shall
hail the name of the illustrious Florus with acclamations ; if only thou wilt extend to them the protection of thy mighty power !"

Florus permitted a smile to distort the mask-like
composure of his face. Without deviating a whit
from his original purpose, he had conceived on the
instant the idea of adding another jewel to his
hoard. A royal wife at my side, he thought within
himself, will increase my power, even as the
worthless cipher set beside the numeral makes it
greater than before. "Depart in peace, princess !"
he said, uxorious indulgence already evident in his
tones ; "for thy sake alone will I relax the severity
of my course toward this rebellious people.—Jove
be my witness," he continued, with a lofty gesture,
"I am not to be moved by threats ! My will
is as adamant ; my purposes are eternal and un-
changing ; yet if future generations shall laud the
clemency of Florus, they shall speak also of the
beauteous princess, who at peril of her life sued

for that clemency at his feet. Princess, I salute thee!"

Berenice bent her proud head to conceal the smile of triumph and of scorn that played about her lips. "Admirable Florus," she murmured, " I thank thee in behalf of the people of Israel—and also for myself. Thou shalt indeed be remembered, as princess of the Asmonean line, I swear it. Thy stern adherence to justice is already known to my brother Agrippa; he shall now learn of thy generous clemency. Doubt not that this day shall be a memorable one both for thee and for me."

The enamored procurator pursed up his lips—after the fashion of Nero when in the company of beautiful women. "A memorable day," he repeated, in tones of fatuous admiration,—"a memorable day for thee and for me."

In the seclusion of his palace the parting words of the princess recurred to his mind. "That Agrippa," he growled to his slave and private adviser, Lotan, "is a smooth and soft-spoken knave; but not to be trusted—curse him! Nevertheless, I will have the woman and the treasure."

" Who is more worthy to obtain both than the illustrious Florus,"—and the slave bowed himself almost to the ground; "yet if I may mention the fact, King Agrippa is already on his way to Jerusalem."

The procurator smote his thigh with a great oath. " The matter must be finished!" he cried.

An hour later the chief priests received the following communication :

" I, Gessius Florus, appointed by the divine Nero to bear rule in his stead over all the provinces of Judæa, do hereby command the people of Jerusalem to submit peaceably to the rule of Rome, as they value their lives and their religion. They have already rebelled and have been punished. And now do I, Florus, solemnly swear to extend to the citizens of Jerusalem a full and unconditional pardon for all offences which they have committed against the divine authority, if on their part they signify their willingness to obey the just and equitable laws of the adored and adorable Nero —whom may the gods preserve ! This submission shall be tendered in the following manner: Two cohorts of soldiers are on their way to Jerusalem from Cæsarea. Now therefore, bid the people assemble at the gate to meet these cohorts with acclamations of loyalty. In this manner and in no other shall they obtain pardon for their heinous crime of treason against the majesty of Rome."

In the same hour he sent swift messengers to meet the advancing cohorts, bearing despatches which informed the commanding officers that Jerusalem was in a state of insurrection. " If ye shall find a mob of lawless citizens in the streets and at the gates upon your arrival,"—ran the message— " do not scruple to cut them down without mercy. Such also is the will of the emperor."

The mourning people were already assembled in vast numbers in the temple; and to them Ananus, as the most venerated of the high priests, addressed himself. The proclamation of Florus had been posted in prominent places in the temple courts, and loud murmurs of surprise and suspicion had greeted it.

"We have broken no law," cried the chiefs of the common people; "why should we kiss the sword that smites us? Rather let us meet the cohorts with such arms as we may muster and exchange our lives for the blood of Rome."

Ananus rent his garments with loud cries of grief. "Submit—submit!" he wailed, "that the tyrant may possess no excuse to continue his outrages!" Whereat, as had been previously arranged, the Levites emerged from their underground music rooms, bearing the golden trumpets and the instruments of sweet music with which they were wont to make melody before the Lord of Hosts. Following the Levites came the priests in long procession, laden with the golden bowls of sacrifice and the holy garments, of white, of scarlet and of blue. "Look upon these sacred objects, which your fathers have revered during the ages!" cried Ananus. "Look also upon this temple which is the place of your solemnities! Would ye behold these things in the grasp of the Gentiles? Would ye see this sanctuary defiled with blood and despoiled of its treasure? If ye rebel against the power of Rome these things

will surely follow. Submit, as becometh men and
patriots, and shortly all these enormities shall be
done away with! Messengers bearing evidence
which will assuredly depose this monster, Florus,
are already on their way to the emperor. Behold
Jehovah of Hosts is our God ; he will also bring it
to pass !"

Immediately the Levites burst forth in grand
chorus :

> " Rejoice in Jehovah ye righteous !
> Give thanks to Jehovah with the harp ;
> Make music unto him with the lute of ten strings !
> Sing unto him a new song ;
> Play skilfully with glad shouting !
> For Jehovah's word is true,
> And all his work is faithful !
> By the word of Jehovah the heavens were made,
> And all their host by the breath of his mouth !
> He gathereth as in heaps the waters of the sea ;
> He storeth the deeps in treasure houses !
> Let all the earth fear before Jehovah !
> Stand in awe of him, all that dwell in the world !
> For he spake and it was done,
> He commanded, and it stood fast !
> Jehovah brought the counsels of the nations to naught ;
> The thoughts of the people he made of none effect !
> The counsel of Jehovah standeth fast forever,
> The thoughts of his heart from age to age !
> Happy the nation whose God is Jehovah,
> The people whom he hath chosen for his heritage !"

Once again the smoke of the evening sacrifice
ascended solemnly into the dumb heavens, and the

people fell on their faces before the altar. Then with the high-priestly blessing yet sounding in their ears they went forth obediently toward the Damascus gate.

CHAPTER XIX.

A DAUGHTER OF THE HERODS.

THE princess Berenice returned to the dreary old palace of the Herods in a frame of mind which bordered upon exultation. She beheld in imagination the city of Jerusalem at her feet in humble thankfulness and adoration, while the fame of her great deed fled away to imperial Rome.

She leaned forward and surveyed critically the face which looked back at her from the depths of a small mirror fastened at a convenient angle to the side of her litter. Time had left no mark, save the seal of a ripe perfection, on that brow and cheek of purest ivory, beneath which the red blood glowed with the delicious color of rose-tinted clouds ; the bow of the scarlet lips parted, revealing the white even teeth within ; then the lips drooped over the lustrous eyes.

"I am more beautiful than ever," she sighed, "—more beautiful ?—Nay, I am most beautiful— why should I not say what is the truth ! The Ro- man yonder devoured me with his basilisk eyes. I read his thoughts. I will hold him in leash, like the beast that he is, till he is powerless ; then——"
She sank back against the gay, embroidered

cushions, dreamily surveying the exquisite outlines
of her form beneath the silken coverlid. "The empress is dead,"—so ran the tenor of her silent
thought—"murdered by a kick from her lord and
master. There are thousands who are eager to
take her place. There is but one woman in all the
circle of the earth fit to grace the imperial throne.
I am that woman. Yet Nero is frightful—bloated
—malevolent; in short, a swine in the guise of
man." She frowned and sighed again. "If only
one might love a god—like the Nazarite yonder;—
nay, why should I not amuse myself with the lad;
'twill help pass away these interminable days."

The slave who walked beside the litter leapt forward as a white hand appeared for an instant between the closely-drawn curtains. "The priest—
the Nazarite; is he with us, as I commanded?"

"He refused to return to the palace, gracious
princess."

"Refused? What sayest thou?"

"The man insisted, admirable highness, that he
must needs return to the house of the high priest."

"Send to the house of the high priest and fetch
the Nazarite to me at once—at once; I command
it."

But it was more than two hours later when
Phannias was ushered into the presence of the royal
lady.

Berenice lay, half reclined, upon a couch of
carved ivory cushioned with palest rose, the un-

bound tresses of her magnificent hair, wound with pearls, descending like a cloud across the dazzling silver of her robe. She raised her lovely eyes at his approach. "Ah, I perceive that thou art not pleased to be summoned to our presence," she said, affecting displeasure.

The young man stared at the vision for a full minute in silence. "Why didst thou send for me?" he asked, abruptly.

A shadowy smile touched the lips of the princess. In truth this gigantic Nazarite—with the clear eyes of a boy—promised exquisite amusement. "Canst thou ask?" she cried, with a fervor born of the conviction. "Did not we stand together on the verge of death? And is it meet that we part as strangers?"

She studied the face before her for a little, then went on with a rapid gesture. "After all, 'tis to thee that the victory belongs. The brute yonder had thrust the eternal laws of Rome behind his back; thou didst hold them up before his face as a mirror, wherein he looked shuddering and beheld his ruin. Yet it soothed his ruffled vanity to promise mercy for my poor sake, that he might not appear to yield to superior force. Come, we will sup together, thou and I, in honor of thy triumph."

"Thou doest me too much honor, princess," stammered Phannias. "Yet I cannot remain. I——"

Berenice lifted her brows. "*Cannot?*—Nay,

that were a word we do not understand. It pleases thy queen that thou sup in her presence ; thou wilt obey."

At a motion of her hand slaves appeared, bearing a small but exquisitely appointed table. " We do as we must in this frightful place," laughed the princess, with a sudden change of manner. ".It is called a palace ; but with all due respect to my royal ancestors it appears to me but little better than a barracks." As she spoke she motioned Phannias to a place at her side.

The face of the Nazarite was a study, as he slowly obeyed. Berenice, stealing a sidelong glance at her reluctant guest, concluded that he was overcome with fear or embarrassment—or both. " Didst thou carry word of our success to the high priest ?" she asked sweetly.

" I repeated to him the promise of Florus— yes."

" And what said he ?"

Phannias looked up to meet the full glance of the beautiful, serious eyes. " He said — many things ; I cannot tell thee all ; it is not true."

" They do not love me—these excellent priests," said Berenice, shrugging her shoulders with an indifferent laugh. " Well, I do not love them ; the account is therefore balanced betwixt us. But thou —Nay, why art thou a priest ? Dost thou love the life ? Tell me truly."

" I wish above all things to serve Jehovah."

"To serve Jehovah—yes; but do the priests serve Jehovah?"

Phannias' black brows met; he looked down without answering at the dishes heaped with delicate viands, which attentive slaves had placed before him.

" Ah, thou knowest full well that they do not!" cried the lady, with a light ripple of laughter. "They bow themselves before a God they know not; they offer unnumbered sacrifices; deck their foul bodies with holy robes; bawl out long prayers on every street corner; haggle and twist the letters of some dead law till their voices sound meaningless as the clink of this goblet; and all the while they despoil the poor—lie—cheat—hate—*murder.* Ay, it is true; I know them. I know enough of all religions—" she continued, after a pause, during which the attendants crowned the pair with rose garlands,—" to declare to thee that all religions are one and the same; a shell of dreary ceremonial masking—rottenness; grave-clothes—scarce covering dead bodies."

She shuddered lightly, then laughed again; a sound as musical and sweet, thought the bewildered Phannias, as the sound of singing birds in the garden at Aphtha.

"No, for myself I do not believe in these religions," pursued the princess, observing with satisfaction the faint smile that flitted shadowlike across the face at her side. " I once heard a Jew called

Paulus, a prisoner in bonds, on his way to Rome to be tried—for what I know not. He had angered the priests by his heresies, perchance, and they hated him for it.—Yes, I remember me now; and to save himself, being a Roman citizen, he had appealed to Cæsar. Poor fool; he tarried in his prison three years, then went forth to his death—not a year ago. Cæsar hates all Christians."

" Christians !" exclaimed Phannias ; " what knowest thou of Christians ?"

" Priest and Nazarite—art thou also apostate? Truly, I could tell thee much concerning Christians if I would. They are a strange folk. And, by the girdle of Venus, I believe that they have seen something that we know not of. This Paul —of whom I spoke—in chains, in rags, and bowed with age, stood up in presence of Festus, King Agrippa and myself, with the people of our train, and spoke for himself right boldly.

"And what said he of Jesus of Nazareth?" demanded Phannias, fixing his eyes upon the face of the princess with unconcealed interest.

Berenice was visibly piqued and displeased. Who and what manner of man was this boorish priest, to whom she had already shown favor for which princes would have knelt; and who had looked coldly upon her beauty, only to kindle at the mention of a dead malefactor. She gazed long into the dark, eager face, framed in its loose-curling locks ; then her glance slipped serpent-wise to the broad shoulders and the light but powerful limbs. "Veil of the Holiest!" she murmured, with a curl of her scarlet lip, "thou hast the face of an Apollo, the body of a warrior and the soul of a puling babe!"

Phannias paled beneath the bold eyes of the woman. "Thou wilt permit an unworthy servant of Jehovah, who has failed to please his queen, to withdraw from her presence," he said deliberately. "I crave also to remind her that I am in the palace of the Herods, not by mine own will, but in obedience to her positive command. Princess, I salute thee! Farewell."

Berenice sprang to her feet with a gay laugh; if her vagrant fancy had hovered like some wandering bee over this strangely beautiful youth, it needed but this to ensnare it.

"No—No!" she cried; "thou shalt not go. I but said it to test thee. Come, I will tell thee of the Christians,—all that thou wilt.—Nay, I command thee. Also thou canst go no further than the door of this banqueting hall, for my soldiers stand before the door."

Phannias sank once more into his place; but his eyes were clouded, and he bent them more coldly than ever upon the smiling woman at his side.

"Shall I—who would be empress, fail to win approval from this clod of a priest?" Berenice asked herself angrily. "See, I will take it for an omen; if I conquer this hind I shall also subjugate

Cæsar." And equipping herself with every weapon
in her armory of fascinations she bent herself to
conquest. From grave to gay ran the current of
her sparkling talk; while smiles, frowns, blushes,
dimples, chased one another across the lovely face
as swift as cloud shadows athwart rich, flowering
meadows.

Phannias was dazzled—bewildered; and—being
altogether human—pleased with the veiled deference of her tones and gestures. Without comprehending the subtle reasons for it all, the Nazarite
held his head with a more stately grace, giving
glance for glance, and word for word in brilliant
repartee.

From time to time he drank from the jeweled
goblet which stood at his elbow; it contained—the
princess assured him, with a smile of delighted
mischief—nothing more nor less than purest water,
stung with spices. And Phannias, through whose
unaccustomed veins coursed the colorless but potent wine of Chios, presently decided that this
princess was in truth the most beautiful and gracious lady in all Jerusalem—nay, in all the world.
Curiously enough at this point in the hidden current of his thought the remembrance of the little
Jewish maiden, whom he had wrested from the
grasp of the soldier, came back to him. He was
astonished to perceive, as he beheld this remembered face, that it was beautiful. Turning to his
royal hostess with a hesitation learned wholly

within the hour, he asked what had become of the girl.

"Of the shopkeeper's daughter?" she asked, a dangerous sparkle in her eyes.

"I know nothing of the maid—whether or no she be the daughter of a shopkeeper," answered Phannias, vaguely discomfited.

Berenice leaned forward and laid her white hand upon his arm. "Tell me truly about the girl," she cooed. "I am no hypocritical rabbi to be offended with a young man because he is not an old one. The little maid is very beautiful; is it not so?"

"I had not thought—" stammered Phannias, proud of dissembling. He dropped his dazzled eyes before the burning splendor of the gaze that was fastened upon him. "I never before saw the girl."

"Thou hast told the truth in that word," observed the princess, with an enigmatical smile; "thine eyes were not yet opened. Verily, the gods are kind to me—and will be kinder. Augusta Victoria!* what sayest thou; is it not a sounding name?—fit to grace triumphant beauty?" She laughed aloud, as one laughs who has won an easy victory.

"I once visited an aged Nazarene, concerning whom I had a curiosity," she continued, after a little silence. "He had wrought strange miracles, it was said; had caused the lame to walk; opened

* Augusta; a title of the Empress of Rome: Victoria; the Latin form of the name Berenice.

blind eyes and the like—all Christians are reputed wizards. I disguised myself as a woman of the people and, attended by a single slave, went to this man's house. It was here in Jerusalem. He was sitting quite alone in a great bare chamber, writing upon a scroll. 'I am lame, good Nazarene,' I whined, affecting to limp as I entered his presence ; 'wilt thou not heal me?' Had he spoken words of incantation, waving his arms aloft, as do the lying magic-mongers of Rome and Athens, I had the intent to fling a coin in his face ; I had no fear of any man—then or now. But he said no word ; only looked at me with his wise, deep eyes, till, I swear to thee, the water of shame stood in drops upon my forehead ; then he turned and read, as if from his scroll ; 'Whosoever transgresseth, and abideth not in the doctrine of Christ, hath not God. If there come any such unto you, receive him not into your house, neither bid him God-speed ; for he that biddeth him God-speed is partaker of his evil deeds.'

" 'Nay, good Nazarene,' I besought him penitently, 'give me a word less harsh to carry into the world.'—Truly for the instant I had the desire to please the man. Again he looked upon me, and with wondrous kindness—I had let down the veil from before my face. 'Daughter,' he said, 'I will give thee a true word and precious ; it is this : 'Love is of God ; and every one that loveth knoweth God.' "

The silver tones sank to a low, musical murmur; and Phannias, shaken to the depths of his soul by the divine truth and beauty of the words, though he wist not anything of the horrible travesty of their utterance, leaned toward his companion.

"Ah, yes," he cried exultantly, "that is true— true! I know it—I feel it. How beautiful to believe that it is true!" He extended his hand mechanically toward his goblet; it was empty.

Berenice raised her hand with an angry gesture. "More wine, slave," she whispered.

Phannias started back before that sibilant utterance as from a blow. "Wine!" he echoed sharply.

The princess bit her lip with vexation. "I did not mean it—truly; 'twas but a slip of this careless tongue."

"No—no! Poor fool that I am to become the sport of a woman! My vow—I have broken my vow!"

"And what is thy trumpery vow more than mine?" demanded Berenice, springing to her feet. "Thou hast broken thy vow? What then; thou hast broken a chain! What hath thy vow done for thee? Has it fed thee,—clothed thee,—warmed thee,—pleasured thee? Nay, I trow not. I too was a Nazarite—why? To please yon rotten priesthood; to gain power and influence for my ambitious brother. I have broken my vow—for love; and thou, my beautiful Phannias—canst thou not forgive me if, when breaking the shackles from my own limbs, I have also made thee a free man?"

Phannias stared dumbly into the exquisite face, lifted so beseechingly to his. "For love's sake, my Phannias," she whispered, and wavered toward him like a tall, sweet lily, bowed before the imperious wind.

He would have caught her with a sob of pain and joy in his strong young arms, but on the instant she recoiled, stiffening in sudden fear and amaze at the sound of hurrying feet in the corridor without. The door of the banqueting hall was flung open. "Agrippa!" she exclaimed; then seeing the blood upon his drawn sword, "What is it—what has happened?"

The man who had thus rudely entered cast a frowning glance about the room. "The people of Jerusalem are crying out for the blood of a certain princess, who has sold them—they declare—to the Roman, Florus," he said hoarsely, bringing his fiery eyes to a standstill on the white face of the woman. "What hast thou done? Answer!"

"I?—But why dost thou speak to me as though I were some base-born slave who had earned thy royal displeasure? Nay, I will answer thee nothing!"

"Thou wilt answer *them*, and that right speedily," said Agrippa, with a significant gesture.

Berenice listened to the ominous sounds from without for an instant. "What—what has happened?" she faltered. "I—I have done nothing—I swear it; save to ask mercy for this howling rabble at the knees of Florus. He promised it me, on the word of his honor."

"The people lie dead in uncounted thousands about the Damascus Gate," answered Agrippa, bitterly; "cut down by the Roman cohorts. The prudent Florus has retired to Cæsarea to gloat over his victims at a safe distance. Wilt thou join him there, fair enchantress? Or hast thou, haply, another affair of more pressing moment in Jerusalem?"

Berenice's eyes flamed with sudden fury. "I hate you!" she cried. Then she turned suddenly upon Phannias. "Go, fool," she said sharply. "Canst thou not see that thou art no longer wanted?"

CHAPTER XX.

"AS BIRDS FLYING."

THE days had passed slowly for Rachel, alone in her cottage at Aphtha. She had received news of her son but once since the morning he left her for Jerusalem ; this was when Ben Huna, smarting with his disappointment, had returned to the village. The rabbi told her gently of the flaw in the line of descent, which at present loomed up in the guise of an insuperable barrier to the illustrious future which the good man fully believed lay before his favorite.

Rachel was somewhat bewildered by the legal phraseology into which Ben Huna allowed himself to stray, in the course of his dissertation on the nature and scope of the priestly office. She understood but one thing clearly ; Phannias could not follow the career which she had herself planned out for him, and which had threatened to sunder their lives so widely. Her eyes brightened.

" Ah, yes," she cried, with a tremulous sigh and smile, " I quite understand ; my poor child has been rejected. Alas, that it is so ! Yet one must bow to the will of God. My son will now return to me, and we shall live here quite happily as before."

"Not so, woman," said Ben Huna, all the majesty of the law in his tone and gesture; "it is
indeed the will of God that we bow to the inevitable; but let us first be sure that it is the inevitable
which confronts us. The lad will remain in the
temple, honorably employed, whilst I fare forth to
look to this matter. I have already collected data
which will enable me to search out—ay, and to
make good this proof which is required."

"But why—" urged the widow timidly, "could
he not remain with me till thou hast succeeded in thy
search. I—I am alone, as thou seest, and——"

"More than once hast thou had opportunity to
furnish thyself with a husband," quoth the rabbi.
"Thou art without companionship because thou hast
willed it. Behold it is written: 'It is not good for
man to be alone.' As for woman, she was made by
Jehovah for no other purpose than to minister to the
needs and pleasures of man; by herself she is as
nothing. This is the law, and it is also good."

Rachel's brown cheeks flushed crimson. If at
any time she had cherished rebellious and un-
womanly thoughts concerning the laws made by
man for man, she had also the grace to be silent
concerning them.

Ben Huna regarded the downcast face of the
widow with a certain kindly indulgence, not unmixed with approval. Rachel was still a singularly
comely woman; and for the rest, there was not a
better piece of land nor a cosier house in all the

village of Aphtha. "Ah well," he continued with
a sigh, and straightened his bent shoulders, " I am
already an old man, and if I would see the sacred oil
on the lad's head before I go hence there are no days
to lose. Farewell, woman ; busy thyself with thy
prayers, and haply God will regard thy petition ; for
so doth the Almighty with wondrous graciousness
condescend toward the humblest of his creatures."

With these parting words the good rabbi went
his way ; and if vague thoughts of a tranquil old
age, soothed and comforted by the gentle ministrations of a beautiful woman went with him, it was
perhaps not to be wondered at. But Ben Huna
had occupied himself too long with the happiness
of other people to think very persistently of his
own, and presently the unaccustomed thoughts
took flight, like a flock of startled doves, before the
prosaic arrangements necessary for a long journey ;
for he had found that in order to compass his ends
he must travel into far-distant cities.

As for Rachel, she did as she was bid ; and truly,
if the yearning petitions of a mother's heart could
have taken visible form, one might have beheld in
those days a cloud of prayers, white as the passionate wings of angels, ascending into the blue
heavens which bent over Aphtha. In doomed Jerusalem the smoke of an altar fire soon to be ex-
tinguished forever also rose, black and ominous,
like the breath of a funeral pyre. Betwixt the two
a human soul wavered in agony.

In her garden at close of day Rachel walked,
musing, dreaming, praying. In imagination she
beheld her child, clad all in white, like an angel,
ministering in the shining courts of the temple.
Would he also remember her, alone in the old garden, where unchanged the stream twinkled pleasantly over its pebbles of yellow and pink and
green, and the blossoming almond boughs wrapped
the moss-grown thatch in a bower of fragrant
silence. The pigeons, already warmly sheltered
from the dew beneath the overhanging roof of the
old house, cooed drowsily to the uneasy nestlings
beneath their wings ; while athwart the gold and
purple of the solemn evening sky, the swallows
came flitting homeward in twos and threes.

Below on the mountain road which ascended from
Bethlehem in long loops and curves like the loose-
flung coils of a rope, a white figure climbed steadily
upward. Rachel's heart leapt to her lips as she
watched it ; then her eyes filled with patient tears.
" He will not come," she said.

The tall lilies, standing like sentinels beside the
worn path, poured forth their gold and frankincense
and myrrh with tremulous haste as one brushed
swiftly past them in the twilight.

" Mother—oh mother !"

The uncounted prayers, white as the wings of
angels—and more strong, had conquered. Phannias was once more at home.

CHAPTER XXI.

THE LAST VICTORY.

IN the year 66—reckoning from the birth of the
man of Galilee, strange things and terrible
came to pass in the Jewish provinces. Agrippa, in
his double character of patriot and diplomat, endeavored to soothe the maddened people, using
now his persuasive eloquence, now detachments of
Roman troops to gain his ends. At the last he
abandoned Israel to its fate, withdrawing to Cæsarea, from which stronghold he watched subsequent
events with the cynical composure of a practiced
gambler. Berenice, somewhat sobered by her narrow escape from the hands of the mob in Jerusalem, accompanied him.

In those days the so-called Zealots threw
wide the gates of Jerusalem to certain wandering
bands of predatory vagabonds which infested the
countryside. " So will we fight fire with fire !"
they declared ; and the brigands—known as Sicars,
because of the cruel curved sword which they wore
concealed beneath their garments, flocked into the
doomed city like vultures, gathering to some ghastly
feast of death. In the space of a month they had
accomplished a frightful work of destruction ; the

palaces of Agrippa and of the chief priests were destroyed with fire ; so also were the public buildings
containing the records and contracts relating to
debts and debtors : there were now neither rich nor
poor in Jerusalem. Antonia, the great fortress of the
Roman garrison, was captured by the mob in a
single night, with the slaughter of the guards to a
man.

Rumors of these happenings spread into all the
provinces; whereat the Jewish nation arose, as a
fierce beast which shakes itself after sleep, and fell
upon the dominant Gentile with a fury born of long
centuries of wrong and oppression.

Cestius Gallus, the proconsul of Syria, was held
to be a wise and prudent man ; one whose actions
were not to be accelerated by undue urging or ve-
hemence on the part of his advisers. " Let them
slay one another for a time," he said, with an air
of weighty wisdom ; " 'twill prove a wholesome
bloodletting, which may serve to ease these turbulent peoples of their disorders."

Yet Cestius was compelled at last to set in motion the ponderous engines of law and war, which,
once started, work out blindly the will of Him who
sitteth—himself unseen—upon the circle of the
heavens. Sending detachments of Roman troops
into the Galilees, and adown the coast as far as
Joppa, Cestius departed from Antioch with the
twelfth legion ; finally reassembling all his forces
at Cæsarea, after successfully checking a number

of threatening insurrections by means of an indis-
criminate slaughter of all Jews who fell in his path.

From Cæsarea the proconsul advanced toward
Jerusalem, by way of the rugged pass of Bethhoron, where, nearly fifteen centuries before, Joshua
had defeated the five confederate kings of the Amo-
rites. At Gibeon, a little further on, he was met by
a certain Sicar chieftain, known as Simon Bar-Gioras, and repulsed with fury. A few days later and
the Roman forces were again advancing steadily
upon Jerusalem, driving the inhabitants of the country before them, as a swarm of locusts is driven
by the fierce west wind.

Seven furlongs to the north of the city, the Olivet range stretches in a long level plateau flung
from its central bulk like the limb of a sleeping
giant; upon this height, known in Jerusalem as
Scopus, the triumphant Romans pitched their camp.

"The war is at an end," quoth Cestius. And
he was the more certain of this when a deputation
composed of the leading men of the city visited
him. This deputation approached the Roman camp
with the greatest secrecy, stealing out from the city
gates by night with the connivance of the gatekeepers.

"We have come to thee, most noble Cestius,"
said Ananus, who headed the embassy, "to proffer
our submission, and to profess to thee our entire
loyalty to Rome. What has already happened at
the hands of the mob, we bewail as the acts of

men bereft of reason and drunk with blood and
rapine. Behold, we ourselves have suffered at the
hands of this common enemy the loss of all that is
dear to us. Now therefore, enter the city, we beseech thee, and restore to our distracted nation that
peace which we may alone enjoy under the powerful protection of Roman law."

This saying pleased Cestius; and having further
received from these men a pledge that the gates of
the city should be opened to him freely, he advanced confidently, only to meet with a fierce resistance from the army of Sicars and Zealots who
crowded the walls with a deadly fringe of archers.
As for the luckless ambassadors, all save Ananus
had been caught by the watchful Zealots, and their
dead bodies were flung piecemeal from the gate
towers into the faces of the advancing Romans.

At this Cestius, being more prudent than wise,
withdrew to his camp to consider the matter at his
leisure, despite the entreaties of his captains, who
saw quite clearly that the city might now be taken
with ease.

Was it a viewless messenger from Jehovah of
Hosts, vested with an authority which could not be
denied, who stood at the side of the proconsul,
saying, "Stay now thy hand; the harvest is not
yet ripe for the sickle—the grain also must first be
separated from the doomed chaff." Or was it a
certain scroll, received that day from his friend and
kinsman, Florus, procurator of Judea. "Suffer

the rival swarms to destroy one another; afterward we will divide the honey,"—ran the enigmatical words of this writing, which was conveyed to
the worthy Cestius by a fleet messenger from Cæsarea Philippi. Certain it is that Cestius broke
camp and fell back to Gibeon; and from thence,
entangling himself with his cumbrous trains of
baggage among the wild fastnesses of Bethhoron,
he fled in a ruck of mad confusion adown the
rocky valleys, pursued by the swarming mountain-
eers, who slew in a single day no fewer than five
thousand of the flower of the Roman army.

And so it came to pass that in Bethhoron, where
Israel had gained its first great victory, it also won
its last. The conquerors laden with spoils returned
to Jerusalem, dragging with them the heavy engines
of war which the Romans had abandoned in their
flight. That night the inhabitants of the holy city
gave themselves up to a mad carnival of joy; fires,
kindled from the saddles of the slain cavalry and
the wooden shields of the foot-soldiers, blazed
fiercely on every sacred height about the city; tumultuous voices shouting pæans of victory sounded
everywhere in the darkness; and in the courts of
the temple crowds of worshipers, delirious with
triumph, bellowed themselves hoarse in honor of
Jehovah of Hosts.

Overhead in the soft dark of the spring night
blazed a mighty sword of fire; the people had
watched its gradual appearance in their familiar

heavens with fear and dread, but now they flung
their arms toward the ominous visitant with exultant clamor.   "The sword of triumph!" they cried.
" The sword of Israel and of the Lord !"

Wild rumors of portent and miracle flew from
mouth to mouth ; it was affirmed that during the
ninth hour of the night before the victory a great
light had shone for the space of half an hour about
the altar of the Holy Place.   Chariots and soldiers
fighting furiously had been observed in the clouds
at sunset.   The Gate Beautiful, which required the
strength of twenty men to move, had of itself swung
wide at the hour of midnight, as though to welcome the incoming hosts of a triumphant deity.
Men looked one another in the face with wild eyes,
half hoping to see in every unfamiliar countenance
the lineaments of the Messiah.   Ay, verily, the
time was ripe !

In certain closed and quiet houses of the city far
other scenes were taking place ; in some, despairing
women wept over their dead ; in others, hasty
preparations for flight were going forward.   There
was no longer any hope of a reconciliation with
Rome ; to escape before the crashing blow of doom
should fall was now all that remained.

In a narrow and crooked street of the Agra,
numerous heavily draped figures sought in the darkness a shabby and ancient house, wherein was an
upper chamber lighted dimly by the flaring light of
a cresset fixed to the blackened rafters.   This light

shone brightly on the bowed head of an aged man who stood directly beneath its glow.

When the room was quite filled with the silent figures, this man lifted his tremulous hands and looked earnestly into the white faces before him. " My children," he said tenderly, " well-beloved and faithful in the belief of our Lord Jesus Christ, the days are come when it is meet to stir up your pure minds by way of remembrance. Already it is known to some of you how that our Lord, before he was crucified spake in this wise to the multitude which was assembled to hear him in the temple. ' Behold,' he said, ' I send unto you prophets, and wise men, and scribes ; and some of them ye shall kill and crucify ; and some of them ye shall scourge in your synagogues, and persecute them from city to city ; that upon you may come all the righteous blood shed upon the earth, from the blood of righteous Abel unto the blood of Zacharias, whom ye slew between the sanctuary and the altar. Verily, I say unto you, all these things shall come upon this generation.'

"When he had said these words, our Lord looked around about upon the people, and upon the temple ; and to those of us who stood by, it seemed that the water stood in his eyes. He stretched forth his arms with longing as doth a mother when she yearneth over an unruly son. ' O Jerusalem, Jerusalem !' he cried, ' thou that killest the prophets, and stonest them which are sent unto thee, how

often would I have gathered thy children together
—even as a hen gathereth her chickens under her
wings, and ye would not! Behold, your House is
left unto you desolate! For I say unto you, ye
shall not see me henceforth, till ye shall say, Blessed
is he that cometh in the name of the Lord.'

"As he was about to quit the temple, certain of
us—marveling at the glory of the place and at the
words which he had spoken concerning it, said to
him, 'See, Lord, what stones and what buildings
are here!' And he answered: 'Verily, I say unto
you, there shall not be left here one stone upon
another which shall not be cast down.'

"In that hour we also remembered the word he
had spoken on the day of his triumph, as the people
brought him with rejoicing into the city, spreading
their garments before him in the way, stripping the
branches from the palms, and crying out, 'Blessed
be the King that cometh in the name of Jehovah!
Peace in heaven! Glory in the highest!' When,
from the heights near Jerusalem, he beheld the
city and the temple, shining white and beautiful in
the sun, he stopped to gaze upon it; and they that
walked by his side heard his voice, as it were heavy
with tears, saying, 'If thou hadst known—even
thou, at least in this thy day—the things which belong to thy peace! But now they are hid from
thine eyes. For the days shall come upon thee,
that thine enemies shall cast a trench about thee,
and compass thee round, and keep thee in on every

side, and shall lay thee even with the ground and
thy children within thee : and they shall not leave
in thee one stone upon another, because thou
knewest not the time of thy visitation !'

" Two days before the passover, in the which he
was put to death, our Lord walked upon the Mount
of Olives, where also he loved to be ; the lilies of
the field flourished there and the shadows of great
olive trees made a cool retreat from the sun ;—ye
all know the place, and love it, for his sake who is
passed from our midst. In this place we who
walked with him at all times came to him privately,
for our hearts were heavy with dread. ' Tell us,'
we said, ' when shall these things be ? And what
shall be the sign of thy coming, and of the end of
the world ?'

" Then he told us freely of all things which were
to happen in the days when he should no longer be
with us. Of these many have already been fulfilled ; wars and rumors of wars have vexed our
ears ; famines, pestilences, earthquakes have visited
the nations. Of them who loved him, have many
suffered persecution even unto death ; of whom also
is Stephen, who was stoned by them that hate our
Lord—and died beholding his glory ; and with him
a great multitude of the saints who have been
scourged, and imprisoned and tortured of wild
beasts—and of men, less merciful than beasts—
both here, and in Judea, and in all the corners of
the earth where the light of Christ hath shone.

These things have been fulfilled; and now behold, the end is at hand. We have seen the abomination of desolation stand in the holy place—for by what other name can the hosts of the heathen be called, which were lately encamped on Olivet, made forever holy by the feet of Him who brought unto us good tidings. Now let them which be in Judæa flee unto the mountains! For the great tribulation is at hand; such as was not since the beginning of the world to this time—no, nor ever shall be! Lo, He told us before it came to pass. It is for us to obey!"

The deep tones of the speaker ceased, and a silence, broken only by the distant shouts of the mad revelers in the streets without, settled like a cloud upon the little company in that upper room. Then a voice, fresh and joyous as that of an angel, chanted softly,

> " Jesus—Christ, glad Light of the Highest!
> Light of the Father, radiant, holy!
> While the night spreads its dim mantle o'er us,
> We worship the light which hath shined—
> Which hath shined in the darkness!"

One by one other voices joined the single glad thread of song. Voices of women, sweet and sad; voices of children, shrill and bright as of downy-throated nestlings; the graver voices of men; all thrilling with life's sorrows, past, present or to come.

" Praise to thee, Father ! Praise to thee, Jesus !
Worthy art thou to be praised of the holiest,
Now and forever ; on all days and eternally,
Beloved of God, who givest us life !''

A few passionate prayers for special help and
guidance in this hour of their sore need, and the
meeting was at an end.

Plans for the future were simple and quickly decided upon by these followers of One who was with
them alway, and upon whose word they leaned as
upon a strong staff. They would take with them
no useless burden of worldly goods ; for the time
pressed, and their Lord had spoken concerning this
also : " Let him which is upon the housetop not
come down to take anything out of his house ;
neither let him which is in the field return back to
take his clothes." Following the counsel of
James, the beloved head of the church in Jerusalem, they settled upon a small town in the mountains of Gilead as the divinely appointed refuge
from the threatening storm. The name of this
place was Pella, which signifies in the Hebrew
tongue hidden—secret—set apart ; and again, deliverance, or escape.

In the gray of the morning they set forth—all
the Christians of Jerusalem who were able to travel.
But James, and with him Rufus, a proselyte, and
certain women who were bereft of home and family
remained behind. " There are the aged ones,"
said the bishop, " and also of them that are sick

not a few—which must perforce tarry; I will not leave them alone."

After he had sent away the last of the travelers with prayers and blessings, James sat in the upper chamber, spent and worn, yet rejoicing because he knew that it would be well with those whom his soul loved. In spirit he went out with the wayfarers along the great Roman road, soon to resound to the tread of avenging hosts, and he pictured to himself the Lord's flock, folded safe in the green pastures and beside the still waters of distant Pella.

As he mused thus in the chilly dawn, one touched him upon the shoulder; he turned to look into the blushing face of a young maid who held before him a trencher containing meat and bread. "I pray thee, my lord," she said timidly, "that thou wilt eat and refresh thyself after the long night."

To the dim eyes of the aged bishop she looked no less than a ministering angel, for the dawn streaming through the lattice touched her bent head with heaven's glory. "Who art thou, my daughter?" he asked wondering.

And she—"I am Merodah; I have heard thee speak now seven times of the crucified Jesus; and truly, I love both him and thee."

"But thou art young and strong, my child," said the bishop tenderly. "Why is it that thou hast not departed with the others from this place of doom?"

Merodah looked troubled. "I cannot leave my father," she said simply.

CHAPTER XXII.

IN APHTHA.

IN the towns and cities of Judæa, news of the splendid victory over Cestius aroused the wildest enthusiasm. Public thanksgivings were held in all the synagogues; while in the humblest cottages, feasting, singing and dancing went forward right merrily. It was positively affirmed that the whole Roman army had been destroyed; that the resistless hosts of heaven had been seen visibly descending from the clouds, and pursuing the flying cohorts with swords and banners of fire. The days of the Messiah were surely at hand, and there remained now only the consummation of the glorious promises so long held out by sage and prophet. The vague reports of the landing of Roman legions at Ptolemais aroused no alarm in the minds of the deluded people.

"Our God is able to overthrow the hosts of the idolaters," they said boastfully, "even as when Sennacherib, King of the Assyrians, set himself against Jerusalem, and the angel of the Lord went out at midnight through his camp and smote of the Assyrians an hundred, fourscore and five thousand, that they died."

Certain of their number, whose eyes were not entirely blinded, called urgently upon the people everywhere to arm themselves; to make strong their walled cities; to fortify the mountain passes; to gather up their harvests and bestow them in places of safety. But to these last futile words of warning the doomed nation paid no heed. When the towns of Galilee began one by one to fall before the fierce attacks of the Romans under Vespasian, the inhabitants of Judea only hugged their delusion the closer. Many of them, it is true, terrified by the lawless deeds of the Zealots, abandoned their homes and set their faces toward Jerusalem with their wives and their little ones. "Behold, in Jerusalem we shall be safe," they said, "and in the city of Zion shall we eat the fat of the Gentiles."

In quiet Aphtha, people still sowed their crops and harvested them; observed the times and seasons of the moon; ate and drank merrily at feasts and danced at vintage, as in the old days. Galilee with the avenging Romans was far away; and Jerusalem, hid among its sacred hills, gave forth no disquieting token of the fire of civil warfare which devoured it. Now and again a traveling merchant would startle the idle peasants who hung about the village inn with wild tales of the Zealots, who had entrenched themselves in the courts of the temple as in a fortress; while below in the defenceless Agra swarmed the dissolute soldiers of John of Gischala.

Strange tales indeed to tell of the City of Solemnities. The children laughed with witless delight to hear how these rioters paraded themselves by night in the garb of women, their faces painted scarlet, their touseled heads decked with rich head-dresses and jewels. But their elders frowned uneasily when their informant whispered of the bloody deeds of these fantastic marauders.

"The priests should not allow these unlawful things," they said with indignation.

"Moses is no longer spoken of in Jerusalem," was the ominous answer; "as for the priests, they also have become warriors."

During these months Phannias remained in the house of his mother. After the first outburst of love and joy with which she had received him, he had said little of his experiences in the temple. "I have broken my vow," he had cried despairingly, on that night of his return. But when on the following day Rachel had begged him to take counsel with the ruler of the synagogue and with the Batlanin, he refused in a tone which silenced her.

"I will have none of them," he said fiercely. "Nor will I again become a Nazarite."

And Rachel, bethinking herself that it was she who had bound him, forbore to urge the matter.

On the third day after his home-coming, the ruler of the synagogue and the ten Batlanin visited the widow. They had heard of the young Nazarite's rejection at the hands of the priesthood, and

were full of curiosity to see how he bore himself.
"'Tis in accordance with the law of Moses and the
will of Jehovah," said the ruler of the synagogue
piously, staring with hard, unwinking eyes into the
young man's gloomy face.   Phannias returned the
look haughtily; but he made no reply.

"Thou art still a Nazarite—God be praised!"
quoth another, "and canst give thy life to the
blessed study of the Talmud and Mishna."

"I am not a Nazarite," said Phannias.   "Nor
will I give my life to the study of what is useless
and unmeaning."

Whereat these righteous representatives of the
law cried out as one man, "Apostate!   The devil
hath seized upon thee for his own!"   After this
they troubled him no more, though there was talk
for a space of scourging his body at the door of
the synagogue, that haply he might be purged of
the evil spirit which had possessed him.   Yet because of his great stature there was no man of
them all who durst undertake the task.

As for the fallen Nazarite, at times he worked
mightily in his mother's vineyard, performing with
ease in a single day labor upon which the slow-
witted peasants would have spent a week.   At
other times he disappeared from the village, leaving home with no word of warning, and reappear-
ing as suddenly.   Once, after an absence of thrice
seven days he returned, exhausted and scarce able
to speak, the reason for which appeared in a

ghastly wound beneath his tunic, which he reluctantly allowed his mother to dress.

"Oh, my son," wailed Rachel, in an agony of helpless love and sorrow, "where hast thou been? What if thou hadst fallen in some desert spot with none to help thee?"

"The ravens pluck the flesh from thrice ten thousand bodies of men slain in battle," answered Phannias gloomily. "I am but one man, and hateful in the sight of Jehovah."

Rachel caught eagerly at the last word. "Jehovah is very merciful," she said timidly; "surely thou hast not forgotten how thou wast cleansed in the temple and restored——"

Phannias broke away from the gentle hands with a harsh laugh. "Cleansed!" he repeated. "Can a flock of vultures whose talons reek with the blood of holy men cleanse one who hath sinned?" He turned suddenly and fixed his burning eyes upon his mother's white face. "Mother—mother!" he cried, "there is no longer any way of cleansing. There is nothing but death—death!—Look you," he continued, after a long silence which Rachel did not venture to break, "I have visited every place where I might find them that could tell me of the man, Jesus of Nazareth.—I swore to do this thing; for myself, I swore it. Mother, what if it be true! The Messiah—rejected—crucified. The blood of the Promised on the head of Israel! My God, if it be true!"

After this for the space of a month Phannias remained quietly at home; during these days he was
more than ordinarily gentle to his mother, whose
bitterness of soul he divined, but could not comfort. If he knew that she spent her days in prayer,
and her nights in secret weeping and humiliation
before the God who seemed so very far away, he
gave no sign. For himself he no longer prayed;
the grand religion of his fathers appeared in his
eyes no better than a loathsome corpse, from whose
ghastly features the cerecloth had fallen away;
while the mysterious ecstatic joy of the believers
in the crucified Nazarene seemed a strange madness upon which he looked with cold dislike.
"If the Messiah has come," he groaned within his
darkened soul, "then is the end of all things at
hand."

He hated and feared himself the more because,
believing this, he could yet spend long feverish
hours dreaming of the fair false princess, who had
made him the plaything of an idle moment, to
spurn him as one spurns a dog whose fantastic
gambols no longer amuse. A thousand times the
mad blood leaped to his brain as he recalled her
face, splendid as some passionate rose, dew-
drenched and sun-flamed. "She loved me!" he
cried, forgetting all but the baleful radiance of her
eyes as she bent toward him, whispering, "For
love's sake, my Phannias."

Once, as he passed on one of his wild journeys

through the mountains, he came upon a group of
refugees, who told him many things that had taken
place in the world. "Nero is dead; Otho is dead;
Vitellius is dead. The legions have declared Vespasian emperor," they said. Then perceiving that
he cared nothing for the information, they fell to
talking among themselves of the slaughters in Galilee, and of the towns in Judæa which yet remained
to be conquered.

After a little one made mention of Berenice, af-
firming that she had visited the camp of the Roman
conquerors, that she might, at the last, save Jerusalem and the temple.

Whereat another— "The woman hath cast her
gilded web about the son of Vespasian that she
may please herself; for Jerusalem and the temple
she cares no more than for her former lovers—who
are legion." With that he laughed aloud and
called the princess a vile name.

The word was his last, for Phannias sprang upon
him like a wild beast. "Liar!" he shrieked, and
choked the soul from the man's lips. The others
drew their weapons; but in the end Phannias
rushed away into the hills, leaving all three behind,
a silent company.

If a man lose his faith in God and in woman on
one and the same day, that day becomes a day of
doom. But Phannias yet believed in one woman;
that woman clung to him with one hand and to
God with the other; and so although his soul

hung over the pit that has not been sounded of men or angels it could not well fall lower.

On a day in Iyar, the bloom month, Phannias labored in the terraced steeps of the vineyard, his strong brown shoulders glistening in the sun as they rose and fell with the rhythmic motion of the spade. Warm gusts of fragrance, exhaling from the new leaves and blossoms of the vines, mingled with the potent smell of the freshly-dug earth. Phannias drew in long breaths of it and was conscious of a primal gladness stirring in his soul. Over the roof of his mother's cottage the almond trees billowed against the sky like nearer clouds of pink and white ; they were alive with bees whose loud joyous humming filled the silences betwixt bird songs.

Below on the steep path which led from Bethlehem there toiled a bent figure, which Phannias knew. His first impulse was to throw down his spade and run to meet the wayfarer ; his next was to hide himself. In the end he did neither, but continued stolidly at his digging.

After a time he heard his mother's voice ; she was calling him, a note of gladness in her tones which Phannias resented. "She thinks that I will obey him," he muttered, with a savage thrust of the spade ; "but I am no longer a child." He affected not to hear the summons, turning his back upon the cottage, and busying himself blindly with the topmost row of vines ; but he must needs acknowledge the authoritative touch upon his shoulder, with which Ben Huna presently announced himself.

Phannias looked up, his black brows meeting over stormy eyes ; he was prepared to face righteous wrath, godly sorrow, and a long dissertation on the law ; but in the eyes that met his own he read only gladness and love—love unutterable, yet full of a strange regret.

He opened his lips to speak, but Ben Huna stretched out his arms with a great cry, " My son —my son ! Thanks be unto Jehovah and unto our Lord and Saviour, Jesus Christ, who hath heard my prayer and hath preserved me alive till I should undo the mischief I have done !—But come, let us descend into the garden; I have much to say to thee—and to Rachel, thy mother."

Phannias threw down his spade and followed his old master with a curling lip.

" Thou wast right, my son Phannias," began Ben Huna, when all three were seated in the thick shadow of the fig tree. " Thou wast right, and I— blind that I was—forced thee into the hoary paths of error, despite thy clearer vision. Look you, I have traveled far since last I saw you, and this much have I learned by the grace of God. Jesus of Nazareth, born in the khan of Bethlehem yonder, was the Messiah of Israel !" The old man spoke these words with a solemn joy that did not escape the watchful eyes of Phannias. He had seen this

look upon many faces; he had not ceased to wonder at it. " If it be true," he said within himself,
" why rejoice ?"

" In Ephesus," continued Ben Huna, after a
silence, during which he seemed, in his old wise
fashion, to be searching among his thronging
thoughts for the best and easiest to be comprehended,—" in Ephesus, I fell in with a man called
John ; he was an apostle of Jesus ; that is to say,
one appointed by the Christ to be his companion
during his earth life and a shepherd of his flock
after he was forced to leave them. This holy man
told me all the story of the blessed life in Bethlehem—in Nazareth—in Capernaum and in all the
places through which the Master traveled, healing
and teaching the people. As much of this as I
was able I have written down.—See, here are the
parchments ; thou shalt help me, my son, to put
them in order. Ah, the blessed life—the blessed
death !"

" The man died upon the cross," said Phannias
gloomily. " What blessing can come from that
which is accursed ? If it be true that the Nazarene
was the Messiah, there can be nothing in that
truth save death and ruin for Israel. For myself I
will not believe it."

Ben Huna turned his mild eyes upon the young
man with a look of dismay and sorrow. " Alas !"
he said, as if to himself—or to another close at
hand, " I did my terrible work too well."

" *Thou* didst it ?" cried Phannias, shaking his
broad shoulders impatiently. " *Thou ?*—Nay, I am
no longer a child—a weakling, to believe blindly
what I am told. Look you, rabbi, I also have
traveled, and have talked with many of the followers
of this man. They all harp on the same string, and
affect a mysterious rapture of belief in the dead man,
who lives, they declare—though they cannot prove
it to the eye or touch of any man. That the temple
is defiled by the presence of evil men they care
nothing ; that the enemies of the nation threaten to
devour it like a swarm of locusts they care nothing;
that the laws of Moses are trodden under foot by
their Gentile proselytes they care nothing. Nay,
they declare that the days of the law are past ; and
they sing and pray to the crucified One, their faces
shining as if anointed, while the sword hangs over
the nation's head !"

Phannias poured forth these words with a feverish energy which brooked no interruption ; and
Ben Huna, comprehending something of the storm
which raged in the young man's soul, remained
silent.

Rachel had spoken no word, but sitting apart
wrapped in her patient sorrow listened with wonder; now she started to her feet with a gesture
of alarm. "There is tumult in the village !" she
whispered, her dark eyes resting with a mother's
keen prescience upon the face of her son.

The sound of swift feet and tumultuous voices

penetrated the calm peace of the little garden. A man, breathless, exhausted as if with swift running, hurled himself over the low barriers at its foot.

"I seek Phannias Ben Samuel," he cried imperatively. "In the name of the holy council of Zealots, show me him!"

"What wilt thou with the lad?" began Ben Huna, extending a trembling hand as if to protect his beloved pupil.

Phannias put him firmly aside. "I am the son of Samuel," he said boldly. "What is it thou hast to say to me?"

The man gave vent to a loud shout of exultation. "High Priest of Israel, elect of the holy council of Jerusalem, I salute thee!" he cried, and threw himself upon his face at the feet of Phannias.

CHAPTER XXIII.

THE HOUSE DESOLATE.

AFTER the suicide of Nero, three emperors passed in rapid succession before the eyes of the Roman people. Driven as it were by the relentless furies, Galba, Otho and Vitellius snatched at the royal emblems held out to them by a blind fate, then passed onward into death and oblivion, with but a shred of the imperial purple clutched in their stark fingers.

During this pageant of royalty and death, Vespasian, with a force of sixty thousand men, was steadily pursuing his task of reducing the rebellious provinces in Palestine. The Galilees had already fallen, with the destruction of all the important cities, whose inhabitants were either slaughtered outright or sold into slavery. The early months of the year 68 beheld the victorious legions advancing into Judæa, crushing in their progress the walled towns one after another with dull, monotonous, resistless blows, which filled the unreasoning populace with abject terror. To the cry, " The Romans are coming !" there was now but one answer, " Jerusalem !"

Jerusalem's gates stood open night and day, like

the doors of a furnace making ready for the burning; into it flocked thousands upon thousands of
terrified Jews, men and women, young men and
maidens, children and babes, who had opened their
innocent eyes upon evil times. Month by month
the net was being drawn closer about the doomed
city, when news of the deposition of Vitellius
reached the army. The legions at once declared
Vespasian emperor; and leaving his son, Titus, to
reduce the Jewish capital, the new-made Cæsar set
out for Rome. So there was respite for Jerusalem
—a year of respite. But the city, like some madman gorged with fiery wine, knew it not.

In those days there were strange sights to be
seen in the temple—that great citadel of Jehovah,
which the Jews believed not less eternal than the
rock on which it stood. The marble courts and
cloisters, which for centuries had echoed to long-
drawn chant and stately ritual, and over which the
subtile breath of incense yet lingered like a prayer,
now resounded to the tread of armed men and to
shouts of drunken revelry.

In the Court of the Gentiles some fifteen hundred
of the Zealot forces were encamped; their beds,
cooking utensils and rough weapons, mixed with
heaps of parti-colored plunder, blocked the superb
cloister of Herod's portico, and were even piled
against the sacred *Chel*, which separated this great
enclosure from the holier regions within. The
Zealots themselves, half drunk and gorged with

food, lay about the marble floors, playing at dice
for Roman farthings ; or swaggered in noisy groups
around the gates, watching the trembling worshipers as they passed in and out. For with character-
istic tenacity the wretched Jews clung to the empty
show of worship in their desolate temple.

Eleazar, the Zealot chief, loudly proclaimed himself a patriot; and while in secret he cared for nothing
but power and riches for himself, outwardly he assumed the role of protector of the pious and guardian of the temple. " The temple is mine," he said
within himself; "if I can hold it I shall presently
become a great prince ; in any event the treasure is
in my hands."

The priests and Levites, who had not already
fled from the distracted city, stayed for the most
part at their posts, and, under the doubtful protection of Eleazar and his band of Sicars, carried on a
ghastly observance of religious rites and ceremo-
nies in that part of the temple left to their use.
Eleazar and his captains had entrenched themselves
in the inner chambers of the Court of Israel, hitherto sacred to the use of the temple officials ; to the
vigorous protests of Ananus and others of the
priestly party they presented the unanswerable arguments of might and possession.

It pleased the Zealot chief at this time to assume
the state of prince and ruler, which indeed he had
the intent to become at no distant day. In token
of this resolution he held his councils of war in the

stately chamber of the Sanhedrim, himself occupy-
ing the central seat of authority. Before him appeared a deputation from the priests bidding him
once more, in the name of Jehovah of Hosts and
of Matthias III., High Priest of Israel, to withdraw
his soldiers from the temple.

"Jehovah of Hosts is on my side," quoth Eleazar, staring fixedly into the face of the spokesman.
"As for Matthias, he is no longer high priest. I
have said it."

"By what authority—" began the representa-
tive of the priests, trembling with rage.

"By the same authority with which I now command thee to be smitten on the mouth," said
Eleazar—and motioned to one of his henchmen,
who forthwith smote the priest across the face with
the flat of his sword. "Bind the fellow and set him
against yonder pillar," commanded the Zealot.
"He shall carry back news to Ananus."

This done, he ordered the list of priests to be
fetched from the chamber of records, and the
names of the high-priestly family to be stricken
from the number.

"Now write the names upon tablets," he said,
"—every name upon a separate tablet; cast the
tablets into the great vessel of the drink-offering."

When this was done after many hours of labor,
Eleazar bade the priest, who had been smitten on
the mouth, thrust his right hand into the vessel of
the drink-offering and take out a tablet.

"I will not," he cried. "What you are about to do is foul sacrilege!"

"Strike off the right hand of this man," commanded Eleazar. And when this was done forthwith, he again addressed the unfortunate priest. "Thrust now thy left hand into the vessel of the drink-offering, and take me out a tablet."

The man obeyed, half fainting. Eleazar took the tablet. "I read here the name, Phannias, son of Samuel," he said. "Therefore, I, Eleazar, declare this Phannias, son of Samuel, to be High Priest. Fetch him hither."

And in this manner was the last high priest of Israel chosen, of the line beginning with Aaron, and descending from father to son through more than seventeen centuries.

On that same day the Zealots fetched Phannias, and brought him to the temple.

Here is the man from Aphtha, my lord," they said, bringing their prisoner into the presence of Eleazar.

Eleazar had been conferring with his captains as to the best method of dislodging the priestly party from the lower city. He had, for the moment, forgotten the circumstance of the morning. "Who is this fellow that ye thrust into my presence unbidden?" he said scowling.

"The high priest, my lord, who was chosen by lot."

Eleazar burst into a loud laugh. "By the double

veil !" he cried, " I had lost sight of the matter in
the multitude of weightier concerns. But the game
shall be played out. Here you, priest, stand forth."

Phannias wrenched himself loose from the hands
that held him. "What is the meaning of this?"
he demanded in a low voice, fixing his eyes upon
the Zealot.

"A pretty fellow, I swear it !" said Eleazar,
turning to one of the bystanders, "tall and well
made ; the high-priestly baubles will set well upon
those broad shoulders. Go fetch them."

Phannias approached a step nearer. "I will
have an answer," he said. " These men have
saluted me high priest. If it be a jest, it is blasphemy. Who art thou ; and by what authority
hast thou done this thing ?"

Eleazar stared into the eyes of his questioner for
a full minute before he answered. Then his face
grew grave and stern. " Thou mayst well ask,
priest," he said ; "these are troublous times, and
authority belongs to him who can best wield the
sword. Know that I am Eleazar, chief in command of them that will have freedom for Israel,—
freedom from the galling yoke of the Gentiles ;
freedom from the not less intolerable oppression
of the priests, who are but swollen leeches upon
the foul body of Rome. 'Jerusalem for the Jews!'
is our watchword, 'The temple for the people !'
Thou hast been legally elected high priest in room
of a thief and murderer. Wilt thou be high

priest; or shall I bid them loose thee in the rabble outside the city walls?"

Phannias was silent. A thousand mad thoughts surged through his bewildered brain. "*Thou* a high priest, who dost no longer believe in the religion of Israel?" cried his accusing conscience. "Become high priest," whispered his ambition, "and thou becomest a prince—a potentate, who may well demand in marriage the sister of Agrippa!" Above these conflicting thoughts rang the sounding words of the Zealot: "Jerusalem for the Jews! The temple for the people!"

Eleazar was watching the face of the young man with a frowning brow. No one knew better than he·the farcical nature of the whole affair. It made not the slightest difference to the Zealot chief whether or not there was a high priest; but it pleased him to trample under foot the waning authority of the priestly party, to hurl, as it were, this last insult into the face of the dying hierarchy. Moreover, he thought to gain popularity with the common people by choosing from among their number this figure-head of a religion, for which he cared less than nothing. "Your answer, priest," he growled impatiently. "Wilt thou be high priest ; or wilt thou not?"

"I will be high priest," said Phannias slowly.

"Done!" cried Eleazar, bringing his hairy fist down upon his knee. "To the Court of the Priests; the matter shall be finished."

Under a strong guard of Zealot troops the new-made head of the temple was conducted to the Hall of Robes, where he was hastily divested of his peasant's garb and dressed in the sacred garments of the high priest. This service was performed by a half dozen silent Levites, who were in manifest terror of the drawn swords of the Zealots. Phannias knew little enough of the sacred office, but he perceived that his investiture was being accomplished with none of the ceremonial prescribed by law. The blood rushed to his face; he set his teeth hard. "I am high priest," he said within himself. "What care I for the law?"

"Fetch him out," commanded Eleazar briefly. "Let him show himself before the people."

Phannias heard the command; his eyes flashed fire. "Stand aside," he said imperiously, "I will go forth to the people."

Eleazar involuntarily fell back before the imposing figure of priestly authority which swept toward him. This high priest was but a puppet—a toy—a creature of straw, which he himself had set up to be the wanton sport of a moment; yet this "boorish peasant"—as he called him in his heart—"this ignorant knave," who comprehended so little of the blasphemous farce of his investiture as to accept it without question, presented in his magnificent robes a picture of regal grandeur, which awed even the coarse-minded Zealot. The bells and pomegranates which bordered the sacred robe clashed musically ; the breastplate flashed a twelvefold gleam of dazzling splendor, as Phannias slowly advanced down the hall betwixt the triple rows of soldiers.

Eleazar suddenly remembered the strange legend of the Urim and Thummim—the mystical communication of God with his people by means of the sacred stones of the breastplate. What did those flaming stones—each graven with the name of one of the tribes of Israel—signify? He followed dumbly, while the new-made high priest advanced toward the altar. It was already the ninth hour, the time of the daily evening sacrifice.

A double line of priests advanced with measured steps along the cloister which divided the Court of Israel from the Women's Court ; at their head walked Ananus, haughty chief of the high-priestly family. Looking neither to the left nor the right, the procession swept on to a position directly in front of the great altar. The trumpets sounded a thrilling blast ; the great bell of the temple clanged heavily. From the subterranean music rooms beneath the Steps of Degrees the Levites emerged, a maze of snowy figures, chanting the evening hymn in deep resonant voices.

Phannias stood alone, his head bowed, his hands clenched beneath the gorgeous robes. The hostile glances of the priests lashed him like the blows of a scourge ; the low murmur of the people sounded in his ears a thunder of impending doom. A High Priest— but pilloried before the mocking eyes of a nation !

Two Levites now approached the place in which he stood, preceded by a priest, who bore the golden vessel of incense.

On a sudden Phannias remembered the law concerning this offering. " If there be one priest in the house of his Father, who hath not yet burned incense in the Holy Place, he and no other shall offer the sweet-smelling savor to Jehovah of Hosts, at the time of the evening sacrifice."

He fixed a compelling gaze upon the priest who was about to pass him without obeisance. " Give me the vessel of incense," he said in a loud voice, "—and the censer ; it is the law."

The priest stared at the resplendent figure with cold, unseeing eyes and passed by without pause.

"Stop !" cried a raucous voice from among the Zealot soldiers, who stood in serried ranks in the Women's Court. " Obey your high priest !' A low, ominous clash of swords followed the words.

The priest turned white to the lips ; he stood still in his place, his venomous eyes fastened upon the face of Phannias. " Wilt thou profane the Holy Place, who art both unsanctified and unclean ?" he demanded in a hissing whisper.

Phannias looked full into the eyes of his questioner ; he knew him for the man whom he had seen in the subterranean chambers of the temple on the terrible day of his novitiate. " If I be unsanctified and unclean," he answered dully, as one in a dream of anguish, " I am neither thief nor murderer."

Mechanically he received the golden vessel of incense and the censer of live coals from the hand of the man who would have slain him, scarce hearing the frightful words of anathema breathed in his ear. Still in a dream of anguish, he ascended the marble steps of the sanctuary. A number of priests who guarded the entrance made as though they would have seized him ; but he swept by them —passed within the double curtains of Babylonian byssus, gay with broideries of gold and purple and scarlet, and stood, at last, alone in the Holy Place.

CHAPTER XXIV.

THE LAST HIGH PRIEST.

ALONE in the Holy Place ! It was as though he had left his mortal body in the world without and had stepped, a naked soul, into the presence of the King of kings. All the doubt and anguish, all the fever and turmoil of the past months fell away, even as the rent mantle of the flesh drops from a liberated spirit. The twilight and silence of the great vaulted chamber descended with exquisite soothing upon his tortured heart. He fixed his eyes upon the curtained space at the further end of the hall—the Holy of Holies. God was there.

He fell upon his knees in a passion of weeping— such blessed weeping as shakes the child, who casts himself upon the breast of his mother, to pour out in that sacred refuge all his sorrow and fear. " Have mercy upon me, who am a sinful man !" he whispered brokenly. " Teach me the truth ! Hast thou sent the promised Deliverer ; and has Israel rejected—slain him ? God of my fathers, show me the truth!"

Then it seemed to the last high priest of Israel that one touched him gently upon the shoulder. He raised his eyes, hot with tears, and behold, the vast curtain of the veiled place had vanished; in its room he looked into a wild, desolate sky, black with hurrying clouds, thrust through and through with darts of livid lightning. Against this background of cloud and fire loomed a terrible shape—the shape of a cross. Upon the cross hung the figure of a man. Despite the darkness, the face of this man shone out clear and distinct, a face whereon God-love and mortal anguish struggled for the mastery; then the mortal vanished, and the glory of the Eternal settled down upon it. There were voices now—voices of the prophets, sad and yearning: "The assembly of the wicked have closed in upon me; they have pierced my hands and my feet!" "Wounded for our transgressions; bruised for our iniquities:" "Taken from prison and from judgment, who shall declare his generation; he was cut off out of the land of the living; for the transgression of my people was he stricken."

Above and beyond the wailing voices sounded a pæan of triumph, sweet and far-reaching—a many-voiced song of angels, dropping—it seemed—from infinite heights of heaven like the light of stars.

"Glory to God in the highest!
On earth peace,—good-will to men!"

Then on a sudden the veil dropped with a sound of thunder, and the voices blent in awful harmony: "We are departing hence!"

When Phannias came to himself, he beheld once more the great chamber of the Holy Place, dim and bare save for the seven-branched candlestick, the golden table of shew-bread and the altar of incense. Before the Holiest Place hung the double curtain of scarlet and purple and white—vast, motionless—veiling emptiness. Upon the floor at his side lay the scattered incense, and the coals from the altar, black and dead.

He arose to his feet and passed out before the eyes of the waiting congregation ; there was a look upon his face before which the sneering priests shrank back in terror. He advanced steadily to the space before the altar and raised his arms high above his head. Instinctively the people fell upon their faces, awaiting the high-priestly benediction. But no empty syllables of blessing fell from those white lips. " Men of Israel, ye have slain your Messiah !" was the sentence which fell from them, each word distinct—terrible, like the blows of a scourge. " The hope of Israel hath gone out, like a lamp that is quenched, and as live coals that perish on the altar ! Hear now the word of the Lord : 'When ye fast I will not listen to your cry. When ye offer burnt offering and an obla- tion, I will not accept them. I will consume you by the sword, and by famine, and by pestilence ! Behold, the house which is called by my name is become a den of robbers in your eyes ! I, even I, have seen it. Behold, there shall not be left here

one stone upon another that shall not be thrown
down !' ''

There was silence for an instant—such silence as
stalks majestic before the presence of the whirlwind ; then a long, loud wail burst from a woman's
throat. Phannias beheld a surging wave of furious
faces, which rose and broke shrieking upon a fringe
of spears. He was dragged backward—downward ;
the priestly robes were torn from his shoulders.

" Accursed of God and man—die. Thrust him
through—quickly !"

Phannias knew the voice and the face, black with
murderous passion ; a mighty strength came upon
him ; he rent his assailant with his naked hands
and flung his limp body against the foot of the
altar.

"Well done, priest," cried a harsh voice at his
side. "Take the sword—thou wilt need it. —Shut
both gates below there ! So, we have beat them
back into the Court of the Gentiles ! Now slay
every priest and Levite within ; the knaves will
betray us else !"

The Zealot chief turned upon Phannias with an
oath. " I was minded to slay thee also, but I have
spared thee, since thou hast shown thyself an honest
enemy to these whining cowards. Come, off with
the priestly gauds, or I cannot save thee from the
swords of the Sicars."

With his own hands Eleazar stripped off the
breastplate and ephod, casting them with a shud-

dering curse upon the smouldering fire of the
altar. " They will be wanted no more if what thou
saidst be true," he growled. " But why saidst
thou it? Thy words were as coals of fire flung
upon chaff."

Phannias shook his head. " Nay, I know not,"
he said dully.

"'Twas the stones yonder; they are accursed!
Look you, if the temple be no longer a temple it
is a citadel and mine. Go now; guard the Gate
Beautiful."

Drawn sword in hand, Phannias made his way
through the Gate of Nicanor, down the Steps of
Degrees, slippery with blood and heaped with dead
bodies, into the Court of the Women. Frightful
scenes were taking place here; the Zealot soldiers
had beat back the assault of the people led by the
priests, and had finally succeeded in closing the
heavy brazen doors. Now they were carrying out
the commands of their chief, hunting down and
killing without mercy the wretched priests and Levites who had been shut into the sacred enclosure.
Cries of mercy, shrieks, curses, execrations arose
from the cloistered courts and chambers where the
pursued had taken a last vain refuge.

Phannias beheld with horror the dead bodies of
women and children mixed with the slain. From
under one of the great treasure chests which stood
on either side of the cloister, a baby crawled,
screaming for its mother. A Sicar reached toward

it with a swoop of his crooked sword. Phannias snatched the child unscathed from beneath the blade and darted away among the cloisters.

"To the Gate Beautiful!" he shouted. "Defend the gate!"

A band of soldiers who were busy breaking open the door of a chamber in the court of the sacrificial wood paused at sound of the cry; then they abandoned their task and hurried away.

Phannias stared helplessly at the burden in his arms; the child looked up into his face and laughed aloud. "I must save thee, little one," he murmured, "—but how?"

He looked despairingly about him, recognizing with a throb of gratitude the spot where he had labored with his hands in the first days of his service in the temple. "Jachin!" he called aloud.

A faint voice answered his cry; then the head of the old priest was thrust cautiously out from behind a pile of knotted sticks. "Praise be to Jehovah, it is thou, Nazarite! Come, thou art a lusty fellow and canst protect me. If they are gone we will get us down to a place of safety; I know the way."

"Take thou the child—for the love of God, and get thee down!" cried Phannias, and rushed away toward the gate. He had now but one desire, and that was to escape from the desecrated temple.

Jachin stared at the babe, which again wept piteously. "By the stones of the breastplate!" he muttered, "shall I endanger my life for a crying brat?" Turning his back upon the child he plunged among the heaped-up wood of the sacrifices. "God of the sanctuary, remember thou the years of my faithful service!" he ejaculated, making obeisance toward the altar—and disappeared down a hidden stairway into the depths.

As for the babe, it shortly found its mother. For the innocent, death is but a single step from terror into joy.

CHAPTER XXV.

THE SHOPKEEPER OF THE AGRA.

THE times were assuredly evil; all men declared it; yet in spite of the times—or perhaps because of them, Ezra Ben Ethan, shrewd,
cautious, far-seeing, was doing a thriving business.
He chuckled to himself often in these days, and
rubbed his dry withered palms together with an air
of stealthy enjoyment. There had been a time,
and that not many years back, when the little shop
close by the Old Wall had been of the humblest.
Few pilgrims had chosen to purchase their Passover bread or their oil cakes for the meat-offering
of Ben Ethan. They had preferred rather to lay
in their supplies of these commodities on the temple platform, where a multitude of rich and prosperous merchants offered a dazzling variety of sacrificial goods; all guaranteed to be legally clean,
and therefore of a certainty acceptable to that Jehovah of Hosts whose shining temple looked down
in solemn grandeur on the bustling thoroughfares
at its feet.

Formerly Ben Ethan had never passed through
these rich market places of the Agra without ex-
periencing a fierce pang of envy. He hated the

16

sleek merchants who lolled indolently behind their
stalls, scarce troubling themselves to cry their
goods to the passers-by. Times were changed indeed ! The fierce soldiers of the Tyrant and the
Zealot—as John of Gischala and Eleazar had come
to be called, had wasted all that prosperous district
with fire and the sword. The sleek merchants had
disappeared to a man. Some had fled at the first
outbreak of the internecine warfare ; others, braver
or more greedy of gain, had stuck to their business,
only to be stripped of all they possessed ; and later
to lie unburied, save for the smoking ruins of their
houses.

"Jehovah is just !" ejaculated Ben Ethan, piously
rending his garments in token of his grief at this
disaster. " He abaseth the proud and he also set-
teth up the humble ; blessed be his holy name !"

As for the small shabby booth near the gate
Miphkad, its owner took good care that there
should be no unseemly display to tempt the cupid-
ity of the soldiers ; a paltry basket of cakes, a
bottle of oil, perchance ; a heap of mouldy olives.
"It is all I have, patriots !" he would cry, lifting
his lean shoulders and spreading abroad his hands.
"All that I have—Jehovah be my witness ! but
such as it is, honored defenders of Jerusalem, you
are kindly welcome to it !"

And the marauders, sleek with stolen provender
and wine, swore with maudlin generosity that Ben
Ethan was an honest man and should not be dis-

turbed in his business. After a time, certain of these worthies found the obscure shop a convenient place of resort. One could always be certain of a skin of good wine there, and the baskets of wheaten cakes were never empty. Little by little it became also the custom to entrust the shopkeeper with certain valuable bits of plunder; which indeed a diligent man could accumulate with such ease and rapidity that the very abundance became at times a matter of embarrassment. It is certain that the owner of a particularly desirable article was frequently forced to exchange his booty for a dagger-thrust in the back, a thing which no man coveted.

Ben Ethan trembled at first under the load of his new eases and responsibilities. It was, for example, far from pleasant for a law-observing and orderly Jew to be forced to witness the killing of a man in his very presence ; and this happened not infrequently when the wine was strong and booty plenty. But there are two sides to every matter— if one will but take the trouble to reflect ; and no philosopher of them all knew better than Ben Ethan that a calamity turned inside out oftentimes displays a blessing. He was therefore not slow to observe that in case a man quitted Jerusalem thus suddenly, neither he nor another ever inquired for his property. And so it came to pass that he shortly found himself the undisputed possessor of a very handsome collection of silver cups, plates, candlesticks, jewels, chains, and the like ; all of which he be-

stowed for safe keeping in certain excavations underneath his house, the secrets of which were known
to no other but himself.

There was one person in the house of Ben Ethan
who regarded these enlargements of his interests
with undisguised alarm and anxiety; this person
was his daughter, Merodah.

"Thou art a woman—which is to say a fool!"
observed the old man sententiously, when the girl
besought him with tears to fly the distracted city.
"Have I lived in poverty all my days to turn my
back upon plenty when it is within my grasp?
Get thee to thy spinning and hold thy chattering
tongue."

Later he presented her with a richly embroidered
robe, which a soldier had flung down in a corner
of the shop and forgotten. But Merodah, observing a jagged rent, deeply dyed about its edges in
the folds which had lain across the wearer's breast,
only shrank away aghast, her dark eyes fixed and
staring.

"What now, woman!" cried Ben Ethan angrily.
"Art thou not pleased with the gift? A rent—eh?
what then; can it not be sewn and the garment
purified? One must be zealous in these days to
keep one's accounts straight with Jehovah!"

By which it will be observed that Ben Ethan had
by no means forgotten his religion; indeed his
prayers, oblations and vows had only grown more
numerous and fervent as the demands upon his

piety increased. It was truly a difficult task for
one to keep himself undefiled and walking orderly
after the law, when the sluggish current in the gut-
ters ran foul with blood, and the odor of corruption
tainted the very air one breathed; but Ben Ethan
accomplished it to his satisfaction.

"Jehovah will make allowance for these evil
times," he reflected, recalling with gratification the
fact that King David and his soldiers were once
reduced to the impious extremity of devouring the
shew-bread from off the altar. It was rumored
that things even more terrible had taken place
of late in the temple, where Eleazar, the Zealot
chief, and his dissolute soldiers held high carnival
in the intervals of battle; but he, Ben Ethan, was
surely not responsible for the misdeeds of others.

Between whiles, when his patrons were busy with
warfare or engaged in the accumulation of plunder,
Ben Ethan pursued the legitimate lines of his business with energy and discretion. The prices of
grain ran ruinously high, but notwithstanding this
fact hundreds of bags of wheat and barley found a
snug resting place in the cellars of the house by
the gate.

Ben Ethan contrived that for the most part this
grain should be delivered under cover of the darkness. For more reasons than one, he was unwill-
ing that his neighbors should be aware of these
transactions. "It is written thou shalt not covet
thy neighbor's goods," he said righteously. "Be-

hold a wise man boasteth not himself; nor will he tempt his neighbor to sin by displaying his goods before the eyes of them which lack."

As the time for the Paschal offering drew on, he became more and more zealous in his pious observ‍ances. Also, he ventured to display in the front of his shop a large quantity of Passover bread, tied up with bunches of bitter herbs; with a brave show of oil cakes, raisin wine, baskets of roasted grain, and other foods and condiments suited to the holy season.

Never were the pilgrims more numerous or more devout, thought Ben Ethan. They poured through the gates in countless thousands, with an anxious haste and silence quite unlike the joyous bustle of former years. All Judæa, it would seem, had flung itself bodily into Jerusalem, like a flock of fright-ened sheep under the lash of the terrible Roman name. "The Romans are coming! The Romans slay and spare not! The Romans will leave no man alive! Our babes will they kill with the sword, and our women will they sell into slavery! The Romans—the Romans—the Romans!"

For the most part this never-ending procession of fugitives were heavily laden with goods and pro-visions; also they brought with them their women and young children by hundreds and by thousands; till, what with the wailing of the little ones and the bleating of unnumbered flocks, which were assem-bled for the sacrifice, Jerusalem gave forth a strange piteous sound, like that of a mighty shambles on the day of slaughter. And this sound ascended to the heavens. But the heavens were as brass.

Ben Ethan, from the open booth in front of his shop, observed this great and ever-increasing multitude with wonder and satisfaction. "Victuals will be hard to find for all of these!" he ejaculated. "But what of the prudent man who hath foreseen this day and hath also made provision for it? Behold, he will reap the harvest of his wisdom, and that harvest will be gold!"

He said something of the sort to a woman who stopped at his stall to buy food for her child; and by way of making his meaning clear, he charged her a double price for the bread.

She paid the money without murmuring. "The Romans are just behind us!" she said, wiping the sweat from her forehead. "Thank God I have reached the city in time!"

"In time—eh?" echoed Ben Ethan; "and the Romans are just behind, sayest thou? They will perhaps shut up the city."

The woman stared at him with a frown. "How can I tell thee what will come to pass," she said wearily. "The Romans cannot get into Jerusalem; that much is certain.—Thou art safe, little one, eat thy bread and be silent!" For the child, terrified at the mention of the Roman name, had begun to whimper and clutch at her gown.

"They will shut up the city!" said Ben Ethan

to himself, snapping his fingers gleefully, as his customer disappeared from view in the crowd. " Ah, what a time for a poor man with a wise heart ! A good time, say I,—a fat, rich, profitable time !"

So pleasantly occupied did he become in calculating the gains certain to accrue to his prudent and far-seeing self in case of a prolonged siege, that he failed to observe the advent of a new customer. He was called to himself by a truculent voice.

" A cup of wine, Jew, and a loaf! Bestir thyself, for I am in haste."

Ben Ethan perceived with some trepidation that his patron was a soldier, also that he was eyeing the interior of the shop with a sharp and covetous gaze. He did not remember to have seen the man before. " Make thy choice of the loaves, honored sir," he said civilly ; " the large ones are a denarius; the small ones yonder in the basket, a penny each. As for wine——"

" A murrain on thee, Jew ! dost think I will pay thee for a bite and a sup?" growled the soldier, fixing his red eyes threateningly on Ben Ethan. " I will eat as I will of the loaves, and do thou bestir thyself to fetch the wine."

" Thou art welcome, patriot," stammered Ben Ethan, backing precipitately into the shop. "—the wine ? yes—certainly ; I will fetch it without delay." Then bethinking himself that his presence might prove something of a check on the rapacity of the hungry man, who had already made serious inroads upon his stock of fresh-baked loaves, he called loudly to his daughter, commanding her to fetch a skin of wine from within. She obeyed at once.

"Girdle of Venus!" exclaimed the soldier, dropping a half-eaten cake to stare at the girl who stood in the open doorway. "The goddess hath after all remembered me. It is the pretty maid I captured on the street a twelvemonth or more ago! Nay, my bird, thou hast not already forgotten Saph, who saved thee from the mob in the square of Antonia! May all the gods bear me witness that thou art handsomer than ever! This time thou shalt not slip through my fingers!"

He pushed boldly into the shop with outstretched arms, as if to seize the girl; but Merodah, who had stood at first transfixed with terror, retreated instantly, locking and barring the heavy door behind her.

For once Ben Ethan could have cursed himself for his miserly folly. He filled a cup with wine and advanced trembling. "The—wine, patriot; thou wilt find it good and strong, I trust."

"Scorpions and furies!" roared the soldier, dashing the cup aside. "I want the girl! Fetch her out to me!"

Ben Ethan's eyes flashed fire; his wizened figure dilated with wrath. "She is my daughter, dog of a Gentile!" he cried shrilly; "and under the protection of Jehovah of Israel!"

The soldier made a motion as though he would

have seized the merchant by the throat; then he fell back a pace and burst into a fit of uproarious laughter. Something in the aspect of the puny Jew seemed to afford him exquisite amusement. It was as if a mouse had suddenly presumed to defy a lion.

"May the gods smite me," he cried, "but thou art more of a fool than one often meets with in these days! What now is to hinder me, swine of a Jew, from crushing thee against the wall of thy shop, as one would crush a fly; and that done, who but this Gentile would be master of thy daughter and thy money-bags.—For thou hast a pretty store hidden away within, I'll warrant me. How comes it that thou art here unmolested, with a beauty like yonder wench shut up to thyself?"

Ben Ethan's face had become the color of clay during this harangue; thrice he attempted to speak, but his voice failed him. "Mercy, patriot!" he stammered at length. "Have I not made thee welcome to all that I have? I am a poor man; I have nothing—I swear it—also,"—his voice gaining strength—"I am under protection of John of Gischala."

At sound of this name the soldier glanced over his shoulder uneasily. "Thou art lying," he said, staring hard at Ben Ethan; "I know thou art lying, for I myself belong to the forces of John. Listen, Jew, I caught the girl on the street a twelvemonth or more ago; she is therefore mine—though she

escaped me for the time by reason of a cursed
priest. I have possessed many women, but this
little one is a thousand times more beautiful than
any of them. I *will* have her; that much is certain! Thou thyself wilt deliver her up to me
peaceably, or thou shalt fight for her with me."
Here his amusement again overcame him, and he
paused to give vent to it.

Ben Ethan wiped the great drops from his forehead and groaned aloud. "Now a plague on a
comely face!" he muttered; "—a comely face and
a lecherous eye hath sent more than one righteous,
law-abiding man to an untimely death." He resolved that this should not be his case, come what
might. Still the girl was his daughter; he would
make an effort to save her.

Aloud he said deprecatingly, "The maid is not
over beautiful, patriot. She is blind of one eye—
alas! Also, she is afflicted with the disorder of
leprosy, which as thou art aware——"

"Lies!" roared the soldier. "What knowest
thou of beauty, dotard? I have eyes in my head
and can see. Fetch out the girl, I say!" With
that he brushed the Jew aside as though he were
an insect, and laid a violent hand upon the door.

To his amazement it was flung wide open, and
Merodah stood upon the threshold.

CHAPTER XXVI.

OUT OF THE NORTH.

WHILE the soldier, who, like most giants, was somewhat slow both of wit and body, still stared open-mouthed at the unlooked for apparition of the girl, Merodah seized her father and drew him within the shelter of the door.

The sound of the heavy wooden bar, as it shot home into its socket, awakened the man outside to the fact that, for the moment, his victims had both escaped him. Obeying his first impulse, he began a furious assault upon the closed door, with but little result beyond a scarce perceptible straining of its stout oaken timbers. Then bethinking himself that there was an easier way to accomplish his wishes, since the Jew could not remain shut within his house for any length of time, he proceeded to amuse his leisure by looting the shop. He passed in this way some very agreeable moments; great handfuls of the delicate cakes finding their way into the street, to the joy of a half dozen starved-looking children, who gathered fearless as sparrows to the scene. Later, having emptied the baskets, this open-handed patriot proceeded to bombard the locked door with a miscellaneous assortment of olives, plates, cups, wooden bowls, oil flasks and the like.

Ben Ethan, cowering just inside, could not be induced to leave the neighborhood of the disaster. "My God," he moaned piteously, wringing his hands, "I shall be ruined! I must go out and defend my property!"

Merodah laid her hand upon his shoulder. "If thou goest out, my father," she said, "I go also."

"Sacred fire, girl! Get out of my sight; 'tis thou and no other who art the cause of it all! Didst thou not disobey me; and is not this the result of that disobedience? Ay—the woman which thou gavest me. 'Tis always the woman—the woman—the woman!"

The sounds outside suddenly ceased; the fact being that Saph, having exhausted the stock of available ammunition, was casting about for some new mischief. Chancing, in his rambling tour of investigation, to arrive opposite the outside door, he espied a couple of his boon companions in the street.

"Well met, comrades," he roared, thrusting his great head out from the booth. "Here's capital sport for us all! An obstinate swine of a Jew, a pretty maid and a skin of good wine. Look you, they be all inside awaiting your pleasure!"

"Better sport on the walls," returned the others. "Come with us; the Romans are in sight!"

Saph hesitated for an instant; then bestowing

two or three thundering kicks on the closed door, he yielded to the superior attraction, promising himself a complete and satisfactory vengeance upon this particular house later on.

An hour after his departure Ben Ethan ventured out from his stronghold. During that hour he had ample time to reflect upon the threatening aspect of his affairs. "God of Abraham!" he murmured disconsolately, his eyes roving about over the scene of desolation and ruin which the soldier had left behind him; "there is no longer any place in Jerusalem for a prudent man who would labor with his hands for the reward of his diligence!" Which indeed was a far truer saying than Ben Ethan in his short-sighted wisdom could guess.

To Merodah the hour had been one of fear and anguish. More than once in her short life she had stumbled upon black depths in the nature of the man whom she revered; depths which in childlike faith and humility she had endeavored to bridge over with love's tender apologies. "Father knows best," she assured herself over and over; "I am a foolish maid and do not understand." She believed firmly that her father was the best and wisest of men; the something within her own innocent soul which now and again rose up in revolt against the man's cowardly nature frightened and tortured her. She longed to lean upon his strength, to love—to worship him.

Ben Ethan accepted this fragrant homage with

as much comprehension of its meaning and value as men of his kind are wont to exhibit. His daughter was his daughter, and for this reason alone presumably possessed of some merit ; she was also the last of his family. He had bitterly resented the fact that his wife had not borne him a son ; but, inasmuch as she had promptly paid the penalty of her mistake with her life, he had magnanimously forgiven her memory. After all the girl had proved herself useful ; she was meek, obedient, and possessed of a skillful hand in the fashioning and baking of the cakes, which up to this time had formed his chief stock in trade. He intended at some time in the future to marry her to a reputable Jew. Indeed, more than once of late he had cast about in the circle of his acquaintance for a possible son-in-law ; but in every case the proposed marriage price had not, on the whole, appeared sufficient to compensate him for the loss of his daughter's services.

To-day as he endeavored to restore his dismantled shop to some degree of order he cursed himself both loud and deep for his procrastination in this matter. "The girl is a positive menace to me !" he muttered ; "I swear that I will marry her within the week—if it be to a beggar on the street corner."

Full of this idea he double-locked and barred the doors behind him, and without speaking to his daughter of his benevolent plans for her future

hurried away into the inner city. He had the intent
to broach the matter of the marriage to a dealer in
sacrificial animals, who conducted his business hard
by the tower of Antonia. This man was a con-
temporary of his own, and a widower for the third
time.

"I will not be over strict in the matter of the
dowry," he said to himself; "the girl is young and
eats more than I,—and God knows every mouthful
will shortly be worth a denarius! Nehemiah Ben
Azor is a worthy man, and ought to be prosperous
this Passover season if never before.—Lord, what
a power of folk in Jerusalem, and a lamb for every
ten!"

He had arrived by this time at the street of the
sacrifices, where dwelt the man whom he sought.
For the first time he noticed the singular stillness
which brooded over the city. It was nearing the
hour of noon, for the sun stood almost overhead,
shedding a blaze of light into the narrow street,
which was choked for a part of its length with the
ruins of fallen houses. Ben Ethan clambered nimbly through one such ruinous building, picking up
on his way a silver anklet and a bronze drinking-
cup, which had escaped the covetous eyes of the
beggars, who followed in the wake of the destroy-
ing soldiers like a swarm of vultures. He surveyed
these articles with an air of satisfaction. "A good
omen!" he ejaculated, and made obeisance toward
the temple. "So doth the Lord prosper the law-

observing !—But what hath become of all the people ? I have seen neither man, woman nor child
since I left my door."

Marveling much within himself at this circumstance, Ben Ethan knocked loudly upon the door
of the dealer in sacrificial animals. " A comely
woman is my daughter," he was saying to himself;
"and for the marriage portion I will give an hundred pence ;—yes, I swear that I will do it, for I
shall want no more cakes baked ; I will sell instead
the naked grain ; and the girl will devour as much
—and more, in a twelvemonth."

When there was no answer to his summons, he
knocked again and yet again. " By the Ephod !"
he muttered, " has the earth then opened and swallowed the inhabitants of the Agra ? Or do they
think it is midnight instead of midday ?" With
that he laid his hand upon the door ; to his surprise
it yielded to his touch, and he stepped without hin-
drance into the courtyard. The place was crowded
with lambs, huddled close together under the hot
rays of the sun.

" The Paschal beasts—and without a guardian !"
cried Ben Ethan aloud. " Ben Azor is either dead
or mad. If he be dead—and verily, men die easily
in these days, the animals must be looked to—and
sold."

Determined to solve the question to his satisfaction, and already uncertain in his mind as to
whether it were better to marry his daughter or fall

heir to a dead man's property, this excellent man
of affairs pushed through the courtyard and began
to ascend the stairs which led up to the inhabited
portion of the house. As he went he called loudly
upon Ben Azor.

" Who is it that calls me?" cried a gruff voice
from above. " Come up—come up—in God's
name, whoever thou art; for I will not come down
in this hour."

"What in the name of the *Chel*—" began Ben
Ethan, wheezing and wiping the sweat from his
forehead as he set foot upon the hot level of the
roof. Then he stopped short and stared in amazement; Ben Azor, his sons, his daughters, his man-
servants and his maid-servants, were one and all assembled at the verge of the battlemented roof,
gazing from under leveled palms away toward the
north.

" What is it?" he cried. " Are ye all mad—and
the house unlocked and unguarded?"

Ben Azor, a tall powerful man, whose beard descended in waves of silvery whiteness upon his
broad chest, motioned to the newcomer authoritatively. " Come thou," he said, hoarsely, "and
behold what the eyes of no Jew hath beheld from
the days of Moses—a hostile army descending
upon the holy city at the time of the Passover.
God knoweth what will be the end of it all!"

" They will shut up the city!" cried Ben Ethan
shrilly. " I have said that it would happen; I knew

that it would happen; and pilgrims from Galilee and Samaria and Perea and from beyond the mountains—and all Judæa to a man. Veil of the temple! There can be no fewer than fifty score of thousands—not counting the children; and the granaries burned with fire!"

Ben Azor groaned aloud and beat upon his breast. "We have sinned," he said, "and our punishment is nigh at hand!"

Ben Ethan chuckled behind his hand. "The Lord is merciful to such as keep his laws and walk orderly after the customs," he said piously; "for myself I fear nothing;—but for my daughter, now, a beautiful maid and the only child of my old age, I feel——"

"Hold thy peace, man, and pray for the deliverance of Jerusalem!" said Ben Azor, turning his back upon his visitor.

And Ben Ethan, deeming it prudent to withhold for the present the object of his visit, approached the parapet and looked forth. He now beheld clearly the reason for the strange stillness which prevailed in the streets and squares of the city. As far as the eye could reach over the vast expanse of housetops, the roofs were crowded with people; their robes of white and scarlet, yellow and blue, glowing like vast beds of flowers beneath the steady radiance of the noonday sun. Over this scene of glowing life brooded a singular silence; there was no sound of shouting from roofs or towers; no

clash of weapons nor martial blare of trumpets from
walls or battlements, though like the housetops
these places swarmed with people. Beyond the
walls lay the familar valleys, dusky with cool shadows; while the mountains stretched softly heaven-
ward, clothed to their tops with blossoming groves
and vineyards, here and there a white-walled villa
or a cluster of cottages gleaming like pearls amid
the surrounding greenery. Over all lay the sunshine of mid April like a benediction.

North and south, east and west, the great Roman
highways wound like silver ribbons among the
smooth green hills. Away to the north, over
Scopus, Ben Ethan could see a great cloud of dust
hanging vast and threatening upon the horizon. In
the front of this cloud a solid phalanx of men and
horses advanced steadily, the sun striking blinding
sparks of splendor from spear-point and standard.

"The Romans!" he muttered, for the moment
forgetting all, save that he was a Jew. "Lord Jehovah deliver us out of their hand!"

From the silent city there arose a mighty, far-
reaching wail that pierced to the noonday heavens,
and echoed in a thousand ominous reverberations
from the sacred heights of Olivet.

There were many who remembered in that hour
the word of the prophet Jeremiah: "Then said the
Lord unto me; out of the North shall an evil
break forth upon all the inhabitants of the land;
for lo, I will call all the families of the kingdoms

of the North, saith the Lord ; and they shall come and shall set their throne at the entering of the Gates of Jerusalem, and against all the walls thereof round about, and against all the cities of Judah. Be astonished, O ye heavens, at this, and be horribly afraid; be ye very desolate, saith the Lord. For my people have committed two evils ; they have forsaken the fountain of living waters and hewed them out cisterns—broken cisterns that can hold no water."

CHAPTER XXVII.

A HIRED SERVANT.

A SOUND of hurrying feet and loud voices in the street below recalled Ben Ethan to the consideration of his own immediate affairs; he shuddered to think that at any moment the gigantic soldier might return with a band of his fellows. "If they break into the house," he thought, the cold sweat starting out upon his forehead, "the girl might show them the cellars."

He looked stealthily at Ben Azor; the dealer in sacrifices was still beating upon his breast, while tears streamed from his eyes and mingled with his beard. Ben Ethan's thin lips curled with contempt. "Thou canst either help an evil matter, friend, or thou canst not," he cried sharply. "If thou canst help it, well; if not, resign thyself to the decrees of the Eternal,—ay, and wring good out of evil, even as men force a fat harvest from stony and barren soil. Hearken unto me, neighbor, the Romans are upon us of a verity, but why weep and beat the breast? Get thee down; sell thy beasts and hide the money till the war cloud blow over. For myself I will—yes, I will do what I can. I am a poor man, yet to see my daughter—the only

child of my old age—safely bestowed in these evil
days, I will give a marriage portion of—of one
hundred silver pence. It will impoverish me—ay,
truly; but I am old and can endure. Take thou
the maid to wife, and increase thy substance and
thy household."

Ben Azor stared at his guest with astonishment
not unmixed with displeasure. "Shall I think of
wives and feasting, and buying and selling in this
the day of Israel's peril?" he said slowly. "Nay,
it is an evil hour in the which to espouse a maid.
Keep thou her safe in thine own house till the
days be finished; and then haply thou shalt give
her to wife, if there be any man left alive to be her
husband."

"Dost thou refuse then?" cried Ben Ethan in a
fury, "—and I have asked thee for no marriage
price; didst thou hear aright?"

"It is a time of mourning, not of merrymaking;
more than that, I am already an old man; I shall
not again wear the marriage crown." Ben Azor
said this with all possible gentleness; for it is truly
an evil thing to refuse an offer of marriage. His
sons and daughters, his servants also, both male
and female, had heard the thing, and after the
manner of youth were eyeing one another with
meaning smiles.

Ben Ethan flung himself adown the stairway, two
steps at a time. "Anathema!" he cried shrilly.
"May the Romans spoil this house!"

He scattered curses of the kind with a lavish hand during the next hour, even as a man sows mischievous seed in the field of the neighbor whom he hates; for of all that he approached on the subject of the marriage not one gave him any answer save that of Ben Azor. " It is not a time for marrying nor giving in marriage."

He emerged from the dwelling of a beater of brass, who had a marriageable son, in a very fury. In this place he had increased the amount of the dowry to three hundred pence, only to meet with the same reply. " My son will defend the temple," said the worker in brass; "if haply he survive, we will again speak of the matter."

Ben Ethan cursed the worker in brass, and his sons and his daughters, his house also and everything that he possessed; he wished moreover that the man might remain unburied after death, and that of his children not one should remain alive.

Being quite absorbed in his own evil thoughts he all but fell upon the body of a man which lay squarely across the street. This man was dead, he observed with indifference, but from beneath his prostrate body peeped out the corner of what looked to be a sack of grain. Upon investigation it appeared that it was a sack of grain—and full to the top.

" Dead men eat no bread," quoth Ben Ethan. " Some Sicar hath thrust the fellow through for his purse; for I perceive by his dress that he is a

Percan." With considerable difficulty he pushed the body to one side and pulled out the sack; it was large and heavy; Ben Ethan could scarcely lift it. "Must I then empty out a part of it," he murmured disconsolately "—and grain worth its weight in silver?"

He looked about him for some solution of the difficulty. Not ten paces away beneath the shadow of an archway sat a man, his head bowed upon his knees. "If he be neither dead nor drunken with wine," thought Ben Ethan, approaching the motionless figure with caution, "it may be that I shall be able to hire him to fetch the bag home for me." He was emboldened to touch the man upon the shoulder, since he perceived by his ragged tunic that he was neither Sicar nor soldier.

The man lifted his head from his knees and looked up. "What wilt thou?" he said hoarsely.

Ben Ethan observed with satisfaction that he was young, and of a pallid and haggard countenance which spoke of hunger. "A handful of the grain will hire him," he thought. Aloud he said, "I have purchased a sack of grain, young man, and find myself unable to fetch it home; thou art a sturdy fellow; carry it for me and I will repay thee."

By way of answer the young man arose—he was of great stature and strength—and flung the sack upon his shoulder. "Where shall I take it?" he asked.

Ben Ethan looked up at him with wonder and alarm. "I—I am armed," he said shrilly, "and can slay thee with ease if thou dost attempt to escape me with the bag. Go thou before. I will tell thee where."

In this manner—the tall young man with the sack upon his shoulder, and the bent, wizened figure of the miser scuttling rapidly along at his heels—the two reached the house by the gate. Ben Ethan unbarred his door with a great rattling and banging. "Set the sack within," he said sharply.

"Thy pay—eh? The task is surely not worth a farthing. Come, I will give thee a mouthful of yesterday's bread, and thou shalt depart in peace."

"Ay, give me the loaf quickly," said the man who had carried the grain. "I have not tasted bread since—Nay, I know not."

"There will be many in thy case before the Feast of Weeks," said Ben Ethan, twisting his grim features into the semblance of a smile. Then his eyes started out of his head with terror; a group of soldiers had turned the corner, laughing and shouting. "Come thou in," he gasped, seizing the stranger by the arm; "thou shalt have bread and wine also. T ou art a stout fellow, and the soldiers yonder will ruin me, if they get into my house." He had fastened the door again by this time, and stood trembling and shaking with abject terror.

"Thou art a stout fellow, I say,—and yes, thou

hast the look of an honest man. Tell me, who art thou, and whence comest thou? who knows but that I may hire thee—that is for a bite and a sup; it is worth no more in these days when grain is as silver, and like to be as gold."

The stranger looked about the dismantled shop with a faint show of curiosity; then he fixed his sunken eyes upon Ben Ethan. "My name is Phannias," he said slowly. "I am from—the mountains beyond. I came to Jerusalem in an evil hour. I have no money. I must work or die."

"Thou canst not get away, of a surety," said Ben Ethan, rubbing his hands with a dry chuckle. "No man can get away; and the mouth will eat——eh? or the bones dry up within the flesh. What a time for the rich who have grain to sell—Lord, what a time!—Not that I have it," he added with trepidation, "I am a poor man. I have a single sack, as thou seest; but I cannot have the house pulled down about my ears by these drunken wretches—may Jehovah smite them! Veil of the temple! I hear them; they are coming nearer. Wilt thou stay with me and look to the place? I have weapons—knives and the like."

"I will stay for the present—yes," said the young man, looking down upon the ground. "But why thinkest thou that I will not destroy thy goods even as others?"

Ben Ethan shrugged his shoulders. "I have no goods," he whined fretfully; "have I not said it? But there is the house and—Stay, art thou a keeper of the law?"

"I neither lie, steal, nor covet my neighbor's goods," said Phannias scowling. " But the law— what is the law, when the ephod and breastplate are burned with fire, and the courts of the temple run red with the blood of its priests? The Messiah is slain; the city and the nation are doomed."

Ben Ethan drew a long breath of relief. "If thou art a Nazarene, thou canst be trusted fast enough," he said briskly; "the knaves will go hungry when they cannot come honestly by a loaf; I have had dealings enough with them to know, that much.—Not that I favor the apostates and their blasphemous sayings concerning the crucified carpenter," he made haste to add; "for myself I keep the law, and my skirts are clear of offence. But come in—come in. The matter is settled betwixt us; thou wilt defend my premises; I will give thee a bite and a sup, as I can afford from my slender store."

Phannias followed his new master into the courtyard of the dwelling house; the place was clean and sweet, he observed with dull indifference, but bare and of desolate aspect. He had scarce time to look about him, when a small figure darted out from the shadowy interior of a room to the left of the yard, and flung itself with a cry upon the neck of the old man.

" Father—oh father ! Thou art alive—thou art

safe! Dear father, I have been so afraid—and the house so silent, and all the people crying out that the Romans———"

"Unhand me, woman," growled Ben Ethan, removing the clinging arms with no tender hand; "'tis little thanks to thee that I am alive and safe. Disobedient one, if at this moment I lay dead in the booth without, my blood would rest upon thy head."

The girl cried out again at these cruel words. "Father—father! Spare me. I love thee so!"

"'Tis not the hour in the which to prate of thy affections," said Ben Ethan savagely. "Come, hast thou no eyes for the stranger within our gates? Bestir thyself; fetch bread and wine that he may eat, as I promised."

Merodah turned her large eyes upon Phannias; then she fell back a pace in her surprise, her scarlet lips apart. "It is,—why it is———"

"I have spoken," said Ben Ethan loudly; "wilt thou again disobey?"

"It is the priest, father,—the good priest who saved me from the soldiers so long ago!—Ay, and from the cruel princess also, who would have scourged me. Afterward she sent me home with a piece of silver. Dost thou not remember, father?"

"Am I like to forget it, girl, after to-day's work? The worth of ten shekels wantonly destroyed! Alas—alas! oil-flasks—olives—cups—bowls—

loaves—everything gone, because of thy accursed folly! But what can one expect of a woman? Go now, and fetch the bread,—there is nothing, thou wilt bear in mind, save the fragments of yesterday's loaves."

"But yes, dear father," said Merodah gently, "there are also the fresh cakes which I have baked this very day. I will fetch them, and water for the hands and feet—yes, and the wine and oil." The girl cast a quick look of gratitude mingled with fear upon Phannias and disappeared within the house.

Ben Ethan stared after her with a muttered malediction; then he turned sharply upon the young man. "Bide thou here," he commanded; "I must speak to the woman, she hath clean lost her wits."

Phannias had listened to the conversation between the old man and his daughter with a rising fire of indignation which looked out of his eyes, as he surveyed the crafty, wrinkled face upraised to his. "Fetch me the loaf that I have earned," he said, "and I will go."

"No—no; it was agreed betwixt us—eh? Thou wilt remain. A priest, declared the girl—but no; she has lost her wits, as I have said; thou art not a priest, man?"

"I was a priest," said Phannias bitterly, "—but what matters that to thee or me; fetch me the loaf, for I hunger even as other men. I will go then."

"But where wilt thou go?" persisted Ben Ethan.
"Not to the temple; the Zealots have slain their
puppet high priest, whom they brought but yesterday from his labor in the fields.—Jehovah will give
them blood to drink, one and all, for the sacrilege.
As thou knowest, the gates are fast shut by the
Gischalan to them that would go out. Hast thou
money?"

"No."

"What then; one cannot live without money."

"I have my two hands—I can work."

"Thou wilt work for me, as I have said—for a
bite and a sup."

The flower-like face of Merodah appeared for
an instant in the doorway; she was smiling, and her
eyes sought those of Phannias with the glad com-
radry of youth.

"A great hulking brute of a soldier attempted
to carry off the maid this very day," whined Ben
Ethan; "and when I would have protected her, the
accursed villain spoiled my goods. Oh, my loaves
—my oil-bottles—my cups—my bowls! And he
said he would return—he swore he would return!
If thou art a priest thou art an honorable man; I
will trust thee with a matter now. I have goods—
some few bags of grain, earned by the painful sweat
of an honest brow; if the soldier return for the
maid—as he swore he would, he might also carry
away my goods. I have no son—woe is me!
Thou shalt remain and fend for me as a son; after-

ward—nay, who knows, when the Romans are departed, I—I will reward thee."

Phannias was looking upon the ground, his dark brows knit in thought. Yesterday, he had told himself, he wished for nothing save death. But when years be few, it is only to-day that counts. A fragment of song, chanted in a sweet treble voice, floated out to him from the house :

> " Jesus—Christ, glad light of the Highest !
> Light of the Father—radiant, holy !
> While the night spreads its dim mantle o'er us,
> We worship the light which hath shined—
> Which hath shined in the darkness."

Ben Ethan frowned. " The girl hath picked up certain blasphemous sayings of the Nazarenes. I let my upper room to the knaves for a time. They meet now on the street below—the few that be left in Jerusalem. Verily, if the holy city suffer at the hands of the Romans, I believe that it will be because of the crucified carpenter and his followers."

Phannias looked up ; a steady light burned in his eyes. " Thou hast spoken !" he said. " And look you, I will remain in this house as long as there is need of my presence."

CHAPTER XXVIII.

THE COMING STORM.

BEN ETHAN'S fears were not immediately realized. As the days went on he began to chafe at his folly; the soldiers were busy upon the walls, it was said; making forays beyond the walls, harassing the Romans at their work of camp-building, and the like. At all events they did not trouble the obscure house in the Agra.

"Another mouth to feed!" groaned the old man as he doled out the scant handfuls of grain, which Merodah ground and fashioned into bread. "A mouth, say I? Nay, rather, a bottomless pit to fill; the fellow hath the appetite of a beast,—Lord, he hath eaten in a week what would suffice me for a month!"

"He is young, father," said Merodah, with anxiety, "and so strong! Thou wouldst never guess, dear father, how easily he lifted the great stones for grinding, which I could not so much as stir."

"What is his strength to me?" snarled Ben Ethan. "And why should I fill the mouth of a stranger in the days when a city cries out for bread? —Ay, but the price is nothing as yet! I will wait— I will wait."

18

Later in the day he came upon the two in the
courtyard, where Phannias, chafing at his enforced
idleness, was busying himself at the grindstones,
in truth all too heavy for the delicate hands of the
girl. Merodah was kneading the meal in a trough
with water, her dimpled arms bare to the shoulder,
her smooth cheeks flushed with scarlet, her childish eyes brimming over with unconcealed happiness.
If the Romans were without, what then? It was
still pleasant to be young, and the sun shone, and
the swallows twittered gaily as ever.

Ben Ethan stared at the scene with tightened lips
and a frowning brow. "Wilt thou do a woman's
work and devour a man's portion?" he said sharply
to Phannias.

The young man looked up. "I would work," he
said stoutly; "and there is nothing else to do."

"I will give thee a task better suited to thy appetite; go thou and look to this matter of the siege.
I know nothing of what is passing. Go to the
temple platform—the Zealots hold it; and to the
upper town—Simon Bar-Gioras is in power there.
Fetch me word of the Passover also; will they kill
in the temple as heretofore? The matter must be
attended to, if I am to keep the law.

Phannias sprang up with alacrity. "I will go at
once," he said. He did not look at Merodah.

"Father," ventured the girl timidly, "our guest
has no sword, and the streets are full of bloody
men."

Phannias looked back into the sweet, anxious face ; something in the imploring dark eyes brought the heart-beats to his throat.

" Thou wilt never return," she murmured.

" Nay, but I will return, and that before the sun sets," said Phannias.

Ben Ethan smiled. "Do not fail," he said dryly, "to visit the upper town ; it is there that thou wilt learn of the siege and our chances of success against the Romans."

Phannias set forth upon his quest with a more cheerful and confident heart than he had carried with him for many a day. During the quiet hours spent in the house of Ben Ethan a soothing balm had been poured with lavish hand upon his bruised spirit. Merodah, with the beautiful innocence of a child and the tender prescience of a woman, had divined his need, and out of the abundance of her soul had ministered to him as an angel might have done.

She had not forgotten him, she assured him. "Ah, no ; I could never do that. Also I have prayed for thee many times each day since that terrible hour. Truly, after I knew the holy Jesus, I prayed more often because, as thou knowest, he was himself like to us and knows therefore all that we need."

Phannias asked the girl many questions concerning Jesus of Nazareth, and she told him all that she had learned in the quiet meetings held in the upper room,—all, and more, for in the silence of her own innocent heart the divine voice spoke ever more distinctly.

"Alas," she said, in conclusion, "they went away long ago—that is, all the strong men and the women who could travel and the little ones."

"Why did they go?" asked Phannias.

The girl's dark eyes grew wide with fear. "The city will be destroyed," she whispered, "and all that dwell therein will perish or be sold into slavery. Yes, assuredly it will happen. *He* said it in his lifetime and it must come to pass. I—I am afraid sometimes."

"Who said this?"

"One who heard the Messiah utter the words. It is just; they slew him on the cross; they cried out: 'His blood be upon us and upon our children!' We are the children."

"Why didst thou not go away with them?" he demanded, after a long silence.

"I? Oh, I could not leave father; he does not believe. But it does not matter," she said, her eyes brimming over with sudden joy; "the Lord is here; he will take care of us. It is only at times that I fear—when I forget; if I pray to him the fear goes away at once and I am happy again. The good Bishop also remained; he is not afraid—ever; but I am only a foolish maid and forget often. There were also Lesbia and Rachel and Rufus and many of the others; they stayed that they might care for the sick and old who could not go."

" Where are these Nazarenes ?"

Merodah shook her head. "I do not know,"
she said sadly; "my father sent them away from
here after a time, and I never go out in these days.
Perhaps they have gone also. I—I hope that they
have."

Phannias was thinking of this conversation as
he hurried away to do the bidding of Ben Ethan.
"It is true," he thought within himself; "the day
of reckoning is at hand!" Words of frenzied en-
treaty to the God of Israel rose to his lips; but he
thrust the petition back. "It is just," he said betwixt his teeth; "his blood is upon us—the blood
of the Messiah!"

He paused at the corner of a square, once devoted to a market place, and looked about him.
The place had long ago been swept bare of its
shops and booths, as had most of the similar
quarters of the city; the dwellings and warehouses
which fronted upon it had been gutted by fire,
and with their black, eyeless windows and crum-
bling walls lent a sinister air of desolation to the
scene. Every foot of ground however was now
occupied with the paschal pilgrims and their baggage. The shrill voices of women, and the loud
crying and shouting of hundreds of children filled
the air.

" They will leave fast enough when they see that
our walls do not crumble at sight of four legions !"
one woman was saying to another, as she rocked

her baby to and fro in her arms. "Hush thee—
hush thee, little one; the Romans will never get
thee! The walls of Jerusalem are mighty—and
we are safe inside!"

Phannias passed on, treading carefully amid
the heaped-up bundles and the crawling babies.
"Canst thou tell me whether they will kill the
passover in the temple?" he asked, accosting a
man who was busy arranging a rude shelter of
sheepskin coats betwixt the hot sun and the head
of a young mother, who sat nursing her baby
against one of the ruined stalls.

The man paused in his occupation and wiped
the sweat from his forehead. "Assuredly, they
will kill the sacrifice in the temple," he said, staring. "Where else? I am going there now with
the lamb, as soon as ever I make the mother and
the babe comfortable. I shall be glad when the
Romans get them away; always before at passover
time we have camped in the gardens without the
walls where it is cooler."

"Thinkest thou that they will leave then?"

"Assuredly!" And this time the stranger strength-
ened his affirmation by a great oath. "Did not
the Gentiles fly before Israel when the defenders
of the holy city were few. Now there are more
than twenty thousand fighting men upon the walls
—to say nothing of scores of thousands of paschal
pilgrims. We are able to fight the Romans were
they ten times as many—ay, and destroy them!

Remember also what feast we celebrate, man. Wait you till to-morrow night and see what will befall yonder heathen company. The Angel of the Lord hath not forgotten how to wield the sword! While we eat the passover, staff in hand and girded as for journeying, that sword will descend; then shall Israel go forth and fall upon the prey.—Jehovah grant that I get my share of the booty, for I am a poor man."

Phannias had no reply for this confident son of Abraham; therefore he went his way, thinking strange thoughts. "These men did not slay the Messiah, why then must the punishment come upon them; upon the women also, and the babes?"

His brow grew dark again, and the heart in his bosom was as lead, as he threaded his way through streets and squares, everywhere elbowed and jostled by throngs of excited people, who were surging back and forth betwixt the temple and the wretched places where they had camped with their belongings.

Everywhere there was a sound of the wailing voices of children; thirsty children crying for water; hungry children crying for bread; lost children crying for their mothers; tired children crying for very weariness; and everywhere anxious-eyed women were feeding and hushing and holding cups of water and hurrying to and fro on endless errands, after the custom of women. The men, after the manner of their kind, sat for the most part comfortably in the shade asleep; or exchanged wise

comments with their fellows on the strange state
of affairs without and within the walls.

None of these people, Phannias observed with
wonder, displayed any alarm; they rather endured
their obvious discomfort as if it were something of
short duration, and therefore not worth the men-
tioning. Here and there a hysterical woman
shrieked out that she could not bear it; that the
Romans would break in upon them in the night.
Such weakness called forth a storm of reproaches
mingled with stout-hearted assurances of safety.

"Hold thy peace, woman;" bawled the wise
male relative of one such apprehensive soul; "hold
thy peace and attend to the young ones. Am *I*
not here? and will *I* not protect thee? Besides,
foolish one, the walls of Jerusalem were not builded
in a day; neither shall they be destroyed in a day."
Which indeed was a true saying, and not less terrible than true.

As Phannias approached the temple platform, he
became possessed of a strong desire to see what
was going on outside the walls; he therefore re-
traced his steps to a point near the Palace of Agrippa,
where arose the magnificent structure called the
Tyropœan Bridge. This bridge, built up on mighty
arches from the valley beneath, sustained a wide
marble causeway which connected the temple platform with the palace; from it one could obtain an
unobstructed view of the valleys and mountains
without the walls. There were few people here, for,

more than once in the past months, this bridge had
been the scene of a bloody struggle betwixt the
fierce Zealots under Eleazar and the soldiers of
Simon, who held the Upper Town.

Phannias, intent only upon his purpose, climbed
to the top of the balustrade in the shadow of one
of the towers with which the bridge was studded,
and looked away toward the Damascus Gate. The
great North Road stretched away through blossoming gardens and orchards over the crest of Scopus;
not even a fleck marred the smooth whiteness of its
surface. To the left gleamed the Dragon Pool,
bright as a bit of blue heaven set in the silvery
green of olive orchards. East of the pool, at the
edge of the upper Gihon valley, a flutter of savage
color, a glint of gold and the raw earth thrown up
in the form of a square, betrayed even to the inex-
perienced eyes of the beholder the location of a
Roman camp. On the opposite side of the deep
valley lay a second and much larger square, from
the midst of which streamed a banner of the royal
purple.

Despite his conviction that the city was doomed,
Phannias could not forbear a curl of the lip as he
glanced from the comparatively insignificant spots
on the mountain side to the great, fortified city which
lay spread out at his feet. Wall within wall, of
enormous strength and thickness, enclosed the
shining heart of the whole—the temple; while at
the angles of the outer wall rose the three mighty

towers builded by the great Herod during his
bloody reign, Phasaelus, Hippicus and Mariamne.
To the left of the temple and connected with it by
two lines of half-ruined cloisters lay the great Roman fortress, Antonia ; and still further to the left,
overhanging the New Town, was a second fortified
castle, Acra.   In front of the bridge the battlemented towers of the Asmonean Palace looked
haughtily down upon the crowded Agra ; while beyond, surrounded by superb mansions and gardens,
Herod's Palace—known also as the Prætorium, a
fortress of immense strength, standing on the his-
toric ground once occupied by the castle of David,
commanded the upper Hinnom valley.

As Phannias gazed upon this splendid scene, all
the ingrained pride of race awoke within him. Jerusalem, the city which had endured from generation
to generation—the city wherein countless prophets
of God had poured forth mysterious messages from
the unseen ! Could it be that the end was at hand—
because the son of a carpenter had died yonder
upon Calvary?   All the old doubt and conflict
closed in upon him once more like a cold, impenetrable mist.

He looked once more at the square patches of
raw earth, about which swarmed thousands of small
red figures no larger than ants ; he knew that these
small red objects were Roman soldiers, at work
fortifying their camps.   Then he turned his eyes
toward the temple, which towered into the intense

blue of the spring heavens, as it were a mountain of fire and snow. To-morrow they would cele-brate the great deliverance from Egypt. Would not the God who had brought Israel out from bondage with a strong hand and an outstretched arm once again remember his people?

The uneasy current of his thoughts was inter-rupted by a caustic voice which hailed him from the bridge; the words were accompanied by a prick from the point of a naked sword, which the owner of the voice brandished in his right hand. "What doest thou here, fellow?"

Phannias leaped lightly down from his place on the balustrade, and eyed the intruder upon his meditations. The man was a soldier plainly enough, and in a truculent frame of mind; for he repeated his question loudly, again flourishing his weapon in an unpleasantly suggestive manner.

"I am looking at the city—and at the Romans yonder."

"Art thou a soldier?"

"No."

"A spy then—from the temple! By the *Chel*, thou art a bold knave. We make short work of your sort, as thou shalt see. Thou wilt come with me."

"I am no spy, fellow," said Phannias indig-nantly. Whereat the other thrust his tongue into his right cheek and winked rapidly with his left eye. "A bold knave," he cried, describing a great flourish in the air with his blade, "but no very proper liar. Can I not see that thou art clothed in a priest's tunic? A bold knave—a blasphemous knave! We shall see what Bar-Gioras hath to say to thee! Come along now, or I will thrust thee through and drop thy carcass into the valley."

CHAPTER XXIX.

BAR-GIORAS.

SIMON BAR-GIORAS, for the moment the most powerful man in the distracted city of Jerusalem, sat in one of the chambers of the tower of Phasaelus listening to the reports of his captains.

The body of the son of Gioras resembled the tower in which he sat, in that it was tall, squarely-built, and of enormous strength and thickness; this trunk crowned with a tawny, lion-like head, housed the soul of a strange being. It was impossible to despise this man; he inspired fear, hatred, love; but indifference—never. Simon Bar-Gioras believed in himself first, last, and absolutely. Thus far he had accomplished his purposes without deviation and without wavering. For this reason, if for no other, he was confident that he would always accomplish them. Men, women, cities, kingdoms, appeared to him but as chaff to be swept away with a motion of his powerful arm.

Once only had the sword penetrated that iron bosom. In the same year in which Cestius had besieged Jerusalem, the Zealots, too cowardly to meet him in open battle, had seized upon his wife, as she passed with her attendants through an ambushed pass to join him in his camp, and had carried her away to Jerusalem. In that moment the fate of the temple was sealed; Bar-Gioras swept down from the mountains with his thousands, filling the valleys outside the city with a murderous war-cloud which thundered and muttered about the walls day and night. As for those who ventured beyond the gates on whatever of business or pleasure, they returned no more, save as ghastly specters, eyeless and handless, crying out in their torments the words which Simon had traced upon their breasts in letters of blood: "My wife—my wife; give me back my wife!"

In those days Simon Bar-Gioras made a great oath, and he swore it by the only name he respected above his own—that of Jehovah of Hosts, that unless his wife should be returned to him unharmed, he would straightway make of that proud city a desolate ruin; that of all her inhabitants, warriors and women, old men and children, young men and maidens, there should not remain so much as one to repeat the story of his great wrong. He caused this oath to be written in letters of Hebrew, and sent it to the chief of the Zealots.

His enemies took counsel together. "This man," said one, "will perform what he hath sworn. Therefore restore the woman that he may go his way."

Others advised that she be put to death and her

body flung from the walls. "Thus shall we avenge those whom he has tortured and slain; as for the city, neither he nor any man is able to take it."

In the end, they commanded the wife of Simon to be set in their presence. She was very beautiful and of a lofty and dauntless carriage.

"Dost thou understand, woman, that although thy husband rages without the walls like a lion bereft of his mate, he cannot save thee out of our hand?" they asked her.

"Only wild beasts and cowards make war upon women," she answered them scornfully: "Slay me if ye will; my husband is able to avenge me, and he will avenge me speedily."

"We do not fear the son of Gioras," they replied. "Jerusalem is ours, and no man can prevail against it. Notwithstanding all this, we will have mercy upon thee. Go thy way, and say this to Simon. Depart out of Judæa and disband thine armies, lest a worse punishment fall upon thee."

Then they set the woman outside the gates unharmed, and she came to her husband and told him what she was bidden. Whereat Simon laughed, long and loud.

"I will depart," he said, "but I will also return. And thou, beloved, who hast been a captive in Jerusalem shall reign over it a queen."

Before the waning of the moon—which was even then at the full, he returned, driving before him into the city the inhabitants of the country around, which

also he wasted with fire and the sword till it was
bare as the palm of his naked hand; then he encamped with fifteen thousand picked men under
the walls of Jerusalem.

Now within the gates were already horrors beyond the telling; all semblance of law and order
had long ago vanished from the distracted city.
The Zealots devoured it as a consuming fire. By
night a flaming sword hung above it in the heavens.
The dead lay unburied in the streets; the living
cowered in their desolate homes, scarce daring to
lift their eyes to the God who seemed to have forsaken them. During this time the iron hand of
Rome was crushing the rebellious Galilees as a
man crushes an empty eggshell. Jerusalem like a
den filled with rabid beasts was left for the nonce
to destroy itself.

Affairs being at this fearful pass, the chief priests
resolved as a last desperate resource to open the
gates to Simon. " The son of Gioras is a mighty
warrior," said the high priest—at this time Matthias
III. ; "he will protect the city against the Zealots
who are tearing out its very vitals. Also, he will
enable us to withstand the Romans, who will surely
descend upon us at no distant day."

They carried out their purpose; and Simon
Bar-Gioras entered Jerusalem in triumph at the
head of his troops. The people greeted him as
their savior and deliverer. " Jerusalem is saved!"
they cried in transports of joy. " The temple

is saved! Hail to the son of Gioras! Hail to the conqueror!"

Bar-Gioras sneered at them openly. What was Jerusalem to him, save a citadel from whose well-nigh impregnable walls and fortresses he meant presently to face the last great obstacle to his power. He was already the uncrowned king, not only of Jerusalem, but of all the surrounding countries over which he had swept like a devastating whirlwind. Rome itself was but a rotten shell of its former greatness; his sword should pierce that shell.

He found that the Zealots had entrenched themselves under their two hostile leaders, Eleazar and John of Gischala, in the temple and the Lower Town. Bar-Gioras forthwith took undisputed possession of the Upper Town, where he presently installed his wife in queenly state in the deserted palace of the Herods.

Some terrible months followed, during which the Assassin, the Tyrant, and the Zealot, as Bar-Gioras, John of Gischala and Eleazar came presently to be called, tore each other like rabid dogs. The clamor of their deadly conflicts filled the city day and night. Lust and murder stalked the streets unveiled. Granaries were burned; property and stores of all kinds were wantonly destroyed. The courts of the temple resounded with blows and curses; its marble floors were slippery with the blood of priests and worshipers; the stench of unburied corpses mingled with the odor of incense; for the fire yet burned upon the great altar, and at morning and evening a sacrifice of slain beasts was offered before the desolate sanctuary.

There had now been peace within the walls for the space of eight days; the combatants sullenly watching the Romans as they worked upon their fortified camps, to the east, the west and the north of the city.

On the fifth day, Bar-Gioras sent a flag of truce to John of Gischala and to Eleazar, with a message. "Let us unite to crush the enemy that is without," ran the words of this writing. "Afterward we will resume our former positions and fight for supremacy within the walls."

The crafty Gischalan agreed to this proposition, reserving to himself his quarters in the Lower Town and the command of his troops. Eleazar shut up within the inner temple refused to make answer. It was impossible to make plans for the defence of the city till he should be dislodged from this important position.

It was this question that Bar-Gioras was pondering, as he sat on this twelfth day of April in the great chamber of the tower of Phasaelus.

One of his captains, Kimosh by name, stood before him. He had been describing to his chief a skirmish which had just taken place between the soldiers of the Zealot forces and the Romans of the tenth legion, who were constructing their camp on Olivet. The Jews had rushed out suddenly from the Women's Gate and had fallen upon the enemy with such fury that they had all but captured the half-fortified camp.

Bar-Gioras scowled. "Fools!" he muttered, bringing down his great hand upon his knee. "Had I been with them, we should have cut the legion into pieces."

"To-morrow is the Passover," said Kimosh tentatively.

"What of that?"

"The Zealots will perforce open the inner temple to the people."

Simon gnawed his beard in silence for a full minute. "By the prophets!" he cried loudly, throwing himself back in his chair, "thou hast said! Send out and capture a priest for me at once; I must know more of the inner temple, lest the knaves entrap us."

"One of the sentinels on the Tyropœan Bridge brought in a certain man this morning," said Kimosh cautiously. "He was dressed in a priest's tunic; but whether or no he be priest——"

"Fetch him."

"Who art thou?" demanded Bar-Gioras, fixing his piercing eyes upon the man, who was shortly set in his presence.

"I am called Phannias," answered the prisoner.

"Art thou a priest?"

"No."

"What then—a beggar?"

Phannias looked into the fiery eyes of the Sicar chief. "I have no money," he said; "but I am not a beggar."

"What wast thou doing on the Tyropœan?"

"I went there to see the Romans."

"Didst thou not know that I hold the bridge?"

"I know nothing of what is doing in Jerusalem."

Simon ran his eye over the stalwart figure before him. "What of the priest's tunic thou art wearing?" he asked, with rising choler. "Thou art either priest or spy."

"I am neither," said Phannias scowling. "The temple is no longer a temple. It is a den of thieves and murderers."

Simon's brow cleared. "This den shall be purged," he said. "Come; thou art no weakling to play either priest or beggar; Jerusalem will have need of such as thou before yonder Gentile dogs be scattered. Serve me."

"And if I refuse?"

"Thou wilt not refuse; I know men, as I know myself; I am never mistaken. Thou wilt serve me; thou wilt serve thy country; 'tis one and the same thing."

Phannais gazed steadily into the piercing eyes of the man before him; he was irresistibly drawn toward this Sicar chief by an influence which he neither questioned nor understood. He felt suddenly sure that life spent in his service would be satisfying. "I will serve thee," he said slowly; "but I must first return to a certain house in the Agra."

"And why must thou do this?"

"Because I have promised; I will go and return within the hour."

The Sicar chief raised his hand imperiously. "They who would serve Bar-Gioras forget their past," he said harshly. "Henceforth thou art answerable to no man save me."

CHAPTER XXX.

"LO, I AM WITH YOU ALWAY!"

IN the old house by the gate, a little maid
watched anxiously for Phannias, from her post
in the latticed window of the upper room. "He
will come before the setting of the sun," she whispered to herself, "—he promised it."

When the sudden dark of the spring night fell
like a curtain over the narrow street, she slipped
from the window seat and looked about the great
bare chamber, shivering a little in childish fear.
Then she dropped to her knees with a cry of joy ;
she fancied that in the dusk she could dimly discover the compassionate face of the Christ, who
had come to be a near and beloved Presence.

"Ah, Master, it is thou," she whispered, clasp-
ing her small hands ; "—and I had again forgotten
that thou art with me always ! Why do I fear
what shall happen to him ? Thou dost love him,
dear Jesus, even more than I." At that she hid
her face in her hands, abashed at her own innocent
confession. "Yet it is right and beautiful to love
every one," she murmured—half to herself, half to
the brooding Presence which never failed to understand her inmost thought. So ran the mingled cur-

rent of praise and petition, pure and untainted as
a mountain stream; sometimes spoken joyously
aloud; again dropping to a low whisper of tender
confidence.

This was not prayer; ah no. To pray to Jehovah, the lawgiver of Sinai, girt with awful light-
nings; seated aloft on a vast throne in the shining
immensity of the unknown heavens—the King
of kings, oftentimes burning with anger, terrible,
swift, merciless;—to pray to this God of Israel,
one must stand with bowed head and face turned
toward the sanctuary. There must be ablutions
and a fringed garment fashioned according to law;
many words also, both long and difficult of utterance, must be said in a loud voice. And, after all,
it was not becoming for a woman to trouble the
ear of the Maker of the Universe too often; she
knew this right well. To the august head of the
family belonged the sacred prerogative of prayer—
with other divinely appointed functions. For a
woman obedience only was necessary.

But to Jesus of Nazareth one might speak freely;
he had never rebuked the women who came to
him with their troubles. Never once had he refused to help them. Merodah remembered the
story of the widow of Nain; of the woman bowed
to the earth with a spirit of infirmity; of the sisters
of Bethany; of the Gentile mother of Syrophenicia;
of the daughter of Jairus. All these and many
other wonderful tales of the goodness of the Mes-

siah to women and children had been told her by
the Christians who had once gathered in that upper
room.   No one was too poor, no one too ignorant,
no one too sinful, to come freely to the Christ,
who had lived and suffered and died that the poor,
the ignorant and the sinful might be saved.   Was
it not a beautiful belief to carry in one's breast ?—
beautiful and delightful beyond expression to be
able to speak to this Jesus whenever one would !

The girl became so absorbed in her happy
thoughts that she did not hear the sound of
stealthy feet on the stair.   Ben Ethan had missed
his daughter from her accustomed place in the
dreary house.   "She is spying into what does not
belong to her," he muttered to himself with angry
suspicion.   "Yes, I am sure of it; she has made
some compact with the beggar who has been devouring my substance.   Together they will strip me of
everything—everything !   Merodah !" he called
sharply, dashing the cold drops from his forehead.
"But no—I will not call the wench ; she shall not
suspect.   I will catch them together ; and then—"
He felt for the knife, which he carried always in
these days hidden beneath his ragged garments.
It was there.

In the upper chamber he heard the low murmur
of a voice.   "Ah—the hussy !" he muttered.   "It
is by the outside stairway then that she will receive a thief into my house !"   He stooped cautiously and applied his ear to the half-closed door.

"There is also my father,"— were the words
which floated out to him—"thou knowest, dear
Master, how wise he is and how carefully he ob-
serves the law; yet I am afraid in his presence at
times; and to-day I even doubted whether—"
The words died away in a low, indistinguishable
murmur.

Ben Ethan stole into the room noiselessly and
approached the window; the dim light from the
crescent moon streamed through the lattice, and
shone faintly on the bowed figure of his daughter.

He grasped her roughly by the shoulder.

"Father! Dear father! How you frightened me!"

"What art thou doing here?"

"I? I—was thinking, dear father,—of many
things. Shall I—yes; it is true—I quite forgot to
make ready the grain for to-morrow's baking! I
will go at once."

"Thinking always of food—like the glutton that
thou art!" snarled Ben Ethan. "But stay, woman,
to whom wert thou speaking as I came up the stair?
—Do not deny it; I heard thee."

Merodah drew a quick breath; her trembling
hands sought her loud-beating heart.

"Answer!"

"I was speaking—to—Jesus of Nazareth."

"What!—Thou?"

"Yes, father; I believe that Jesus was the Messiah. I should have told thee before; but—I was
afraid."

There was a breathless silence in the room for the space of a minute; then a terrible look crept over the face of the man; the darkness mercifully hid it from the girl's beseeching eyes. His hand closed upon her tender arm.

"Father!"

"Come."

"*Dear* father—let me tell thee more of this Jesus —I beseech of thee! It is so beautiful—so blessed to believe!"

"*Come!*"

At the courtyard door Ben Ethan loosed his hold long enough to unfasten the heavy bars which secured it.

"Father!" shrieked the girl, throwing herself half-fainting at his knees. "Father! What—what are you going to do with me?"

The man tore away the clinging hands; then, without a word, he lifted the light figure and thrust it into the street.

This done he locked and double-barred the door and went into his house—alone.

CHAPTER XXXI.

AN OPEN GATE.

PHANNIAS found himself a close prisoner in the barracks of the Prætorium. Kimosh, the officer in command, had evidently received some special orders concerning the newcomer, for after furnishing him with the rough clothing of a common soldier he caused him to be locked up securely in a small bare chamber off the guard-room.

In this place the hours dragged slowly by. There was ample time for reflection, but after a little, reflection became an active torment; the more Phannias thought of his past, the more gloomy and forbidding did his future appear to him. "I am like a withered branch," was his bitter conclusion, "driven hither and yon at the will of the witless winds. I have failed in everything that I have undertaken."

Toward evening Bar-Gioras sent for him a second time, and without preamble put a number of short, sharp questions concerning the structure of the inner temple—its courts, corridors, chambers and subterranean outlets.

Phannias answered as well as he was able from

his limited knowledge of the once-sacred precincts. The Sicar chief was evidently disappointed
with the amount of information which he had
gained ; but he said nothing beyond a curt word of
dismissal.

" Stay," said Phannias ; " I also have a question
to ask. Why am I a prisoner ?"

Bar-Gioras scowled. " Take the man away,"
he said peremptorily, " and put him in the outer
court."

The outer court proved to be a large, gloomy
enclosure, paved with stone and surrounded on all
sides by high, blank walls. " What are my duties
in this place ?" asked Phannias of the soldier who
had conducted him thither.

The man grinned. " What you see," he replied
briefly.

" I see nothing."

" Then it appears that thou art in rare luck.
Sleep and be idle. If that does not suit, the more
fool thou." The sound of heavy bolts clattering
into place on the outer side of the door announced
his departure.

Phannias looked about him with care ; to be a
soldier in the service of a successful general was
one thing ; to be locked up like a criminal was
quite another. He had already resolved to quit
the place at his earliest opportunity ; that the opportunity had not yet presented itself, he shortly
assured himself by a careful examination of the

courtyard. There were numerous doors sunken into the massive walls; all were securely fastened. Plainly, there was nothing to be done but to await further developments.

As the young man paced restlessly up and down the confines of his prison he reviewed once more his hardly-gained knowledge of the mysterious Jesus of Nazareth. His vision in the Holy Place he deliberately set aside as being the result of an overwrought condition of mind and body. Point by point he compared his rabbinic teachings concerning the long-expected prince with what he had learned of the slain carpenter of Galilee. The remembrance of the beautiful child-faith of Merodah and her flower-like face, as she poured forth the story of the cross, brought with it a smile and sigh. "It is a tale meet for credulous women and children," he thought; "how can it be true? The declared mission of the Messiah—as set forth by the Bible, the Talmud and the Mishna—is to deliver Israel; this man of Nazareth not only failed to convince Israel that he was the Messiah, but he perished miserably, having accomplished nothing,— nothing, save the alleged healing of a few sick folk, most of whom are already dead. He possessed nothing. He left nothing behind him but empty words,—which the next generation will forget, with the man and his accursed cross."

His mind reverted to the strange sayings of Ben Huna on the day of his return. "It is the same

story," he said aloud, with an impatient gesture;
"one and all of them insist that the crucified man
is still alive—that they are able to communicate
with him, and he with them. Impossible! If he
be alive, why does he not appear openly and demand the allegiance of all Israel—ay, and save it
gloriously out of the hand of the Romans?"

"Speak for yourself, friend, to this Jesus who
was dead and is alive again; he will himself reveal
to thee the truth so that thou canst not gainsay it."
The words sounded in his ear as though spoken by
a living voice. Who had said this—and when?
He shook his broad shoulders angrily: Ah, he
remembered now; it was the Gentile who had
helped him out of the temple wall. Gentiles,
women, publicans, fishermen—yes, these were the
believers in the crucified Nazarene.

It seemed to him further—as he drifted idly upon
the unhappy current of his thoughts, that the Galilean had met and thwarted him at every point of
his career, as if indeed he were a living Presence.

After a time darkness settled softly over the
place, and Phannias looking up beheld two or
three bright stars, which looked down at him from
the limitless roof of his prison like familiar and well-
loved eyes. The garden at Aphtha; his mother's
face—as he had seen it last—white and full of fear,
flashed before him like a picture. She would have
died to save her child—he knew it right well. With
the picture came certain strange words—words of

the man slain upon the cross, and repeated to him by the daughter of Ben Ethan. Jesus had said these words, she told him, to a very wise man—a rabbi indeed, who afterward believed. " As Moses lifted up the serpent in the wilderness, even so must the Son of man be lifted up, that whosoever believeth in Him should not perish but have eternal life. For God so loved the world that he gave his only begotten Son, that whosoever believeth in him should not perish but have everlasting life."

Strange words indeed ; did the man then know from the beginning that he must die the accursed death ? " Lifted up," as the brazen serpent on the pole, that the eyes of the dying Israelites, prone upon the desert sands in their last agonies might rest upon it—life for a look ! For an instant the wonderful significance of the cross blazed before his startled eyes ; then he hid his face from the light with a loud cry.

A sound of voices, the trampling of many feet and the flaring light of torches announced abruptly that his solitude was at an end. Phannias drew back into a shadowy corner of the courtyard that he might observe the newcomers, himself unnoticed. There were at least fifty of them and in the highest spirits ; they had evidently just come in from a successful foray, for they were loaded one and all with booty.

There was a confused shouting for fuel ; for more lights ; for wine. " Here you, comrade," said one, casting a careless eye upon Phannias, "take your axe and make firewood of yonder door, while I cut up the meat here ready for roasting. Passover lamb, man ; my mouth waters at the thought of it !"

Within the half hour every man of the fifty was sprawling before a roaring fire, busily engaged in roasting a great piece of succulent meat which he had spitted upon his sword. No one had questioned the presence of Phannias; he could have slipped away with ease through any one of a half dozen openings which the ready axes of the hungry soldiers had made in his prison ; but he reflected that he knew nothing of the interior of the palace, and that he was more than likely to be caught in any premature attempt at escape.

He decided to remain where he was, and boldly joined a group near an open door. "Just in, comrades?" he asked, affecting a yawn ; "and how went it outside?"

The soldier next him dropped his meat into the flames, then swore roundly that the newcomer had shaken it off. "Come," he roared, "I'll not go supperless to sleep after such a fight; get me another piece, man, or I swear I will roast ye on my spit!"

"There's plenty of meat in the corner yonder," growled another. "Take what thou wilt and hold thy peace.—We got the temple," he added, glancing carelessly at Phannias. "By the *Chel*, it was

neatly done! We went in disguised as pilgrims—
our swords hidden beneath our cloaks—two thousand strong; with as many more of the soldiers of
the Gischalan. The Zealots were but half armed
and looking for nothing save the slaughter of Passover lambs. At the moment when the priests
beckoned to the people to fall upon their faces, our
chief blew a single blast upon the trumpet. It
was the signal. After that I remember nothing
save forcing my way over fallen bodies toward the
inner temple. It was all done within the hour;
Eleazar and his men slunk like foxes into their
burrows beneath the altar; but they came out
peaceably enough when they found that they must
surrender or die. The city is safe now."

"What of the worshipers?" asked Phannias, his
voice shaking with the horror he could not conceal.

"There are some six or seven thousand of them
who will eat no Passover," said the soldier coolly.
"They failed to understand the matter and got in
the way of our swords. We gathered in a few
lambs as we came out—all neatly dressed and
ready for the spit. Have a morsel, comrade, and
a cup of wine to celebrate the victory!—Hail to
Bar-Gioras! Confusion to the Romans!"

A great shout greeted this cry, and the mirth
speedily grew fast and furious. Phannias, who had
drawn back again into the shadow sick at heart,
gathered from the chance words which came to his
ears that the enemy without the walls were actively

engaged in making ready for the siege; and also that an attack of some sort was planned for the following day. He listened to the rough carousal which followed in a maze of unhappy thought which at last merged into heavy slumber.

The first faint beams of morning light which struggled into the murky air of the courtyard aroused him to the fact that the day of the Pass-over had dawned. The great, holy feast of the Deliverance—how eagerly he had looked forward to it in the happy days of his childhood. He looked about him with a shudder of fear and disgust. The revelers of the night before were all sleeping heavily about the ashes of the dead fires; while heaps of bones, empty wine-skins and fragments of half-eaten meat littered the filthy stones on which they lay. At the sudden bray of a trumpet in the corridors without, the man nearest Phannias raised his head. "What, daylight already!" he cried with an oath. "Come, comrade, help me to get these fellows onto their feet; they are as deaf as the dead in the temple yonder."

Phannias hesitated for an instant; then catching up a sword and shield which lay within reach, he obeyed.

Fifty men presently filed out into the square in front of the palace. The place was already crowded with troops. Bar-Gioras, armed to the teeth and surrounded by half a dozen officers, stood upon the raised platform known as the judgment seat. He

ran his piercing eye over the dense mass of soldiers.
" The city is ours, men," he said, in a sonorous
voice that sounded in every ear like the blast of a
trumpet. " The enemy within is subdued. The
enemy without must also be faced and conquered.
Will you follow me ?"

" Hail to Bar-Gioras !" shouted a strident voice.
The cry was repeated in a great deafening roar;
then the detachments began to move away at a
rapid pace.

Phannias found himself marching in the front of
a column which after a time broke into a confused
mass, as it plunged into the dark, narrow streets of
the New Town. He understood presently that the
enemy was making ready to attack the Third Wall,
between the Jaffa gate and the tower of Psephinus ;
and also that the populace, horrified by the massacre in the temple, wished to surrender the city before the siege commenced.

The troops had come to a standstill, evidently
awaiting further orders from their chief. These
came without delay, and Phannias was astonished
to perceive the ponderous gates, before which his
column had halted, swing wide, and to find the
company, of which he was an insignificant unit,
rushing out into the face of a Roman battalion
which was stationed less than a third of a mile
away.

Voices from the gate towers were calling upon
the Romans to draw near. " We are ready to sub-

mit!" they cried. "We have thrust out from our gates them that desire war. Draw near and fall upon them. Then enter the city which we open freely."

"Cowards!" exclaimed Phannias, "what does this mean?"

"Hold thy peace, fool, and observe what follows," growled the man next him.

A number of rapid maneuvers ensued, during which Phannias doggedly followed the man in front, without understanding in the least what it all meant; their company advanced impetuously toward the Romans, as if to attack; then fell back in disorder beneath the shelter of the walls, only to receive a shower of stones and missiles from the towers above their heads.

Bewildered as he was by the apparent folly of the officers in command, Phannias observed in these moments a thousand details which he afterward recalled with a sense of wonder. The country for miles about was swarming with Roman soldiers, who were busily occupied in a widespread work of destruction; villas, mansions and cottages had become blazing heaps of ruins; blossoming groves, vineyards and gardens were vanishing under the blows of thousands of axes. Already the scene, which but the day before had presented a vision of smiling beauty, had assumed the haggard aspect of war and death.

Between the city and the scattered soldiers en

gaged in this work of devastation were drawn up strong bodies of troops. One of these battalions directly faced the open gate; at a single blast of the trumpet it hurled itself forward as one man, cleaving the irregular masses of Jewish troops as a sword might cleave a wave of the sea. But like a wave of the sea the Jews closed in behind it with loud exultant shouts. Fresh troops issued from the city where they had been lying concealed; while from the towers which flanked the gate a swift avalanche of javelins, stones and arrows poured down upon the heads of the advancing Romans.

Phannias found himself fighting fiercely and shouting like a demon when the enemy, demoralized by the suddenness and fury of the attack, broke rank and fell back in wild confusion. A Roman, who had turned to fly, stumbled and fell just before him; he drove his weapon into the man's back with savage joy. A blaze of scarlet, and a second figure loomed suddenly before him like a swift vengeance; death looked out of the savage eyes; then the lids dropped. Another—and yet another! He felt suddenly that he could kill them all—all those insignificant scarlet figures which he saw just ahead on Scopus, running hither and yon like frightened ants.

Some one shouted in his ear; then a compelling hand caught him by the arm. He turned with a savage imprecation to find the lion head of Bar-

Gioras at his shoulder. "Back, man,—back to the gates! We shall be cut off!"

An hour later the victorious troops were reassembled in the square of the Prætorium. The Sicar chief himself reviewed them carefully, company by company. "We have lost scarce twenty men," he announced to the officers who walked at his side; "while more than a hundred dead Romans lie without the walls." His keen eyes swept the ranks with a well-satisfied air, which penetrated to the breast of every man who beheld it. Those strange, colorless eyes—transparent windows, as it were, through which the will of the man looked out unhindered—rested full upon a certain man in the front of a company which had once been fifty. "Stand forth," he said.

The man obeyed.

"How came you in this company?"

"I was a prisoner within; this company spent the night in the place where I was imprisoned. In the morning when they went forth, I also went; no man questioned me."

"I commanded the prison till thy words concerning the temple should be made good. They have been made good. Also, thou hast proved that thou art a brave man. The captain of this company lies without the walls; henceforth thou art captain in his room."

Phannias raised his head proudly; his eyes kindled into flame. It was worth while to have lived, if only to die for this master of men.

CHAPTER XXXII.

THE WISDOM OF FOOLS.

BEN ETHAN, shut into his ruinous old house like a spider within his web, paid little heed to what was passing in the city. The price of grain was steadily rising and that fact filled his whole horizon. He rubbed his dry hands glee-fully as he counted his bags. "Lord, thou hast been gracious unto me," he cried, addressing as from long habit the being whom he supposed be-nignantly interested in his personal affairs. "Surely, I have kept thy law, and observed thy statutes; therefore thou hast given me wisdom above my fellows."

There was a certain difficulty however in the matter of selling; he could not open his shop with a display of grain bags. There were always the soldiers to be considered, though these were seldom seen in the upper Agra of late; Ben Ethan piously concluded that they were providentially employed elsewhere during the latter weeks of April. As for the stranger within the gates, he was already rap-idly nearing the point where he was willing to part with all that he possessed for food.

The worthy merchant finally hit upon a plan of

disposing of his wares which proved entirely successful. Concealing as large an amount of grain
about his ragged clothing as he could conveniently
carry, he sallied forth day by day in the guise of a
mendicant, visiting only those portions of the city
where he was little known, and disposing of his
store by the handful among the foreign Jews who
crowded the squares and market places.

He set out on such an expedition one morning
in early May, and after some reflection made his
way into Upper Bezetha, as the northeast portion
of the outer city was called. He had been told
on the previous day that the Romans were about
to attack the wall near the Jaffa gate ; he wished
to ascertain the truth of this report. If the outer
walls were taken the people must perforce crowd
into the stronger defenses within.

He had not proceeded far on his way when he
perceived a woman, sitting in the shadow of a wall.
She was hugging a sleeping baby to her breast ;
while several half-naked children played about her
in the sunshine, as careless and happy as sparrows.
Ben Ethan approached this group quietly and stood,
leaning on his staff, regarding the mother with
speculative eyes. He had dealt with hundreds of
such during the past week.

"Thou art blessed of Jehovah, woman," he
whined, waving his lean hand with an expansive
gesture of greeting. " Peace be with thee, mother
of sons."

The woman looked up. "I have nothing," she said wearily, "—nothing. My children hunger for bread which I cannot give them."

"I have not asked for alms. Where is thy husband?"

The woman's face contracted with a soundless sob. "He is dead—it must be that he is dead, since he does not return to us. He was in the temple at Passover time."

Ben Ethan raised his brows. Then he smote his breast and rolled up his eyes toward heaven. "And did he leave thee no money with which to buy food for the little ones?"

"I had my necklace," replied the woman dully; "but it is gone—all is gone. My God! What shall I do?" Her misery overcame her and she sank back weeping convulsively. The little ones frightened at the sound gathered about her, and all burst into loud crying.

"Go away, wicked man!" cried the oldest of the brood; "go away—I will hurt you with a stone!"

Ben Ethan turned his back upon the group with a scowl. There was no business to be done here, and time was money in these days.

He wondered a little as he made his way toward the nearest market place,—where he felt tolerably sure of finding customers, as to what had become of his daughter. He had quite succeeded in convincing himself long before this of his own entire blamelessness in the matter. "The girl had blasphemed,"—he assured himself for perhaps the thousandth time—"She was undeniably apostate. Now if I, a law-abiding son of Abraham, had continued to feed and shelter a blasphemer and an apostate, would I not have become partaker in the guilt? Being therefore blameless in the eyes of Jehovah, was it not meet that I should sacrifice my daughter to the law, even as Abraham offered up his son Isaac and was blessed therefor? God will also bless me because I have done this thing."

There were strange sounds to be heard in the Bezetha on this bright morning in the Bloom month, sounds which penetrated even to the dull ears of Ben Ethan, and brought him at last to a standstill near the open door of a courtyard. He drew near to this door and peered in; the persons within, women chiefly, were making hasty preparations for flight—if one might judge by the huge bundle of goods and provisions which the two men of the party were already loading upon their backs.

"Whither away, neighbors?" inquired the dealer in grain, inserting his hatchet-shaped visage into the yard.

The woman nearest him screamed aloud. "Holy patriarchs—how you frightened me!"

"I can abide nothing more," she whimpered in reply to one of the men, who had ventured a soothing remonstrance. "God knows I am ready to swoon with terror,—and the children! Whatever

shall we do!" She screamed again as one demented, and thrusting her fingers into her ears
rushed into the street.

The mysterious sounds were growing momently
louder—dull, heavy, crashing blows, recurring with
the regularity and precision of a machine. There
were terrible cries too, rising from the northeast.

"The rams are at work again," cried one of the
men; "go you after the mother, boy: we are
coming!"

Ben Ethan looked after the departing group;
he was half minded to follow them; then his eye
fell upon a bright object which one of them had
dropped upon the stones of the courtyard. He
picked it up and thrust it into his bosom with a
chuckle. "The heavens rain gold in these days,"
he muttered, and got him into the street again. It
was empty, but at the corner below he perceived a
crowd of flying figures with bundles upon their
backs.

The loud, terrified crying of a child greeted his
ears as he turned into a narrow alley which led toward the Gate of Ephraim in the Broad Wall. Ben
Ethan had by this time determined that prudence
demanded his immediate return to the Agra; he
therefore resented the positive grasp with which a
small brown hand clutched at a corner of his abba.

"Let me go, boy," he growled angrily, looking
down to meet the gaze of a pair of tearful dark
eyes.

"I am lame—I cannot walk," wailed the child, "and they have forgotten me! Oh, take me with you!"

"Am I a beast of burden then to carry cripples —who are already accursed of God?" Ben Ethan hurried faster than ever after he had shaken off the small brown hand. Something in the imploring eyes had reminded him unpleasantly of Merodah. He cursed the Romans aloud as he stumbled over a roll of sleeping-mats, which some fugitive had dropped in his unreasoning haste. Also, he cursed all soldiers, dead and alive, as he was forced to squeeze himself into an angle of the wall while a troop of Sicars, covered with dust and blood, rushed by; one of their number fell almost at his feet and expired without a struggle.

"What has happened?" he demanded of the gatekeepers, as he passed through into the inner city. The man was helping to close one of the side portals, and made no reply.

"Why do you bar the gate at midday?" shouted Ben Ethan.

The keepers had made fast the ponderous bars now; one of them turned at sound of the strident voice. "The Third Wall has fallen," he said with a curse; "the Romans are in Bezetha. Jehovah save us, it is the beginning!"

During the days that followed, Ben Ethan divided his time pretty equally betwixt the transaction of business,—which had never been more prosperous, and frenzied entreaties to Jehovah for the Second Wall, against which the Romans had already brought up their heavy engines of war. If this wall went down before the terrible rams, the enemy would pour into the defenseless Agra ; then what would become of his precious bags of grain ? This question must be answered and at once. Already the inhabitants of the Inner Low Town were beginning to pour into the upper portion of the city, doubly defended by the almost impregnable heights of Zion and Moriah.

The thunder of the rams, the sound of rushing bodies of troops and the clamor of conflict filled the air night and day. There was no longer any doubt that the Second Wall was doomed ; it had become a question of hours; Ben Ethan paced up and down the courtyard of his house in an agony of despair. " Have I not kept thy laws ?" he demanded fiercely of his deity. " Am I not blameless? And must I be ruined because of these Gentiles ? Lord, hast thou forgotten Jerusalem ? Wilt thou suffer thy holy city to be defiled with the feet of idolaters ?"

As the hours went by and there was no answer to these frenzied demands upon omnipotence, he ventured to open the door of his house and peer out into the street. A soldier turned the corner at a run. As he drew near Ben Ethan recognized with astonishment the man whom he had hired to protect his property. " Stop !" he cried out with an air of authority. "Where are you going?"

The soldier stopped short. "I have found you at last," he said, "—and thank God in time!"

"*Found me?* What mean you, fellow; did I not hire thee to protect my property? Where hast thou been?—Idling away thy time with wine-bibbers, I'll warrant me. But come in—come in; I will say no more at present. There is work to be done. The grain must be moved at once. It is worth—Lord, I cannot tell what it is worth in gold at this moment! I suppose there is no chance of saving the wall?"

Phannias looked about the bare place impatiently. "Curse the grain!" he cried; "this is no time to speak of gold. Where is the maid?—I have been here, seeking you both, many times in the past days; when the house seemed empty each time, I hoped you were already safe inside the defenses."

"But the grain, fellow! I tell thee that people are starving! I will not leave it to the Romans—I swear I will not leave it!"

"Thou art right; we must take what we can," said Phannias, his eyes roving about with ill-concealed impatience. "I will take you to a place of safety, afterward I will fetch my men; we will save what we can of it. Call the maid quickly; there is no time to be lost!"

Ben Ethan tore at his ragged garment in a frenzy. "Fetch your men!" he echoed, —"call a

pack of rascally thieves to take away my property!
'Tis like your impudence to propose such a thing!
It must be carried away at dead of night, man ; I
will hire a house inside where to bestow it in
safety."

"The maid—the maid!" interrupted Phannias,
who during this harangue had flung open door
after door. "Where is Merodah?—Answer."

Ben Ethan shrank back into a corner before the
fierce eyes of his questioner. "I—I do not know,"
he stammered. "The girl has left me."

"Where has she gone?"

"I—I cannot tell.—But what right hast thou to
question me, fellow? Wilt thou do my bidding
concerning the grain or wilt thou not?—Sacred
fire! What a crash! Now, if the wall— Mercy
—Have mercy!" His eyes started from his head
with terror before the gleaming blade of the sword,
which flashed ominously in the glaring light of
noon.

"I swear I will slay thee on the instant if thou
dost not answer me," said Phannias, deadly intent
manifest in every line of his white face. "What
hast thou done with thy daughter?"

"I have done nothing—heaven be my witness!
I caught the girl praying aloud to the crucified
malefactor, Jesus of Nazareth. She has gone to
her own."

"To the Nazarenes?"

"Thou hast spoken."

" Where are they ?"

" How should I know. The girl hath forsaken me in my old age—left me alone, as thou seest—to consort with blasphemers. And now thou, my hired servant, who shouldst do my bidding after the law of such——"

Ben Ethan stopped short; the man to whom he was speaking had disappeared. Words of execration rushed to his lips, but they were never uttered; the dull monotonous crash—crash of the battering rams had suddenly ceased. There were loud cries; the sound of rushing feet; then silence—broken only by the distant notes of a trumpet.

Ben Ethan's face became the color of clay. " The wall has fallen," he muttered. He stood for a moment irresolute, then with a snarl like that of a hunted animal turned and plunged into his cellars.

The darkness and silence of this familiar haunt exercised a soothing influence upon his disordered nerves. Within the hour he succeeded in convincing himself that in this underground retreat he was quite safe. He had made fast the doors of the place from within, after a device of his own contriving fashioned in the days of the civil war. He congratulated himself on his cunning and forethought, as he passed from room to room of the intricate maze of chambers—in some places lying one below the other in the very bowels of the rock, their entrances skilfully concealed from the eye of the casual observer.

The more he considered his position the more confident and cheerful did he become. "I have food," he said aloud, snapping his fingers, "and wine—plenty of it. Also I have money. But no one will look for it here. There is nothing above —absolutely nothing. It is the house of a poor man."

CHAPTER XXXIII.

A MEETING OF THE SANHEDRIM.

TO the amazement of his troops Bar-Gioras ordered an instant retreat into the Upper Town, as soon as the loud crash of fallen masonry announced that the Second Wall had fallen.

Phannias, who found himself with his company under the direct command of Bar-Gioras, overheard Kimosh inquiring of his chief as to the meaning of this maneuver. "The breach is but an insignificant one," he asserted; "we could hold it, —ay, and drive them back."

Bar-Gioras sneered openly at this remonstrance. "Thinkest thou that I am afraid of the Romans?" he asked. Then, as Kimosh made no reply, "Wait for a day before you question me further."

Titus, marveling at the ease with which he had made this second advance, entered the breach at the head of a thousand picked men; and meeting with no resistance from those of the terrified inhabitants, who had been unable to reach the Upper Town, he gave his men leave to plunder, ordering them to kill no one save those who resisted. The soldiers with the confidence born of long-continued triumph quickly dispersed among the narrow, intricate streets of the Agra, while the son of the emperor with his officers and guards, some two hundred heavily-armed soldiers, advanced boldly into the market place of the wool buyers, there to hold a council of war.

The Roman commander had been directed to spare the city and the temple if it were possible ; he therefore determined to once more offer advantageous terms of peace to its defenders. He was not ignorant of the difficulties and dangers which would attend a continuation of the siege. "What we have already accomplished," he said, "is but the stripping of the outer husk from the nut ; the hard inner shell remains to be cracked."

These and other matters being in full tide of discussion, a long strenuous blast of the trumpet followed by two shorter notes announced interruption.

Some hundreds of quiet figures had been stealing along the dark alleyways leading from the Old Wall ; one figure always in advance of the rest ; now pausing like a stealthy cat under a dark archway, now clambering through the ruins of some ancient building, again running swiftly past bright sun-lighted squares. This figure, huge, threatening, now stood on the confines of the wool mart. He raised his hand, and the whirlwind—which had gathered so quietly that the quick-eared Roman sentries had heard nothing of it—burst forth.

Twenty-four hours later, Bar-Gioras, breathing

deep-throated curses, stood again within the shelter of the Old Wall. "I have failed," he said.

"We have slain no fewer than five hundred of the enemy," cried Kimosh boastfully; "we all but made an end of their leader. They have ceased fighting because they are afraid."

Bar-Gioras ground his teeth. "We should have slain five thousand of them," he said bitterly. "As for their gilded general, I held him, as a man would hold a fly, but like a fly he escaped out of my hand ere I could crush him. Their gods fight for them."

Nevertheless Simon, and with him John of Gischala and Eleazar, the Zealot, united in stubbornly refusing to consider the question of surrender. And this despite the fact that their granaries were so nearly exhausted that rations were issued to the troops but once in three days. All semblance of military discipline was now at an end; the soldiers came and went at will, depending largely upon the wretched inhabitants of the city for their food. The methods by which they obtained these rations became a matter of horrible ribaldry in camps and barracks.

Phannias sought out Bar-Gioras on the tower of Hippicus one morning in early summer. There had been no fighting for nearly three weeks.

"What is to be the end of this?" he asked abruptly.

"Am I a god?" answered the Sicar.

"Thou art at the head of the army and canst

surrender the city if thou wilt. The people are starving by hundreds and by thousands."

" Let them leave then—or die ; there will be the more food for those that remain."

Phannias was silent for a moment. " Look yonder," he said at length in a choked voice ; "there be more than five hundred crosses on Olivet, each bearing the starved body of a Jew, whom famine has driven beyond the walls. The Roman hath set them there for thine eyes."

Bar-Gioras laughed aloud. " I will also show thee another sight," he said.

The two descended in silence to the level of the wall. There were soldiers there. A hundred paces distant a battalion of Roman troops was working upon an embankment.

" Bring out the traitors," commanded Bar-Gioras.

Other soldiers led out from a door in the tower nineteen men in chains. They were emaciated to a horrible degree.

"Seven days since," said Bar-Gioras loudly, "these men were caught communicating with the enemy. They would have surrendered the city without my permission. Matthias, sometime high priest of Israel, thou art condemned to die on the walls which thou art too cowardly to defend. But thou shalt first behold the death of thy three sons, who were with thee in this crime."

Matthias raised his haggard face to the sky.

"And it was I," he murmured, "who admitted this monster to the city !" He turned his eyes upon the Sicar, with a gesture full of dignity and pathos. "I am ready to die," he said slowly. "I shall haply forget the misery which I have brought upon my family and my nation. But these men who stand with me, the last remaining members of the holy Sanhedrim of Israel ; and these, my young sons, have committed no crime. Spare them, I beseech thee, as thou wouldst thyself be spared in the day of thy doom."

Bar-Gioras seemed not to have heard. With the careless nod of one who dismisses a trifling complainant, he motioned to the guard.

The three young men—scarcely more than boys—died first ; then the fifteen members of the Sanhedrim, without a protest—without a murmur. After all the others Matthias, last of the high-priestly line, bowed his gray head to the sword— and was gone.

Bar-Gioras had surveyed the scene without a quiver of his iron visage. "Signal to the Romans yonder to approach within hailing distance," he ordered. And when three mail-clad figures had cautiously approached within twenty paces of the wall, he seized the ghastly head of Matthias and swung it aloft. "Bid Titus receive these noble Jews, who will make terms with him for the surrender !" he cried, and hurled the head into the faces of the Romans.

Phannias felt a deadly faintness overpowering him. In the blazing heat of the summer noon the figure of Bar-Gioras loomed monstrous, horrible, before his dazed eyes ; the sound of the harsh metallic voice rang dully in his ears. He was conscious of nothing save a burning hatred for this man, whom he had followed—ay, and loved, for more than three months. Flinging down his sword and shield in the midst of a pool of blood, he staggered blindly down the steep stairway which led to the street.

CHAPTER XXXIV.

THE BLACK FAST.

FOR nearly three weeks the Romans labored steadily on huge embankments confronting Antonia, Hippicus, Phasaelus and Mariamne. The material for these outworks was obtained from the Agra itself; in the course of ten days hundreds of houses were torn down, and the vast heaps of debris thus accumulated grew as if by magic into ominous mountains over against the frowning towers which they threatened.

This work was not carried on without a desperate resistance on the part of the Jews; the soldiers of Bar-Gioras rained a spiteful storm of stones and javelins from their engines, captured in the war against Cestius; while their sharpshooters, posted on walls and battlements, planted their arrows with deadly effect among the toilers. The Zealots were not less industrious, though they were not visible to the enemy.

Unlooked-for results followed the destruction of certain of the shabby and ancient houses of the Agra. It was as though some populous ant-hill had been suddenly laid bare by a pitiless foot. Hundreds of living creatures sprang out of the dark cellars which underlay the empty houses, and ran shrieking and crying hither and yon like distracted vermin. The soldiers cut down the flying figures with relish ; afterward, they searched the lairs from which they had risen.

In one such cellar near the gate Miphkad were found more than five hundred bags of grain ; together with a prodigious store of cups, plates, chains, jewels and money. The centurion who discovered it vowed a score of the broad gold pieces to the goddess Fortuna on the spot. " The gods love me !" he swore with a great oath ; " I have had nothing but good fortune of late !"

The grain was carried to Titus, who straightway added it to the rations of the army. As for the industrious owner of this particular house and treasure ; his body lay in the cellars which he had loved more than his own flesh and blood. Body and cellars alike being emptied of their valuable contents, they were never again disturbed by the hand of any man, whether friend or foe.

The embankments and wooden flanking-towers being at length quite finished, the Romans proceeded to mount their great engines of war ; also some hundreds of troops took up a position ready for the attack. It was confidently hoped that with the taking of Antonia, Hippicus and Mariamne all resistance from within would be at an end.

But scarcely had the first stone been hurled from the Roman ballistæ, when a series of ominous sounds were heard from beneath; the embankments suddenly collapsed with a fearful crash, carrying towers, engines and troops with them; an instant later and the ruinous mass was wrapped in flames, out of which arose the wild shrieks of the imprisoned soldiers.

From the walls and towers of Jerusalem, other voices pierced the murky air with fierce cries of triumph and joy. The Zealot chief, leaving the work of harassing the laborers to Bar-Gioras, had undermined the wall and constructed extensive galleries and chambers directly beneath the embankments. These excavations were supported upon timber work, which at the last was smeared with pitch, then set on fire.

On the day after this disaster Titus gathered his officers about him and laid before them three plans for the capture of the city; the first of these proposed to take the walls by storm; the second, to rebuild the outworks; the third, to establish a strict blockade, thus increasing the pressure of the famine within, which it was said had already slain upwards of six hundred thousand of the Jews.

This third project was decided upon; and no sooner decided upon than carried into execution. The work was assigned to the legions in shares; it was begun at once, and accomplished with incredible swiftness. The whole army was already maddened by the long-continued and obstinate opposition of the starving enemy; more than this, they were

determined to speedily avenge their comrades who
had lost their lives in the burning of the embankments. Legion vied with legion; cohort with cohort; decurion, centurion, tribune and even general
officers labored with not less fury than the common
soldiers. Titus himself surveyed the work hour
by hour. So it was that midnight of the third day
beheld a trench and a wall of wattled earth, five
miles in length, beginning and ending at the tent
of Titus, girdling 'the hemmed and famishing Jerusalem.'

Thus were fulfilled the words of the slain Carpenter of Nazareth: "The days shall come upon
thee, that thine enemies shall cast a trench about
thee, and compass thee round, and keep thee in
on every side."

But the end was not yet.

On that hot and breathless midnight which saw
the wall of circumvallation completed, the full
moon stared down out of a brazen sky, ashamed
and afraid at the scenes her pitiless light revealed.
In the streets of the city lay countless dead, which
the crowded cemeteries refused to harbor, even had
the living been able to cover them out of sight. In
closed and silent houses where whole families had
shut themselves in with their misery; under dark
archways and in foul alleys where animal-like they
had crawled to hide their death-throes; in the choked
burial-places, where they crouched upon the graves
of the fortunate who had died earlier ; on the roofs

of houses, their ghastly faces turned toward the
shining temple; in open squares; on street corners; in every possible place, in every possible attitude of frozen agony, this terrible multitude was
gathering.

As fast as they were able the starving soldiers,
working under the directions of Bar-Gioras, carried
the dead to the walls and cast them into the ravines
without. But Famine worked yet swifter than the
soldiers; more than once it happened that he who
bore a burden to the wall was himself cast with it
into the depths below. These burden-bearers
worked silently and with slow, languid movements;
no one spoke to his fellow. There was no longer
clamor of any kind heard in the streets; like the
houses from whose closed doors and windows ex-
haled the terrible effluvia of mortality, the city preserved an ominous silence both by day and by
night.

Through one of these silent streets of the inner
city a half-naked figure ran swiftly; the white
moonlight shone clear on the dark heaps which lay
here and there in his path, so that he neither paused
nor faltered in his course. On and on, through
street and alley, through square and market place,
he ran as one demented; then on a sudden, without
a groan, without a sigh, the swift motion ceased
and one more black shadow lay motionless in the
midst of the white moonlight. There were two
other figures moving on this street—a man and a

woman. The woman had seen the swift runner
and his fall. "We must look to this," she said;
"I have still water left in my pitcher."

"It is so little that we can do," said her companion sadly; "and thou art already exhausted, my
child."

The woman had not waited to hear this remonstrance; she had lifted the limp head of the fallen
man. "We must do what we can—to the end,"
she said gently, and poured a few drops of water
into the half-open mouth. Then with a little cry
she bent to look more narrowly into the white face.

"What is it?" asked the man, also stooping to
inspect the fallen body; then he started back with
a loud exclamation. "It is Phannias—my son
Phannias! And he is dead."

"No," said the girl quietly, "he is not dead—
but perhaps dying. Go, call help; it may be that
we can yet save him."

An hour later the starving man languidly opened
his eyes into the anxious faces which bent above
him. A look of great astonishment and joy dawned
in their depths, then he again sank back uncon-
scious.

It was little enough that his rescuers could do to
fan the flickering flame of life which had so nearly
gone out; famine had laid its icy touch upon one
and all of them weeks since; but love is a compelling power, and by degrees Phannias came back
again into a full realization of his surroundings.

The faces which at first seemed but the vague im-
aginings of fevered dreams grew at length pitifully
distinct in their wan outlines. On the third day, he
pushed away with decision the transparent hand
which would have placed a morsel of bread dipped
in water between his parched lips. "No—no," he
said; "I will not eat. Thou art thyself starving."

"No," said the girl, smiling through her tears,
"truly, I am not. I have eaten.—To think," she
cried in rapture, turning to the others in the room,
"he has already the strength to push my hand
away. Is it not wonderful! He will live now;
will he not?"

No one answered. Who could say in the midst
of that carnival of death that any one would live?
The girl glanced in piteous appeal from one to the
other of the ashen faces. "The Master is with us,"
she faltered. "Surely you do not doubt it?"

The man who stood on the other side of the bed
looked up at this with his slow, wise smile. "Nay,
my daughter, Merodah; we have not forgotten;
but there is also a more glorious life beyond, when
this mortal shall be swallowed up of immortality;
it may be that life eternal shall dawn for every one
of us ere long."

Before sunset of that same day Phannias learned
more fully into what company he had fallen; he had
indeed recognized two faces of the many which had
bent above him in loving ministry, but the others
were strange to him.

"These are the Christians who remained behind in Jerusalem to care for the sick," Merodah explained to him. "Yes truly, my Lord was with me on the night when my father thrust me out into the street; he led me straight into the arms of the good Lesbia yonder."

Phannias was pondering a word of hers in his weak brain. "Didst thou say that thy father thrust thee out into the street?" he asked presently.

"I was speaking aloud to the Master," said the girl simply, "and he heard me. He did not believe; to him I was no better than a blasphemer." Then another thought came to her. "Hast thou seen him?" she asked breathlessly; "is my father safe?"

Phannias scowled. "I saw him—a long time ago, before the falling of the Second Wall. I do not know what has become of him.—I went to his house to save you, if it were possible," he added, in answer to the imploring question which looked out of her eyes; "he was there alone; he refused to leave his goods."

Ben Huna's presence with the Christians of Jerusalem was even easier of explanation. "I followed thee to the temple, my son, on the day in which the Zealots declared thee high priest, and was wounded in the terrible massacre which followed. These disciples of the Master ministered to me, and I have remained with them since. They told me that thou wast slain within the hour of thy investiture," he added after a pause. "Yet often have I gloried in the thought of thy testimony to the truth in that terrible hour."

Phannias moved uneasily upon his couch. "I was mad in that hour," he said weakly; "I knew not what my lips uttered." Then he staggered to his feet. "If ye have ministered to me, supposing that I am of your number, ye have erred; I do not believe—I cannot believe. I—I will go now."

Ben Huna's authoritative hand was upon his shoulder. "None the less art thou one for whom Christ died," he said slowly; "and therefore dear to us all and beloved."

After a little they told him how all through the fearful months of the siege they had ministered as they were able to the sufferers about them. More especially to the women and children, on whom the burden of Israel's sin lay heaviest.

The Bishop had fallen peacefully asleep in the earliest days of summer, and they had laid his worn body to rest with tender rejoicings because that he was spared the terrible days to come. His mantle seemed to have fallen upon Ben Huna, to whom henceforth they turned for guidance and direction. The good rabbi with far-sighted wisdom had purchased, immediately after his arrival in the city, a large supply of grain and other provisions; and these he had placed at the disposal of the brave workers. Of late it had become necessary to dispense this charity with extreme caution; nay, in spite of their utmost endeavor their gifts to the suffering poor had more than once been followed by appalling consequences.

A poor widow who had been accustomed to come to them daily for food had been found dying in her house, surrounded by her wailing little ones. Soldiers had broken in, she told them, and had taken the new-baked bread. After they had devoured it, they asked her where she had obtained the flour; this she refused to tell; whereat they tortured her with fire and the sword.

"I kept the faith," she gasped, with a smile of triumph—and died.

"We can do little now beyond soothing the misery of the dying," said Ben Huna. "Many drop with exhaustion in the hot glare of the sun where they are unable to obtain water.—There is still water in abundance, thanks be to God who hath spared us this final agony."

It was many days thereafter before Phannias discovered that his generous hosts had all but exhausted their store of provisions; he had been led to suppose that they were prompted by worldly wisdom to eat little or nothing, in order that they might not become objects of suspicion in the eyes of the soldiers, who were by this time more terrible than beasts of prey. It was Rufus who revealed to him the true state of affairs.

The Greek had obtained employment as a servant in the family of a rich Jew from Samaria, who
had taken up his residence in the city shortly before
the appearance of the Roman army. During the
earlier days of the siege the Christians had seen
little of the young man, who nevertheless failed not
to bring from time to time the full sum of his wages
to add to the common store. One morning late in
July he appeared among them with a white, agonized face.

"My master is dead," he gasped; "and of his
household I only remain alive!"

It was the old story; the house of the Samaritan
had hitherto escaped plunder by reason of large sums
of money passed over day by day to Bar-Gioras,
who in turn detailed a special guard for its protection. But gold rears a feeble barrier against
death. In the dead of night Famine and Death
entered the house of the rich man hand in hand.
"It was the guard who did it," cried Rufus; "shall
one set starving wolves to protect a store of food?"

Toward evening this new member of the household went away, returning in the morning with a
handful of green herbs and a piece of fresh meat;
this contribution was received with joy and surprise
by the women and shortly converted into a nour-
ishing soup, of which all partook with thankfulness.
Rufus offered no explanation as to the source from
which this unlooked-for provision had been obtained, and no one questioned him.

" The good Lord sent it to us," said Merodah simply. " He has not forgotten us ; he will not forget. Also he promised that the days should be shortened '*for the elect's sake.*' He knew that some who believed would be here ; it will soon be over now."

The girl's joyous faith was like sunshine and fresh air to the somber little company. They took good care to keep the more frightful incidents of the siege from her ears ; of late she had been persuaded to remain much within doors, and she did this the more readily since the good Lesbia fell ill and required careful nursing.

" The woman is near her end," said Rufus to Phannias, as the two young men walked slowly down the quiet street. " Of the others, the old man from Bethlehem cannot last long. I would that all were over,—that we slept as soundly as does this poor woman and her babe." He paused as he spoke to glance at the white peaceful face of a dead mother who still clasped her child to her withered breast.

The rams had begun the day before to play against the walls of Antonia and their dull thunder filled the stagnant air ; a haze of dust obscured the heavens through which the sun stared like a red eye ; the heat was intolerable.

" And does Jehovah slay women and children by thousands because certain scribes and Pharisees a generation since crucified the carpenter's son ?"

said Phannias thickly. "—Nay, hundreds of Jews have rotted on the accursed tree since Passover; is it not enough?"

Rufus looked apprehensively into the face of his companion. "It is not for us to ask," he began slowly; then he stopped short and looked thoughtfully up and down the street. "I believe," he said, "that the end is near; if we can but hold out a few days longer;—meantime, upon us rests the sustenance of the household; there is nothing left save a handful of meal and a cup of oil. Go thou and buy, if thou canst, from the soldiers of Eleazar; they are still strong and well fed from the temple stores."

"I have no money," said Phannias.

By way of answer the Greek held out a full purse. "Fare thee well, my brother," he said, gazing steadfastly into the haggard face of his companion. "If I do not return, look to their welfare as thou lovest thy soul.—Take care of the little maid"—the brave voice faltered. "I—I shall not come back unless I succeed."

"Where art thou going?"

"To the gate; between the trench and the wall there are still green herbs to be had. Also, it has happened more than once that a beast of burden from the Roman lines has strayed within reach."

"And if thou art taken?"

The Greek made a rapid sign in the air.

Phannias shuddered. "I will go with thee—thou shalt not attempt this terrible task alone."

" Not so, my friend ; I have accomplished it once in safety. Go thou to the temple ; there is a chance —a chance that thou mayest obtain food there. The Lord be with thee—Ay, He *is* with thee now and alway !"

Phannias stood quite still for a time watching the retreating figure of the Greek. Then he turned his face toward the temple, whose shining towers gleamed through the lurid dust with the unearthly beauty of a dream.

CHAPTER XXXV.

A MORE EXCELLENT WAY.

BEFORE taking a single step toward the temple, Phannias knew that to seek food in that direction was useless. He looked dully at the purse which the Greek had thrust into his hand. " It is of less value," he muttered, " than the stones beneath my feet; what man will sell his flesh for gold?" Nevertheless he concealed the purse in his girdle, and moved resolutely toward the Tyropœan Bridge.

As he again raised his eyes to the commanding heights of Moriah he was astonished to behold great volumes of saffron-colored vapor pouring out from the cloisters of Herod's Porch. The colonnades connecting Antonia with the temple were also smoking; and now scarlet tongues of flame darted up through the billowing masses of murky cloud.

The bridge was crowded from end to end with a ghastly and silent multitude. Here and there one beat feebly upon his breast as he gazed upward; few had strength for even this token of mourning, but stared motionless with lackluster eyes. Phannias accosted one of these ghostly figures, his own

voice ringing strange and hollow in his ears.
" Has the temple fallen ?"

The man to whom he had spoken turned his face
upon his questioner; his parchment lips, stretched
tightly over yellow teeth, widened in a terrible
smile. " No," he said; "the Zealots themselves
are burning the cloisters. Antonia is in the hands
of the Gentiles."

" Four walls; the temple falls !" cried out a harsh
metallic voice, in the words of a saying current in
Jerusalem from time immemorable.

The multitude burst into a low wail of poignant
anguish; at the sound some cast themselves over
the railing of the bridge into the valley below;
others sank in their places without a word. Phannias pushed his way through the death-stricken,
moaning crowd and presently found himself in a
steady stream of humanity, which was moving up
the steep incline leading to the temple area.

This silent and slow-moving procession was
frightful to look upon; it was composed of men,
women and children, half-naked, withered, emaciated, leaden hued; resembling dead bodies, urged
feebly onward by some power outside of themselves. It poured through the open gates into the
Court of the Gentiles, sweeping onward without
pause into the Women's Court, where it merged
into the great multitude within. This multitude had surged upward into the cloistered chambers above the Court of Israel and inward as far as

the great altar, which rose cold and bare out of the seething, struggling masses at its base. Overhead the rays of the August sun beat down into the murky air with the intolerable fury of a furnace seven times heated.

Phannias had followed, with unmeaning anxiety, a tall figure whose head was bound about with a turban of snowy whiteness, which shone conspicuous in the midst of the dust-begrimed and ragged multitude. This man had steadily made his way into the Court of Israel; he stopped there with an air of determination. Phannias recognized with a shock of surprise the face which was turned toward him. "Ben Huna!" he exclaimed; "why art thou here?"

The old man looked vacantly at his questioner. "Hast thou forgotten that this is the day of mourning for Israel, my friend?" he replied, in his old gentle fashion. He seemed not to have recognized the face before him.

"Do you not know me?" cried Phannias.

Ben Huna shook his head with a piteous smile. "I have known so many persons in Jerusalem," he said; "and of late my eyes have failed me. I am an old man—an old man. Thou art perhaps better able to see clearly, my friend; tell me, have the Levites assembled as yet? I cannot hear the sound of the trumpets. Nor can I even say whether the sacrifice be offered. There is a large congregation to-day.—Ay, it is well that Israel should humble

itself before Jehovah of Hosts. I have kept the
fast for many days now—for many days ; may my
sins be forgiven me !"

Phannias laid hold upon his master's arm with
sudden determination. "Come," he said, "we will
go. The sacrifice has been offered. All is over.
The congregation is about to disperse."

Ben Huna drew back with evident displeasure.
"I perceive that thou art not a keeper of the law,"
he began ; then shook his head sadly, and passed
his hand wearily over his eyes. "But it is difficult
for the young—a long and difficult lesson—the law.
I would that there were an easier way. I have
heard something of late—but it has escaped me
now. An easier way—a more excellent way—of
cleansing."

Phannias hesitated for an instant, then he approached his lips close to the old man's ear ; words
which Ben Huna himself had repeated in his hearing only that morning suddenly came back to him.
He had deemed them unmeaning, impossible—
almost blasphemous, but now as he looked upon
the empty altar, and the crowd of death-stricken
agonized faces which surrounded it, they took on
a new and wonderful significance. He repeated
them slowly—distinctly: "The blood of Jesus
Christ, his Son, cleanseth us from all sin."

A sudden glory of joy descended upon the gray,
ashen face of the listener. " ' *The blood of Jesus
Christ—his Son,*' " he repeated slowly, " ' *cleanseth*

—us—from all sin.' An easier way—a more excellent way !"

He seemed not to notice that Phannias had
passed an arm about him, and was slowly forcing
a passage through the dense multitude. Not far
away the dull impact of rams hurling themselves
upon unyielding masses of masonry could be heard ;
and with the beat—beat of that terrible heart of
war mingled frightful cries, the clash of swords and
the savage voices of trumpets. The smoke was
momently growing thicker, and the sharp, crackling
sound of devouring flames arose to the left and
right of the Women's Court.

Ben Huna looked about him with a sudden gleam
of comprehension, then sank back white and breathless upon the breast of Phannias.

The young man lifted the emaciated form in his
arms ; for the moment he felt all his old strength
swelling within his veins. Setting his teeth hard,
he pressed steadily onward step by step. Suddenly he stopped short ; not ten paces away, mow-
ing down the helpless multitude like withered grass,
a solid column of Sicars was rushing toward the
inner temple. Phannias saw and recognized the
colorless eyes and tawny lion head of their leader ;
Bar-Gioras was cursing the people, as he cut and
thrust among the groaning crowd. In another instant they were gone, and the throng closed sullenly over the broad, red track which they had left
behind them.

Phannias found himself at last standing before the door of the house which he had left that morning. How he had reached this door he did not know; he had a vague remembrance of horrible faces; of blows, cries, curses; of flames; of stifling smoke; of red, dripping swords; of dazzling sparks of fire floating confusedly before his eyes; through it all he had clung with savage tenderness to the burden which he had lifted—was it ages or moments since? The burden stirred feebly; he dropped it upon the threshold, then with a loud cry fell against the door.

Ben Huna was dying, they told him at sunset; with difficulty he dragged himself to the bedside of his master. The face on the pillow was calm and peaceful; the sunken eyes closed. Phannias threw himself upon his knees with a choking sob.

"My son,"—the low tones were full of gentle authority, as in the old days; Phannias involuntarily raised his head to listen. "There is but one law"—went on the failing voice—"that law is love. But one sacrifice; that sacrifice has been accomplished on the cross. But one way of cleansing; that way is the blood of Jesus, slain for the sins of the world."

There was a long silence, broken only by a tranquil sigh. The wise master was gone.

CHAPTER XXXVI.

VICTORY.

O N that black day of mourning, observed through six centuries, in which the glorious building of Solomon was destroyed by Nebuchadnezzar, King of Babylon, the temple was burned and pillaged by the Romans. The horrors crowded into that terrible fifth of August—the day of the great vintage of wrath, cannot be recounted. It had been decided on the previous day in a solemn council of war held by Titus and his officers that the temple must be spared at all costs. But it was not so written in the inexorable decrees of heaven : "Verily I say unto you that there shall not be left here one stone upon another which shall not be cast down." This was the sure word of prophecy, and it was fulfilled.

A common soldier of the Roman line was the chosen instrument of vengeance. Shrieking out curses upon the heads of the Jews and upon their temple, he seized a flaming brand from the cloisters and hurled it into one of the chambers of the sanctuary. Instantly the flames leapt upon their prey ; within the hour the whole magnificent building was burning fiercely. Titus himself rushed to the spot, calling loudly upon the legionaries to extinguish the fire; but the clamor of furious voices, the crackling of the flames and the groans of the dying drowned his word of command. The steps of the great altar were drenched with the blood of the slain, whose bodies lay in uncounted hundreds on and about it, while over all rolled the black, shrouding smoke of the perishing sanctuary.

In the light of those terrible flames the Romans fetched their eagles; and having set them up in the sacred precincts, they offered sacrifices to their pagan deities, saluting Titus as Imperator with acclamations of joy and triumph.

With the temple fell the city in the midst of that "great tribulation" of blood and fire and death, "such as was not since the beginning of the world to this time—no, nor ever shall be."*

But the days were shortened "for the elect's sake," according to the promise.

---

* Eleven hundred thousand persons are said to have perished during the siege, while nearly a hundred thousand were made prisoners at the time of the taking of the city. Of these, the old and feeble were put to death on the spot; numbers of the strong men were distributed among the provinces for gladiatorial victims.—In Cæsarea and Berytus alone, where, shortly after the downfall of Jerusalem, the conqueror celebrated the birthday of the emperor with great magnificence, no fewer than four thousand of these Jewish captives were butchered in the arenas. All of the other prisoners were sold into slavery in various parts of the world.

In that same year Rome witnessed the final scene in this drama of nations. On a certain day in November the bright autumnal sunshine shone gayly on miles of streets blazing with life and color; rich stuffs, flung lavishly from doors and windows, festive garlands and bunches of greenery were interspersed with thousands of pennants and banners of scarlet and purple and yellow and white, which danced and fluttered in the fresh breeze like joyous spirits of victory.

It was the day of the great pageant of the imperial triumph, and all Rome in holiday attire and in the wildest spirits had assembled to witness it. The country folk for miles about had been pouring in through the seven and thirty gates since long before daybreak. Already it had become impossible for anyone to so much as set foot anywhere along the line of march, for the eager spectators filled every inch of available space. In the midst of the wide streets, gorgeously appareled marshals caracoled up and down, their magnificent horses appearing fully aware of the important part they were to play in this spectacle of human grandeur. " Without us "—they seemed to say, with every toss of their proud heads—" this could not be."

From the garlanded windows and balconies of the marble palaces which lined the Via Sacra, haughty faces looked down with languid interest upon the heads of the ignoble multitude. From time to time liveried slaves scattered sweetmeats,

fruits and small coins among the people ; interspers-
ing, at frequent intervals, these tokens of patrician
benevolence with lavish showers of perfume, intended to overpower the vulgar exhalations of the
masses which tainted the exclusive air breathed to-
day by rich and poor alike.

In a certain dim and luxurious chamber in one
of these lofty mansions, a woman lay half reclined
upon a couch drawn up in the embrasure of a window. At her side an ingenious arrangement of mir-
rors enabled her to view the street, without so much
as raising her beautiful, indolent head from the
cushions. Great masses of violets, purple and
white, in golden bowls and vases, filled the air with
their delicious odor, seeming in their own mysterious way to diffuse about them an ethereal atmosphere of joy and love ; this subtile felicity rested
full upon the face by the window, adding to its ripe
beauty the last lingering touch of perfection.

At the foot of the couch stood a young girl, clad
in a tunic of scarlet and white and wearing about
her neck a ring-like collar of red gold. She was
looking eagerly out into the street, her small hands
tightly clasped, her dark eyes full of fear and
anguish.

Her mistress presently observed this expression,
and it seemed to displease her. " How now, girl,"
she said with a slight frown ; "thou hast not the
look that I would see on those that serve me.
What ails thee ?"

The girl turned her head wearily. "I am a slave, princess," she said. "My city is in ashes; my friends are dead. How can I rejoice?"

The woman on the couch flung out her hand with a little impatient gesture. "Thou art but a witless child," she said petulantly; "and wert thou not so beautiful I swear I would send thee to the slave-mart to-morrow. Did I not snatch thee from starvation and death—or worse, as one would lift a lost jewel out of the mire? Thou art mine— body and soul; smile therefore and be happy. The gods have been gracious to me and I am no niggard—even with my slaves. Besides, child, I have promised to remove that hated ring from thy neck on my wedding-day. That day is near at hand." She smiled as she spoke the last words; then sighed—the deep-drawn, rapturous breath of one who has attained triumph after long and ex- hausting effort.

The slave girl made no reply; her eyes were still fixed upon the street. "They are coming," she said at length, and hung her head that her mistress might not see the two big tears which dropped stealthily into her bosom.

A sudden roar of anticipation and delight from the waiting spectators mingled with the distant notes of a trumpet; then the clatter of hoofs an- nounced the approach of a body of cavalry. After the cavalry followed a company of musicians, sing- ing and playing hymns of victory, especially com-

posed for the occasion and celebrating the deeds
and virtues of the emperor and of his son, Titus,
Conqueror of Judæa, "the darling and delight of
all the world."

Berenice repeated the words softly. "The darling and delight of all the world!" Then she
smote her exquisite rose-tinted palms together with
the abandon of a child. "Look, Merodah," she
cried, "never in Jerusalem did thy foolish eyes
behold such a sight!"

The girl stared with a blank, unseeing gaze at
the great platforms now passing, upon which mimic
scenes from the late war were presented with wonderful accuracy. Here was a walled town, the
battering rams playing against its towers, while
battalions of pigmy soldiers, clad in the uniform
of the Roman army, were engaged in the various
military operations of a siege. Following this were
other cities, towns, fortresses—assaulted, captured,
in flames, the inhabitants vainly supplicating the
victorious and remorseless enemy. Last of all
came a vast representation of the city of Jerusalem,
borne by more than a hundred men; its triple
walls, its towers, its glittering temple—in flames
and overrun with Roman troops. Behind this
platform walked the rival generals, Simon Bar-
Gioras and John of Gischala, magnificently attired
and loaded with chains.*

---

* Arrived at the Capitol, it is said that the procession
halted, while the executioners dragged Simon Bar-Gioras to

The multitude burst forth into a roar of cheers and applause, in the midst of which the girl at the window quietly sank to the floor. Berenice motioned to the slaves who waited in the background. "Take her away," she said coldly. Pushing the mirror impatiently to one side, the woman leaned eagerly forward to look out. Ships, captured at Joppa and Tarichæa, mounted on wheeled trucks and laden with magnificent spoils of every description, were passing now; and following them came a long procession of priests, leading the snow-white bulls with gilded horns, adorned for the imperial sacrifices with garlands and fillets of scarlet and purple. Then came seven hundred Hebrew youths, selected from among the prisoners for their lofty stature and beauty of face; all splendidly dressed and in chains.

Berenice's black brows contracted as she looked down upon her fallen countrymen; they held their heads haughtily, looking neither to the right nor the left, seeming unaware of the insulting words and gestures of the crowd. A company of lictors, having their fasces wreathed with laurel, followed hard after the captives. Then in slow and pompous fashion came persons dressed in white, bearing the purple Veils of the Holy of Holies; the golden

---

the place of death in the Forum. When it was announced that there was an end of him, the multitude gave vent to a joyful shout.

John of Gischala was condemned to life imprisonment.

Table of the Shew-Bread; the seven-branched Candlestick—and last of all the Book of the Law.

The people cried out afresh at sight of these trophies, calling with loud acclamations upon the powerful gods of Rome who had thus triumphed gloriously over the one paltry deity of Israel.

The woman at the window clenched her white hands till the nails penetrated the flesh. "He should have spared me this," she muttered; "he swore upon the word of his honor that yonder holy things should not be further desecrated!"

Then she laughed aloud—a gay triumphant laugh. "But what care I? Henceforth thy people are my people; thy gods my gods. Jehovah is a myth—a dream, else this could not be!"

She turned again at sound of the prolonged, deafening shout of joy which burst from thousands of throats. The warrior-emperor, Vespasian, clothed in the imperial purple and crowned with laurel, was passing in his gilded chariot; but the dark eyes of the woman leapt eagerly to the face in the second chariot. "My Titus," she murmured, drawing her superb figure up to its full height, "'the delight and darling of all the world!'"

The conqueror stood erect in his chariot, himself guiding the spirited horses, the bright sunshine resting full upon his handsome, laurel-crowned head.

The woman leaned forward to look after him, all her proud soul in her eyes, while the steady, mo-

notonous tramp—tramp of thousands of feet and
the quick imperative voices of trumpets announced
the presence of the scarred and war-worn legionaries.

"The next triumph," she murmured, "will be
mine." Sinking back upon her couch she gave
herself up to delicious retrospect, mingled with yet
more glowing visions for the future. In fancy she
beheld herself the bride of Cæsar, receiving the
adulation and homage of princes and potentates,
while the sparkling diadem of an empress closed
the dazzling vista. "All this," she cried aloud,
"and love beside !"

So absorbed did she become in these delightful
thoughts that she did not hear the sound of a
hurrying foot on the stair without; nor did she
even so much as raise her heavy-lidded eyes when
the door opened and unannounced a man entered
her presence.

He stood for a moment staring at the beautiful
woman before him with a look of mingled scorn
and pity. "Ah, princess," he observed in a loud,
harsh voice, "it would seem that pleasant dreams
visit thee while the victorious legions of Rome pass
by."

Berenice looked up. "Is it thou, Agrippa?"
she said, a shade of displeasure in her silvery tones.
"Why art thou here?"

"And why not, my hospitable sister?" retorted
the man, sinking carelessly into a chair, and fixing

his merciless eyes on the haughty face of the woman. " I have a trifling errand with your highness which may be said in a word; then I will leave you to your meditations. Make ready to leave Rome to-day, carrisima; our presence is no longer desired here."

Berenice started to her feet with a cry. " Leave Rome !" she exclaimed; then the victorious color rushed back to cheeks and lips. " Your jest is unbecoming, highness," she said coldly; " for myself, I am in no mood for witless pleasantries."

Agrippa shrugged his shoulders. " By the gods, woman, I also am in no mood for either jests or pleasantries; what I have said is neither one nor the other. The emperor and the senate have learned of the wishes of the Conqueror and have voted him titles, moneys, provinces, estates; but to his contemplated marriage with the daughter of Herod Agrippa they raise insuperable barriers. In a word they have forbidden it. This being so, we leave Rome to-day."

The face of the woman was more colorless than the pillow of snow-white byssus against which it leaned, but her voice was clear and steady as she made answer. " He who laid low the walls of Jerusalem is also able to level the barriers of which thou hast spoken."

Agrippa laughed aloud. " The walls of Jerusalem were indeed well builded, my fair sister; but the wall of Roman pride is yet stronger, as thou

wilt presently discover.—Come, princess, thou art
no puling, lovesick girl to shed tears over the inevitable; this is but one misadventure out of a
thousand victories; there are other kings and
princes to be enchanted, and thou canst yet boast
of the fairest face in all the circle of the earth."

"Leave me !" cried the woman fiercely, her eyes
blazing like lurid fires. "I will hear this thing from
his own lips.—Nay, it is not true—it cannot be true!"

Agrippa stared with scornful curiosity at the con-
vulsed, quivering face. Then he turned away with
a short, hard laugh. "Can it be possible," he
ejaculated with affected amazement, "that Eros has
succeeded at last in lodging one of his poisoned
darts in that heart of adamant?" He paused at
the door and blew a light kiss from his jeweled fingers. "Farewell, divinity," he said softly; "remember that whatever befalls, thou hast in me a
faithful friend and lover."

Three hours later, Berenice, attired with the magnificence of a reigning queen, was sweeping restlessly up and down her chamber. Sparks of soul-
less fire shot out from the jewels which wreathed
her dark hair, but the eyes beneath burned with
the flame that consumes. From time to time she
paused to glance impatiently into the great mirror
whose polished surface gave back coldly the tense,
white face with its blazing eyes. "Am I beautiful,
girl?" she demanded, pausing before Merodah, who
was again in attendance upon her mistress.

"Very—very beautiful, dear princess," said the girl softly. "But——"

"But what, slave?"

"If thou hast a desire—a—a wish—" The girl faltered and hung her head.

"Well, if I have a desire—a wish; what then?"

"We may ask what we will of—of Jesus of Nazareth; he will give it us—if we but ask aright."

Berenice laughed aloud. "Did he deliver Jerusalem at thy request, girl?"

"I did not ask him for that."

"Why not?"

"It was his will that the city should be destroyed."

"And that thou shouldst become a slave?"

"Yes, truly; since it has come to pass."

"What then dost thou ask at the hands of this dead carpenter who resides with the gods?"

"I have asked him for the life of one whom I love," answered Merodah, with simplicity; "this I shall receive."

"How dost thou know it?"

The girl shook her head. "It gives me great peace here to love the Messiah," she said, laying her small hands upon her bosom; "I may also speak with him whenever I will; and he is able to bring all things to pass which are needful and good."

"Could he make me Empress of Rome?"

Merodah looked troubled. "Yes, truly," she said at length; "Jesus of Nazareth is able to do anything."

Berenice shrugged her shoulders with a harsh
laugh. "I do not find it in my heart to love this
crucified prophet," she said, "but thou mayest
speak with him, if thou wilt, in my behalf. I have
also ordered sacrifices for every altar in Rome.
We shall see—What have you, Arnon ?—A letter ?
Give it me !"   .

"There are also five and twenty Hebrew slaves,
worshipful lady, each wearing a chain and collar
of gold, which were sent with the letter," said the
servant with an obeisance.

Berenice was opening the packet, with fingers
which trembled not at all. On a sudden she seemed
frozen into stone. Her eyes devoured the words
which were written within ; then without a sound
she sank to the floor, as one who had received a
dagger-thrust in the heart. The perfumed parchment, with its seals of amethyst and gold, fluttered
from the nerveless fingers and lay upon the floor
at her side, white and innocent as the wind-blown
petals of a flower.

The man stooped and picked it up with an air
of deference. "Attend to thy mistress, slave," he
said with authority, and placed the letter upon a
table, but not before his rapid eye had seized upon
the words within. They were these :

"Titus Vespasianus to the princess Berenice,
Greeting. The Fates, ever more powerful than
Eros, have decreed that we meet no more. A laurel-

crowned victor, I yet find myself more unhappy than the slave who walked at my chariot wheel. For thy sake I have refused the title Judaicus, which the Senate decreed me this day. I am permitted to do no more. Farewell, most beautiful of women. May the gods protect thee !"

Six weeks later the soldiers of the Roman garrison, now the sole inhabitants of the dreary ruin once called Jerusalem, were astonished to behold a large and brilliant retinue approach the city. They were still more astonished when they learned that the princess Berenice, who had bewildered the legions by her lavish magnificence in the days of the late war, had returned to this desolate spot to perform a vow.

It was shortly whispered among the legionaries that the royal lady had once broken a similar vow with disastrous consequences to her after career ; hence the spectacle—at which they stared with relish—of a beautiful woman bareheaded and with naked feet, who stood each day at midnight and at noonday among the ghastly ruins of the temple, crying aloud in an unknown tongue upon an unseen God. This continued for the space of thirty days ; then the lady and her attendants disappeared as suddenly as they had come.

It was surmised that a part of the penance which the unhappy princess had laid upon herself consisted in the liberation of thirty slaves, one for each day of her vow. Certain it is that thirty collars and chains of solid gold were found on the day after her departure, hung up within the blackened walls of the Court of Israel. These the superstitious soldiers refused to touch, and for many months they remained there, a last, vain offering to the unknown God of the Hebrews.

In a certain quiet village—which, notwithstanding its proximity to Jerusalem had escaped the horrors of the war—the long, level rays of the setting sun shone brightly on the moss-grown thatch of a cottage, set on the green mountain-side like a nest. In the frost-bitten garden, shaded by two gnarled and ancient almond trees, a woman walked amid the dead stalks of the lilies. At morning and at evening for many long months she had prayed for death; but the Death-angel was weary with his labors and came not.

It was now winter. Below in the ruinous khan of Bethlehem the grandchildren of the innkeeper were hanging up green garlands of the olive and the fir in the manger where the carpenter's son first saw the light. There was no one to say them nay in these days. They stopped in their joyous labor long enough to inform two wayfarers that the widow of Samuel was yet alive and dwelt in her house in Aphtha.

It was a man who asked for this information, and his face shone with joy as he rejoined his companion who waited, modestly-veiled, in the courtyard of the inn.

"My mother is alive," he said. "Thank God!"

The woman drew her veil about her face more closely. "I am glad," she said softly; "ah, He is good to give us what we ask!" After a little she stopped short. "I—I will go no further. I will stay here. I shall perhaps be able to find work in some of the vineyards hereabouts."

The man also stopped, and stared at the small figure at his side with astonishment and dismay. "Merodah!" he cried. "What meanest thou? Stop here?—Not go with me to my mother! Nay, but thou must go!"

When there was no answer to this masterful assertion, the tall young man stooped and drew the shrouding drapery from the downcast face. "Merodah," he whispered, "Christ-maiden, who hast taught me to know and love the world's Burden-bearer; to whom dost thou belong in all the wide, lonely earth if not to me? Beloved, do not say me nay."

And so it came to pass that both joy and love returned to the cottage on the hillside. And Rachel, who had prayed in vain for death, lived to thank God that all her prayers had not been answered.

To all three, in the serene and happy years that followed, came such understanding of the terrible events which had shaken the world as the great Master is able to make plain to those who come to him in the simplicity of loving faith. They comprehended that although their city was destroyed, there was also a New Jerusalem, 'wherein they that dwell shall be forgiven their iniquities'; that although their sanctuary was perished, it was but the shadow of the heavenly temple, into which they might enter with joy, made forever white and clean through the blood of Christ, who was in truth "an High Priest of good things to come, in a greater and more perfect temple—a High Priest who was set forever on the right hand of the throne of the Majesty in the heavens; a minister of the sanctuary and of the true temple, which the Lord hath builded, and not man."

www.ingramcontent.com/pod-product-compliance
Lightning Source LLC
Chambersburg PA
CBHW021106270326

41929CB00009B/752